Conte s

62

82

88

94

108

118

FRONT COVER:
Junkers EF 128 by
Daniel Uhr

ALL ARTWORKS: Daniel Uhr
WORDS: Dan Sharp
DESIGN: Lucy Carnell - atg-media.com
PRODUCTION EDITOR: Pauline Hawkins
PUBLISHER: Steve O'Hara
ADVERTISING MANAGER: Sue Keily,
skeily@mortons.co.uk
PUBLISHING DIRECTOR: Dan Savage
MARKETING MANAGER: Charlotte Park
COMMERCIAL DIRECTOR: Nigel Hole

PUBLISHED BY: Mortons Media
Group Ltd, Media Centre, Morton Way,
Horncastle, Lincolnshire LN9 6JR.
Tel. 01507 529529

DANIEL UHR THANKS: Claudio Lamas,
Dan Sharp, Ditero Sigmar Uhr, Isaac
Uhr, Isis Uhr, Sérgio Adriano Menezes,
Veronica Carvalho

DAN SHARP THANKS: Elizabeth C Borja,
Steven Coates, Olivia T Garrison, Carlos
Alberto Henriques, Becky S Jordan,
Paul Martell-Mead, Ronnie Olsthoorn,
Alexander Power, Stephen Walton and
Tony Wilson

PRINTED BY: William Gibbons and Sons,
Wolverhampton

ISBN: 978-1-911276-69-2

Development

Germany ploughed huge resources into scientific research during the late 1930s – resulting in massive financial and industry backing for new forms of aircraft propulsion. This led to development programmes which would produce the world's first fully operational jet and rocket fighters.

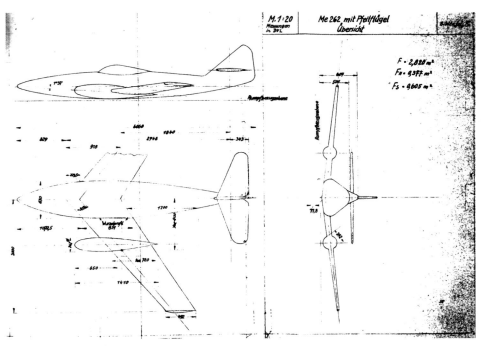

ABOVE: A radically different Me 262. This drawing shows a model that was tested in the DVL's wind tunnel in July 1942. Even at this stage Messerschmitt was making plans to improve the aircraft's aerodynamics.

The turbojet was invented in Britain during the 1920s – but where the British government hesitated to provide the financial support needed to develop it, the Nazi government had no qualms about taking a gamble on this potentially revolutionary engine. Money was also made available in large quantities to pursue intensive research on liquid-fuelled rocket motors and pulse jet engines for both missiles and aircraft.

It was an age of unprecedented technological discovery and scientific progress right across Europe and the arms race that precipitated the slide into war only accelerated the rate of advancement.

At the beginning of 1939, the Reichsluftministerium (RLM) issued the world's first specification for a turbojet-propelled fighter aircraft and in the months leading up to the Second World War the Germans flight-tested both the world's first turbojet aircraft and the world's first liquid-fuelled rocket-propelled aircraft.

The German aero engine industry was actively encouraged to invest in research on new turbojet and rocket motor designs and companies including BMW, Bramo, Daimler-Benz, Junkers and Heinkel each had

GERMAN JET DEVELOPMENT TIMELINE

• **November 9, 1935**	Hans von Ohain is granted a patent for Germany's first turbojet design.
• **Early 1936**	Dr Herbert Wagner begins developing gas turbine engines for Junkers.
• **April 15, 1936**	Von Ohain is hired by Ernst Heinkel to work on his jet engine.
• **Circa February 28, 1937**	Von Ohain's first working jet engine, the HeS 1 is completed and installed in a test rig.
• **Early 1938**	Design work begins at Heinkel on an aircraft that can be powered by von Ohain's new engine. At Junkers, Wagner begins construction of his own turbojet engine.
• **Autumn 1938**	German aero engine manufacturers Daimler-Benz, BMW, Brandenburgische Motorenwerke (Bramo) and Junkers are encouraged to look at turbojet development by the RLM.
• **Early 1939**	Junkers' Rückstoss-Turbinen-Strahltriebwerk (RTO) or 'Reaction Turbojet Engine' runs up to 6500rpm on a test stand. It is designed to reach 12,900rpm.
• **January 2, 1939**	Alexander Lippisch and his team transfer from the DFS to Messerschmitt AG at Augsburg. They form Abteilung L or 'Department L' and develop the DFS 39 as 'Projekt X' which receives the designation Me 163.
• **January 4, 1939**	Heinkel and Messerschmitt each receive a contract to begin work on the design of single-seat fighter aircraft with single turbojet propulsion – 'Jagdflugzeuge mit Strahltriebwerk'.
• **April 1, 1939**	Following preliminary studies, Messerschmitt's main project design team set to work in earnest on their first draft of a single-seat twin-jet fighter, project P 65 – later referred to as P 1065.
• **April 12-13, 1939**	Abteilung L produces the first single turbojet designs in what will become its long-running P 01 jet and rocket fighter series for Messerschmitt.
• **Circa June 1939**	Heinkel begins work on two mock-ups of its projected twin-engine turbojet fighter.
• **June 7, 1939**	The Messerschmitt P 1065 design, intended to be powered by two wing-mounted BMW jet engines, is submitted to the RLM. The RLM asks Messerschmitt to produce a mock-up of the design.

LUFTWAFFE

Secret Project Profiles

Daniel Uhr
& Dan Sharp

**DETAILED PROJECT
DESIGN HISTORIES**

**EVERY PROFILE BASED
ON ORIGINAL DRAWINGS**

COLOURS &
MARKINGS
FROM 1939
TO 1945

ISBN: 978-1-911276-69-2

£7.99

Preface

The jet engine was a 'secret project' like no other. Developed for the most part while the largest air war in history was being fought with piston-engined aircraft, it was at the centre of a technological arms race hidden from all but those with the highest military clearance.

Once the first operational jets – the Messerschmitt Me 262 and Me 163 – had been identified by Allied intelligence (the term 'jet' covering both turbojet and rocket propulsion), all service personnel were notified of their existence and the word quickly spread. When jet aircraft were finally revealed to a public brought up on propellers, they acquired an enduring mystique.

Immediately after the war, when hundreds of thousands of captured German aviation industry documents were assessed by the Allies, it became clear that Germany had poured huge resources into researching jet engines and designing the aircraft that would be powered by them.

In January 1946, Squadron Leader Horace Frederick 'H F' King, known to his friends as Rex, produced A.I.2(g) Report No. 2383 German Aircraft: New and Projected Types, which he introduced saying: "Although not exhaustive [this report] is believed to give a fair cross-section of German design technique. Some of the later proposals are of special interest, particularly the fighters and supersonic research aircraft with turbojet, liquid rocket or athodyd propulsion. There are some ambitious designs for jet-propelled long-range bombers and multi-seat fighters, and among the rotating-wing aircraft is a fighter entirely novel in conception. 'Mistel' composite aircraft, specialised tugs for launching jet bombers, jet-propelled army-support aircraft and a 'glide-fighter' are also in evidence."

The report includes 174 illustrations, 108 of them jets, and in fact the accompanying text mentions a grand total of 315 types, including all sub-types and some designs that aren't illustrated – more than half of them jets. King had worked for *Flight* magazine before the war, having joined in 1931, and rejoined it after the war, writing several articles on the advanced German designs he had seen. He and others like him helped to feed the British public's curiosity about the development of 'enemy' jets and what types might, under different circumstances, have been unleashed to battle Spitfires and Mustangs during the final stages of the war.

While interest in these German projects waned in Britain and America during the 1960s and 1970s, in Germany it underwent a revival. Authors including Heinz J Nowarra and Karl R Pawlas uncovered previously unseen designs and photographs and during the 1990s they were joined by others, including Horst Lommel, Manfred Griehl, Walter Schick and Dieter Herwig, who each discovered yet more previously unknown designs.

I first became aware that Second World War aircraft designs might go beyond the likes of the Hurricane, Bf 109 and P-47 Thunderbolt in 1991 with the release of LucasFilm Games' Secret Weapons of the Luftwaffe game for the PC, which featured a pair of Horton 8-229 flying wings on the cover. Then in 1998 a friend drew my attention to Dan Johnson's Luft46.com website, which opened my eyes to the huge number and variety of German 'secret projects'.

Perhaps the most striking aspect of this website was the incredible 'Luft Art' section. Here more than a dozen talented artists had transformed the flat black and white period drawings into 3D renders, showing how the project aircraft might have looked had they ever been built. Among those artists were Ronnie Olsthoorn – who would later go on to provide the cover and contents page illustrations for my Luftwaffe: Secret series, Marek Rys, Jozef Gatial, Gareth Hector and... Brazilian artist Daniel Uhr.

Having been aware of Daniel's work since those early days of Luft46, I was surprised and delighted to get to know him personally through working on my British Secret Projects 5: Britain's Space Shuttle (2016) book – he provided such a stunning cover that I had no hesitation in commissioning him to produce profile artwork for my Luftwaffe titles and the cover of my RAF: Secret Jets of Cold War Britain (2017) publication.

The various titles in the Luftwaffe: Secret series have been illustrated primarily with drawings scanned directly from original German documents and from period microfilmed copies of original documents, and I always felt that the various colour profiles commissioned to sit alongside them received insufficient space to really be appreciated. Now that imbalance can finally be corrected.

Luftwaffe: Secret Project Profiles features more than 200 of Daniel Uhr's excellent profiles – each one based firmly on design drawings produced during the Second World War. Daniel has used genuine wartime camouflage and colour schemes to bring them vividly to life, including examples as they might have appeared if 'captured' by the Allies or the neutral Swiss, or operated by other Axis nations. Seeing the designs fleshed out this way provides a unique perspective on types that have previously only ever been seen as pure black and white line drawings and evokes the spirit and fascination of Luft46 in imagining just what those oddities of German aircraft design might have really looked like. ●

ALSO AVAILABLE
Luftwaffe: Secret Jets of the Third Reich (2015)
Luftwaffe: Secret Bombers of the Third Reich (2016)
Luftwaffe: Secret Wings of the Third Reich (2017)
Luftwaffe: Secret Designs of the Third Reich (2018)
Visit www.classicmagazines.co.uk to order.

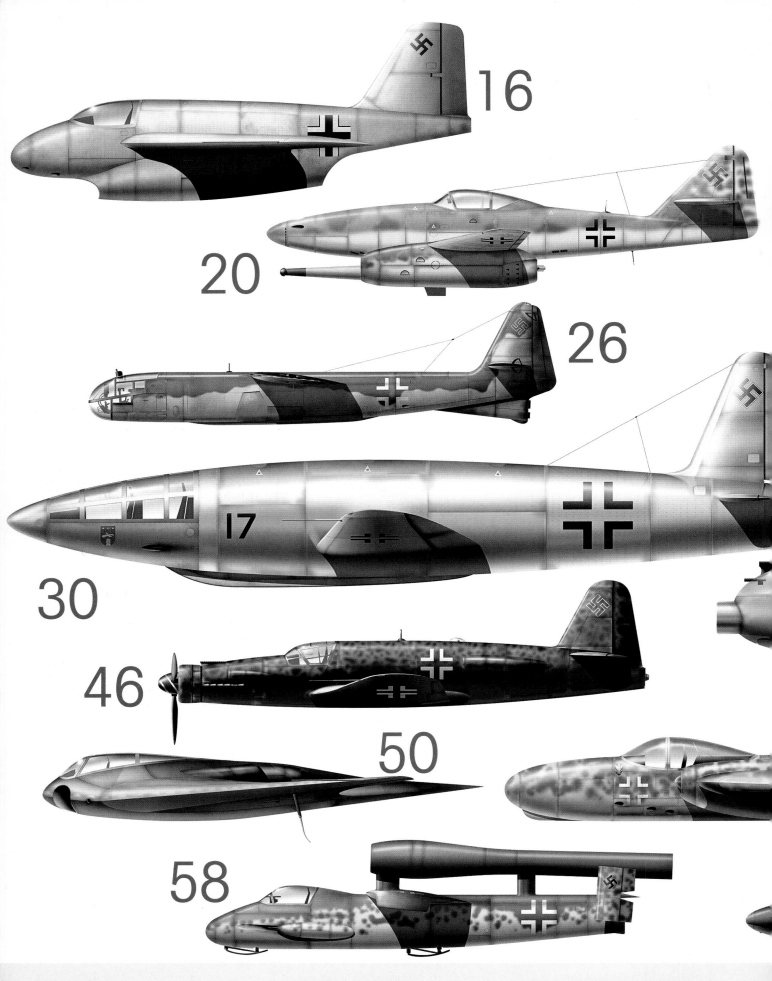

16

20

26

17

30

46

50

58

overload

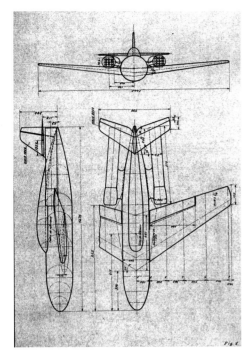

ABOVE: Messerschmitt paid for the AVA to conduct wind tunnel tests on models of its Me 328 with swept wings in July 1943. This drawing is from a French translation of the report.

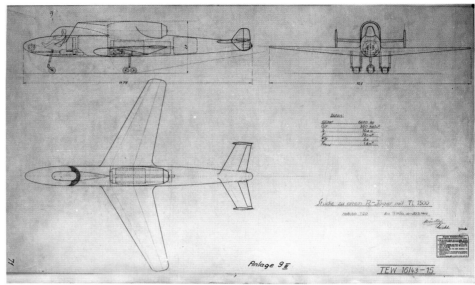

ABOVE: During March 1943, Arado came to the conclusion that a combination of rocket and jet propulsion would be best for the fighters of the future. The result was this: the K-Jäger.

their own separate jet research programmes under way by the beginning of the war.

Creating a turbojet or rocket motor which worked reliably and which provided any significant power gains over a piston engine proved to be more difficult than expected, however. When the war began, only the two largest privately owned aviation concerns were actively working on jet and rocket aircraft – Heinkel and Messerschmitt.

The former appeared to have all the advantages, having been responsible for both of those 'world first' flights in 1939 with the rocket-propelled Heinkel He 176 and turbojet-powered He 178, but the latter caught up quickly thanks to the efforts of government-owned Junkers in building a third-party turbojet engine that could withstand the rigours of operation under real-world conditions for more than a few minutes.

The twin-jet Messerschmitt Me 262 arose out of that early 1939 specification for a "schnelles Jagdflugzeug / Heimatschuetzer (Interceptor) – einsatz gegen Luftziele" – a 'fast fighter/interceptor – for use against aerial targets'. And the rocket-powered Messerschmitt Me 163, which does not

seem to have had a Heinkel competitor, was initially developed purely as a research design that only later became 'militarised'.

Both projects were begun during peacetime and neither was intended to meet a specific military need – indeed, their respective development programmes were so protracted and fraught with difficulties that every time a specific need did arise, the moment passed before either aircraft was ready to meet it.

The Me 262 might have made a real difference had it been built specifically as a fighter-bomber and been available in sufficient numbers to oppose the Allied landings in Normandy on D-Day, as Adolf Hitler had wanted. And the Me 163 B

▶

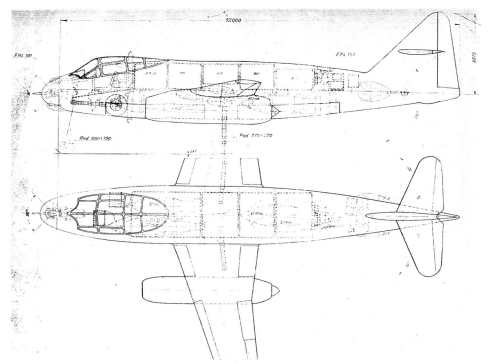

ABOVE: One of two different versions of the P 1100 fast bomber designed by Messerschmitt during early 1944.

could only be used to intercept enemy bombers flying close to its base because its endurance was too poor for ordinary fighter missions or dogfighting combat.

The third jet design to see active service during the Second World War was Arado's Ar 234. It was designed from the outset as a reconnaissance platform and performed this role admirably – but by the time it entered service Germany was in no position to do anything useful with detailed aerial photographs of military facilities in England.

At the point when these three machines were ready to enter service – early 1944 – the Luftwaffe urgently needed jet aircraft capable of intercepting the RAF's fast high-flying de Havilland Mosquito reconnaissance aircraft, destroying Allied shipping, bombing Allied air bases, locating and destroying the RAF's night bombers and inflicting damage on the USAAF's daytime bomber fleet.

The Me 262 and Me 163 B were certainly able to do the latter but there were simply too few of them to do the sort of damage that might result in the Americans halting their attacks or even rethinking their daylight bombing strategy all together. And there were other problems. The Me 262

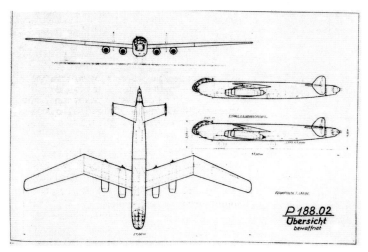

ABOVE: Towards the end of 1943, Blohm & Voss submitted this design for the Strahlbomber competition. There were five P 188 designs and all had the same distinctive rotating M-wing.

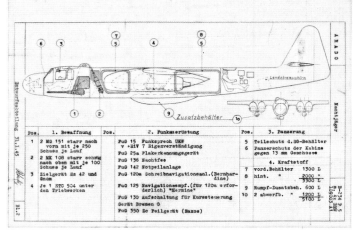

ABOVE: Germany desperately needed jet-powered night fighters as Allied bombing intensified during 1944. Arado's answer was the Ar 234 P-5.

GERMAN JET DEVELOPMENT TIMELINE

- **March 30, 1941** — The Heinkel He 280 V2 flies under its own power for the first time.
- **April-July 1941** — One of Abteilung L's designs, the rocket-powered P 01-114, is given the designation Me 263.
- **April 8, 1941** — Messerschmitt's P 1065 is given an official RLM designation – Me 262.
- **April 18, 1941** — The Me 262 V1, PC+UA, makes its first flight, albeit powered by a Jumo 210G piston engine.
- **Spring 1941** — Unpowered flight testing of the Me 163 V1 prototype begins.
- **July 14, 1941** — Following the invasion of the Soviet Union, Hitler issues Führer Directive No. 32 (Supplement), restricting the allocation of non-war-essential military equipment development contracts. Work on new jet fighter types for the Luftwaffe comes to a halt. It is anticipated that victory in the East will be swift.
- **August 13, 1941** — First rocket-powered flight of Me 163 V1.
- **August 27, 1941** — Lippisch proposes the 'Li P 05' interceptor, an up-scaled development of the Me 163.
- **October 2, 1941** — Heini Dittmar becomes the first man to fly faster than 1000km/h, at the controls of Me 163 V4.
- **October 1941** — The Horten brothers witness test flights of the Me 163 at Peenemünde.
- **October 24, 1941** — Arado has finally come up with a concrete proposal for the RLM's bomber/reconnaissance jet requirement – the E.370/IVa. It is examined by the RLM and an initial batch of 50 aircraft is ordered.
- **November 1941** — Design details of the Me 163 B are finalised. All existing Me 163s become Me 163 As.
- **November 1941** — Two BMW P 3302 prototype engines are delivered to Messerschmitt for installation in the Messerschmitt Me 262 V1 prototype.
- **November 17, 1941** — Lippisch supporter Ernst Udet commits suicide.
- **February 1942** — Arado's E 370 design is allocated the official RLM designation Ar 234.
- **Spring 1942** — The Horten brothers begin designing a twin-jet flying wing, the H IX.

RLM JET REQUIREMENTS WITH COMPETING DESIGNS

JAGDFLUGZEUGE MIT STRAHLTRIEBWERK
As of late 1939
Messerschmitt P 1065 (Me 262)
Heinkel He 280

SCHNELLSTBOMBER (1000 X 1000 X 1000)
As of September 28, 1943
Lippisch P 11
Horten IX
As of December 19-20, 1944
Lippisch P 11/Delta VI
Horten 8-229

STRAHLBOMBER
As of January 1944
Arado E 395
Blohm & Voss P 188
Junkers EF 122 (Ju 287)
As of February 1944
Junkers EF 122 (Ju 287)
Heinkel Strabo 16 to (formerly P 1068, later He 343)

1-TL-JÄGER COMPETITORS
As of September 8-10, 1944
Heinkel P 1073
Messerschmitt P 1101
Focke-Wulf Nr. 280 ('Flitzer')
Blohm & Voss (no proposal)
As of December 19-21, 1944
Heinkel P 1073 ('He 162 development')
Messerschmitt P 1106

Focke-Wulf Nr. 279 ('Huckebein')
Blohm & Voss P 209.02
Blohm & Voss P 212.02
Junkers EF 128
As of January 12-16, 1945
Heinkel P 1078
Messerschmitt I (P 1106)
Messerschmitt II (P 1110)
Focke-Wulf I (Nr. 279)
Focke-Wulf II (Nr. 30)
Blohm & Voss P 212.03
Junkers EF 128
As of February 27-28, 1945
Heinkel P 1078
Messerschmitt P 1101
Messerschmitt P 1110
Messerschmitt P 1111
Focke-Wulf I (Nr. 279)
Focke-Wulf II (Nr. 30)
Blohm & Voss P 212.03
Junkers EF 128

VOLKSJÄGER
As of September 14, 1944
Arado E 580
Blohm & Voss P 211
Heinkel P 1073 (simplified version)

OBJEKTSCHÜTZER
As of November 21-22, 1944
Bachem BP 20 Natter
Heinkel P 1077 'Julia'
8-263 (Junkers Ju 248)
Messerschmitt Me 262 with supplementary

rocket propulsion
As of December 19-20, 1944
Bachem BP 20 Natter
Heinkel P 1077 'Julia'
Junkers EF 127 'Walli'
8-263 (Junkers Ju 248)

LANGSTRECKENBOMBER (TL-GROSSBOMBER)
As of February 25, 1945
Horten XVIII
Junkers Ju 287
Messerschmitt P 1107

SCHLECHTWETTER UND NACHTJÄGER (2-TL-JÄGER)
As of February 26, 1945
Blohm & Voss P 215.01
Dornier P 252/1
Dorner P 254/1
Me 262 two- or three-seater
As of March 20, 1945
Arado I
Arado II
Blohm & Voss P.215.02
Dornier P 256
Focke-Wulf II
Focke-Wulf III
Gotha P-60C

LORIN JÄGER
Heinkel P 1080
Skoda P 14

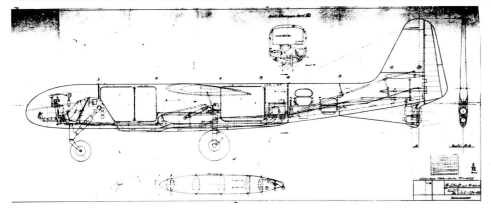

LEFT: Proposals were drawn up to turn both the Ar 234 B and the Me 163 into short-range high-speed rocket-powered battlefield reconnaissance machines. The Ar 234 would have had to swap its turbojets for an internal rocket engine.

was made almost entirely from light metal alloy – a material in perilously short supply in Germany by the beginning of 1944 – and it required two expensive and difficult-to-build turbojet engines to fly. The Me 163 B, while somewhat more frugal on materials, was still difficult to build and dangerous to operate. Carelessly handled, its volatile fuel could cause a catastrophic explosion and its skid landing gear meant every touchdown ▶

• **March 1942**	Drawings and proposals for the Me 163 C and Super 163 Interceptor are drafted.
• **March 25, 1942**	A first flight of the Me 262 V1 is attempted but quickly ends after both of its BMW engines fail.
• **April 1942**	The RLM orders six Ar 234 prototypes. Work on the first prototype Me 163 B is completed.
• **May 29, 1942**	The RLM reduces its Me 262 prototype order to just five examples.
• **June 26, 1942**	First towed flight of the Me 163 B V1 by Heini Dittmar.
• **July 5, 1942**	Flight testing of the He 280 V3, using two of von Ohain's HeS 8A jet engines, begins.
• **July 18, 1942**	Me 262 V3 flies for the first time with Jumo 004 engines. It completes 25 minutes of trouble-free flying.
• **September 1942**	Although Me 262 V3 has been wrecked in an accident, its reliable performance convinces the RLM to reinstate the type's formerly cancelled additional prototypes.
• **September 13, 1942**	The first P 11, a two-seater fast bomber powered by two turbojets, is designed by Handrick.
• **November 5, 1942**	Focke-Wulf produces drawings for a jet-engined Fw 190, using a powerplant of its own design.
• **November 6, 1942**	Lippisch presents a talk on his Me 163 A to members of the exclusive Deutsche Akademie für Luftfahrtforschung, including Siegfried Günter of Heinkel and Hans Multhopp of Focke-Wulf.
• **November 18, 1942**	The RLM reduces its He 280 prototype order to just six examples plus one unpowered aircraft for high speed testing.
• **December 2, 1942**	A second P 11 twin jet bomber is designed by Handrick. He makes it a single-seater.
• **December 10, 1942**	With the tide of battle in the East turning against Germany, and with no imminent victory in sight, Erhard Milch orders into effect "an urgent development and production programme under the code word Vulkan. The programme encompasses jet-propelled aircraft and guided missiles, including associated equipment and the ground organisation necessary to support these activities". The aircraft given top priority for procurement of equipment are the Me 163, Me 262, He 280, Me 328 and Ar 234.

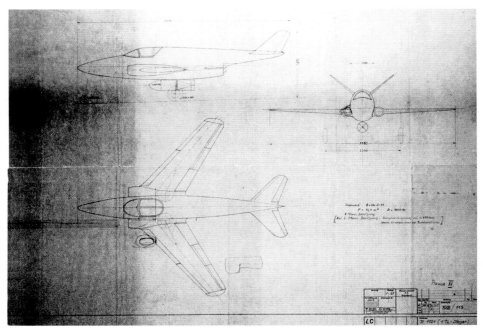

ABOVE: Messerschmitt's first entry for the 1-TL-Jäger competition was the P 1101 – this is how it appeared when presented at the first comparison meeting in September 1944.

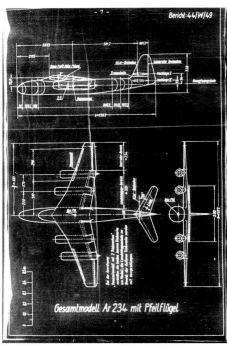

ABOVE: Throughout 1944, Arado attempted to design and build a crescent-wing version of the Ar 234 but it was hampered by a lack of wind tunnel capacity and the prototype was reportedly destroyed by bombing before it could be completed.

carried a risk of spinal injury for the pilot.

However, the Me 262 and Me 163 B did serve to demonstrate the raw potential inherent in turbojet and rocket-propelled aircraft. Awareness of this potential grew during the latter half of 1943, particularly as the Jumo 004 engine proved itself time and again to be both reliable and powerful enough to give the Me 262 previously undreamt-of performance.

By the end of 1943, plans were already in place for the development of a new jet bomber that would take the fight to the Allies and yet more proposals were being put forward for jet-propelled fighters and bombers that would perform the tasks that the existing designs could not. And these new aircraft would need to be made as cheaply as possible and from 'non-strategic' materials too – steel, wood and glue.

Fortunately, Nazi Germany had already developed the greatest concentration of

aviation research and development facilities in history, including 63 wind tunnels plus another 15 in occupied countries. The budget for aviation research and development was RM 500 million in 1945, compared to RM 340 million in 1943, and the number of personnel involved in development work was 8000 in 1945, compared to 7000 in 1943.

JÄGERSTAB AND EHK

A new organisation was formed in March 1944: the Jägerstab or 'Fighter Staff'. Its goal was to significantly increase the number of fighter aircraft being built in Germany and in doing so it transformed the German aviation industry. Production facilities were decentralised, with small urban workshops such as furniture makers being retasked to build aircraft components, which made it much harder for the Allies' bomber fleets to halt production by bombing the large well-known aircraft factory sites. In addition, the

number of aircraft types in production was dramatically reduced, freeing up production capacity and focusing efforts on the materials and tooling required for manufacturing fighters, rather than bombers, seaplanes, transports, trainers or reconnaissance types.

On September 15, 1944, ultimate responsibility for decision-making on new aircraft developments was taken out of the hands of the RLM and given to a new development commission – the Entwicklungshauptkommission (EHK) under the chairmanship of Luftwaffe chief engineer Roluf Lucht. Starting with the Panzerkommission for tank development in 1941, Albert Speer and the head of his ministry's technical department Karl-Otto Saur had steadily established more

GERMAN JET DEVELOPMENT TIMELINE

• **December 28, 1942**	The RLM increases its order for Ar 234 prototypes from six to 20.
• **January 4, 1943**	Focke-Wulf designer Julius Rotta sets out how the company will approach future jet design and suggests an aircraft layout similar to what will eventually be produced as the Heinkel He 162.
• **March 1943**	The RLM orders the Horten brothers' Sonderkommando LIn 3 to cease all work.
• **March 1943**	Focke-Wulf designs its '1. Entwurf' single jet fighter.
• **March 9, 1943**	The RLM decides against series production of the Heinkel He 280 – primarily due to the minimal ground clearance of its low-slung engine pods. This is officially confirmed in a letter to Heinkel dated March 27, 1943.
• **March 20, 1943**	The RLM orders that Lippisch's Department L should be effectively dissolved and absorbed into Messerschmitt.
• **April 28, 1943**	Lippisch officially leaves Messerschmitt. He takes up his new appointment as head of the Luftfahrtforschungsanstalt Wien (LFW) in Vienna, Austria, three days later.
• **May 1943**	Lippisch presents the RLM with his proposal for an aircraft that can fly 1000km at 1000km/h carrying 1000kg of bombs – the P 11.
• **May 22, 1943**	General of Fighters Adolf Galland flies the Me 262 at Lechfeld.
• **May 25, 1943**	Galland convinces Hermann Göring to let Messerschmitt drop its latest proposed Bf 109 replacement, the Me 209, in favour of all-out production of the Me 262.
• **June 1943**	Focke-Wulf designs its '2. Entwurf' single jet fighter.
• **June 22, 1943**	Messerschmitt's plan for series production of the Me 262 is approved.
• **Early summer 1943**	The first Ar 234 prototype is completed and taxiing trials begin.
• **June 7, 1943**	Junkers begins wind tunnel testing its swept wing EF 116 design against that of the Ar 234.
• **June 15, 1943**	Arado makes its first report on a series of flying wing studies designated E 555.

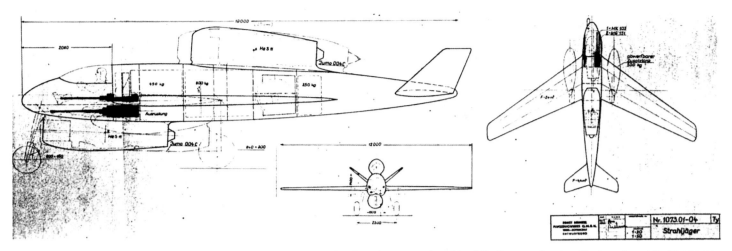

ABOVE: An early two-engine version of Heinkel's P 1073. A single engined version was entered for 1-TL-Jäger and a simplified version of that became the Volksjäger – the He 162.

and more commissions to cover all aspects of military procurement, with the EHK being the twelfth and almost the last.

Under interrogation by the Allies in June 1945, Saur explained: "The formation of the Speer development commissions arose from the necessity for closer co-operation where technically similar problems came from different users.

"For example, the army places an order with a firm for the developing of a new Pak [anti-tank gun]; the Air Force orders the development of a new cannon; the Navy orders the development of a cannon for use against sea and air targets. All three sections of the forces worked in different groups and in most cases against each other, and it could thus happen that development contracts for one and the same job were placed two or three times.

"Then, since each engineer formulates the same matter rather differently, it came about that three different equipments were introduced. To take another example, the Navy and Air Force collaborated in the development of the same gun, namely the 12.8cm flak; later ammunition was developed along different lines and was

no longer interchangeable. One type of ammunition was badly tested so that at the end of 1944 half of the 12.8cm guns in a unit were useless because the ammunition was too bad. Only from this date was Naval flak ammunition used for Air Force flak.

"Military requirements from the three armed services and other users were first put through the filter of the appropriate development commission to the specialists, to achieve as much unification as possible in order to limit the number of different developments undertaken. It was, for example, forbidden to run more than two developments of the same thing except in difficult cases so that not more than two firms were engaged on one and the same job unless it was a reasonably considerate undertaking.

"Two main tasks of the commission were: 1) to avoid the issue of development requirements and their working out in practice without the series production specialists being consulted. 2) to avoid over-elaborate designs leading to an excessive consumption of time and material during development and in building up production. It was found in practice that if 100% of effort was required to meet a specification 100%,

```
TLR/Fl-E
Fl-E 2 Nr. 9776/44 (IIIA)          Berlin, den 15.9.44.

                    Besprechungsniederschrift.

Betrifft: Jagdeinsitzer.

Am 14.9.44 fand bei Fl-E 2 eine Aussprache über
1 TL-Volksjäger-Hochleistungs-Otto-Jäger und
1 TL-Jäger (Ablösung Me 262) statt mit anschliessender
Abschlussbesprechung bei TLR/Fl-E-Chef. Das Ergebnis der
Aussprache wird wie folgt zusammengefasst:

Projekte wurden vorgelegt von den Firmen Arado, Blohm & Voss
und Heinkel. Nach Ansicht der beteiligten Firmen ist die
Startstreckenforderung - Rollstrecke 500 m - nicht
erreichbar. Die Firmen Arado und Heinkel hatten entgegen
der Ausschreibung nur 20 Min. statt mit anschliessender
30 Min. vorgesehen, um die Startforderung annähernd zu
erfüllen. Das Projekt der Firma Blohm & Voss ist bestechend
in seiner Bauweise und erscheint in dieser Form äusserst
billig und zweckmäßig für den vorgesehenen Bau. Es
verwirklicht ebenfalls bestens die Forderung auf weitgehende
Verwendung von Holz und Stahl. Unabhängig davon, welche Firma
den endgültigen Auftrag erhält, sollten die Gesichtspunkte
des Projekts B&V weitgehendst berücksichtigt werden.
Eine Fertigungsüberprüfung des Projekts B&V wird in den
nächsten Tagen vorgenommen. Alle Beteiligten waren sich
bei der Abschlussbesprechung bei TLR-Fl.-E-Chef darüber
einig, dass ein derartiges Flugzeug unbedingt geschaffen
werden sollte, wenn hierdurch der Me 262 keine Kapazität
entzogen wird, wenn es gelingt, durch Sondermaßnahmen in kürzester Zeit
eine grosse Stückzahl zum Einsatz zu bringen. Die
Einsatzmöglichkeiten eines derartigen Flugzeugs sind
selbstverständlich beschränkt. Die Frage des Brennstoff-
menge - 20 oder 30 Min. - wird endgültig zwischen
Chef TLR, TLR/Fl-E-Chef und General der Jagdflieger
geklärt. 20 Minuten Flugzeit sind wahrscheinlich
zu gering.

.................
```

ABOVE: This historically important document is a report of a TLR meeting on September 14, 1944, which refers to the three fighter programmes then in development – 1-TL Volksjäger, Hochleistungs-Otto-Jäger [high-performance piston engine fighter] and 1-TL-Jäger (Me 262 replacement).

• June 24, 1943	First rocket-powered flight of the Me 163 B V1 prototype.
• July 1943	Lippisch receives a RM 30,000 development contract for his P 11, effectively making it a low-priority project.
• July 30, 1943	The Ar 234 V1 is successfully flown for the first time.
• August 1943	The Horten brothers, Walter and Reimar, send their proposal for a 1000 x 1000 x 1000 jet bomber based on their Horten IX design to Göring.
• August 11, 1943	Arado produces a report outlining the possibilities for building a two-seat jet bomber.
• August 17, 1943	Me 262 production is delayed when a US bombing raid destroys fuselage construction jigs at Messerschmitt's Regensburg plant, prompting the firm to move key departments to Oberammergau in the Bavarian Alps.
• September 28, 1943	Reichsmarschall Hermann Göring increases Lippisch's P 11 contract to RM 500,000 and commissions the Horten brothers with the same sum to build the Horten IX.
• September 30, 1943	Wind tunnel testing of the EF 122 swept wing bomber design begins at Junkers.
• November 1943	Focke-Wulf designs its '3. Entwurf' single jet fighter.
• December 1943	Focke-Wulf designs its '4. Entwurf' single jet fighter.
• January 1944	The first production batches of Me 163 B-0 and B-1 airframes are completed but no engines are available.
• January 1944	Focke-Wulf designs its '5. Entwurf' single jet fighter.
• January 1944	Junkers is awarded a contract to build at least one prototype of its EF 122 fast bomber design under the designation Ju 287. Heinkel is ordered to develop its P 1068 jet bomber design as a matter of the utmost urgency so that it can be rushed into production, combining it with the work already carried out by Arado on its E 395 to ultimately create the He 343.
• February 1944	Focke-Wulf designs its '6. Entwurf' single jet fighter.

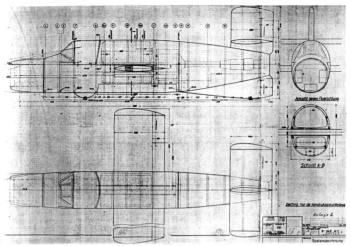

ABOVE: The Bachem Ba 349 A-1 Natter was an entrant for the 'Objektschützer' competition, which commenced during the autumn of 1944 – to find a more effective replacement for the Me 163 B.

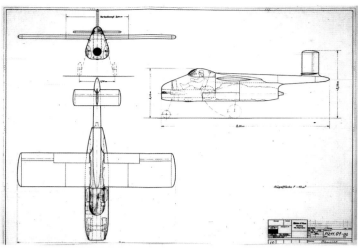

ABOVE: Blohm & Voss's Volksjäger contender was the P 211.

only 30% of effort was needed to meet 90%."

The EHK subdivided into nine special commissions, each directed by a major 'specialist' in the German aviation industry: Willy Messerschmitt was director for day fighters, Kurt Tank – night fighters, Heinrich Hertel from Junkers – bombers, Friedrich Fecher from Siebel – training aircraft, Robert Lusser from Fieseler – special aircraft, Günther Bock from the DVL (Deutschen Versuchsanstalt für Luftfahrt) – airframe construction, Walter Schilo from BMW – engines, planning and installation of equipment – Rolf Stüssel from Lufthansa, and planning and installation of armament – Walter Blume from Arado.

Having so many specialists on board ought to have gone some way towards achieving Speer's goal of avoiding wasteful overlapping of effort but in practice it seems to have made little difference. The usual practice of aircraft requirements resulting in a competition between manufacturers continued – only now some of those competing manufacturers had been set in positions of seniority over their rivals, which made it increasingly difficult for anyone to make a firm decision.

NINE COMPETITIONS

The first jet competition had been a straight contest between Messerschmitt's P 1065/Me 262 and Heinkel's He 280. Development of Arado's Ar 234 commenced in 1940 without a competitive tender. In May 1943, the RLM gave Me 163-designer Alexander Lippisch an RM 30,000 contract to develop his P 11 twin-jet design, which became a second jet competition in September 1943 when Reichsmarschall Hermann Göring upped the contract to RM 500,000 and commissioned the Horten brothers, Walter and Reimar, with the same sum to also build a twin-jet flying-wing type aircraft.

Shortly thereafter, a third competition was begun: to design a four-engined 'Strahlbomber' fast jet bomber which resulted in the construction of a Ju 287 flying mock-up. The fourth competition was for a '1-TL-Jäger' single-jet fighter to replace the Me 262, begun in July 1944. At this time, another uncontested jet project was begun, to develop an experimental turbojet aircraft for the German Research Institute for Sailplane Flight or Deutsche Forschungsanstalt für Segelflug (DFS). The project for Heinkel's rejected Strahlbomber entry was revived and continued in development as the DFS P 1068.

The fifth jet competition, beginning in September 1944, was to create a cheap and easy to build and fly single-jet 'Volksjäger' or 'people's fighter'. The sixth, also starting in September, was to develop an 'Objektschützer' point defence fighter to replace the Me 163.

The seventh was effectively a re-run of 'Strahlbomber' but under the designation 'TL-Grossbomber' or 'Langstreckenbomber', with the Ju 287 again in the running, while the eighth jet competition was to build a twin-jet night fighter to replace the various piston engine types then in service. Details of the ninth competition – to design a fighter that would use ramjet propulsion – are sketchy but evidence suggests that Heinkel and Skoda-Korba were each commissioned to design rival ramjet fighters in the spring of 1945.

JET OR PISTONS?

Even as all this work was proceeding, there were still serious doubts about whether it was preferable to switch entirely to jet

GERMAN JET DEVELOPMENT TIMELINE

• March 1, 1944	The Jägerstab (Fighter Staff), a committee of industrialists and RLM officials, is established with the goal of reinvigorating Germany's flagging aviation industry. This effectively ends the RLM's direct involvement in aircraft production, allowing it to focus on research and development.
• March 1, 1944	The unpowered H IX V1 glider is ready for its first flight, which it makes four days later.
• June 1944	The first 20 pre-production Arado Ar 234 B-0 aircraft are delivered.
• Late June 1944	Construction of the Horten IX V2 begins at Göttingen.
• July 1944	Focke-Wulf designs its '7. Entwurf' single jet (turboprop) fighter, also known as 'Peterle'.
• July 11, 1944	The RLM issues a specification for a new single jet fighter aircraft, a '1-TL-Jäger'. The aircraft must be powered by a single HeS 011 turbojet, take-off weight should be 3500kg, fuel tanks in the fuselage must be protected from 13mm rounds (.50 calibre) and it must be ready to fly on March 1, 1945.
• August 8, 1944	The Ju 287 V1 is flown for the first time.
• September 1944	Dr Rudolf Göthert at Gotha begins work on a flying wing design with the intention of supplanting the Horten brothers' 8-229, which Gotha has been charged with building.
• September 8-10, 1944	A meeting is held at the Messerschmitt facility in Oberammergau where the four firms invited to tender for the RLM '1-TL-Jäger' requirement of July are supposed to present their initial designs for assessment. Messerschmitt, Heinkel and Focke-Wulf make presentations but the Blohm & Voss submission is deferred since it is not yet ready.
• September 10, 1944	Just as the '1-TL-Jäger' meeting draws to a close, the RLM invites Arado, Blohm & Voss, Fieseler, Focke-Wulf, Heinkel, Junkers, Messerschmitt and Siebel to tender submissions for a new requirement designated 'Volksjäger' or 'People's Fighter'. This calls for a lightweight fighter built from existing components and powered by a single BMW 003 jet engine.

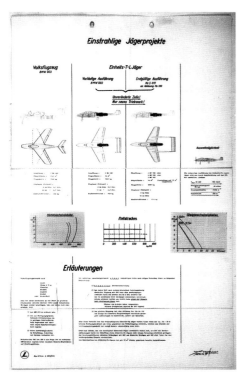

ABOVE: Focke-Wulf's Volksjäger entry, pictured on the left of this pamphlet, was submitted too late for serious consideration. Previously published versions of this document have always left off the little 'Peterle' design on the right.

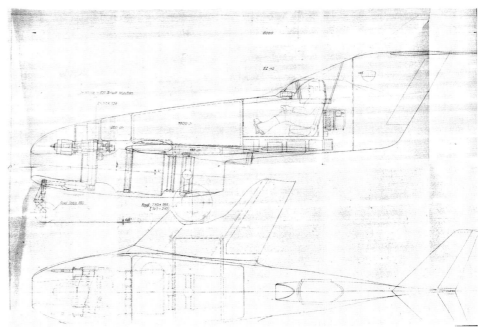

ABOVE: The Messerschmitt P 1106 was a later entry for 1-TL-Jäger, submitted during December 1944.

aircraft production or to continue with piston or 'Otto' engines – Otto being the contemporary German way of referring to the piston engine, after pioneering German inventor Nikolaus Otto.

At a meeting three days after the formation of the EHK, Lucht stated: "On the basis of the aforementioned advantages and disadvantages, the single-engined pusher-propeller Otto fighter, which can perform the role of the Do 335 at approximately half the cost, is very economical for use against bombers at all heights.

"It is equally suitable for deployment against enemy Otto fighters at all altitudes. Thanks to its endurance the Otto fighter is the type most suited to protecting any given area of airspace. And due to its economical cruise capability, the Otto fighter performs better at all heights in bad weather and blind-flying conditions than would a jet-powered aircraft.

"Furthermore, it is the most suitable fighter for operation in greater numbers when circumstances call for massed formations. In our opinion, and in the light of the above, the Otto fighter at its most advanced stage of development with pusher propeller is indispensable for aerial defence duties above and behind the front lines.

"And thanks to its being less susceptible to ground fire, it also lends itself to use in the fighter-bomber and ground-attack roles."

But this was not a view likely to gain much support from the aircraft manufacturers themselves, who realised that there was little left to gain from continued development of piston engine aircraft.

Arado director Walter Blume wrote on November 2, 1944: "To increase the speed of Otto-engined aircraft requires more time and expense in every way. This is because, with Otto engines, it is a matter of fighting for a percentage increase in the output and performance of every one of their component parts, with very little end result to show for all the work involved."

According to the minutes of the EHK meeting on December 19-20, 1944, opening the first item up for discussion 'piston or jet fighter?' Willy Messerschmitt "refuses the Otto fighter, without giving details, only with reference to speed superiority, also with regard to bombers where he considers a speed of 1100km/h is possible, because we could do it now".

It is often stated that Germany worked on too many jet designs, particularly during the final year of the war, and that it would have been better to simply build

● September 14-15, 1944	A meeting is held at the RLM's offices in Berlin and three of the seven firms invited to tender for the 'Volksjäger' requirement present their designs – Arado, Blohm & Voss and Heinkel.
● September 15, 1944	A new main development committee, the Entwicklungshauptkommission (EHK), led by Luftwaffe chief engineer Roluf Lucht, is established by Germany's minister for war production, Albert Speer, to oversee work on new aircraft types.
● September 17, 1944	Another meeting is held to discuss the two most promising 'Volksjäger' entries – Heinkel's P 1073 and Blohm & Voss's P 211. No decision is reached.
● September 19, 1944	Yet another meeting is held to discuss the 'Volksjäger' finalists and all the original entries are reviewed – along with new entries from Fieseler, Focke-Wulf, Junkers and Siebel.
● September 23, 1944	Hitler orders Heinkel's P 1073 design into mass production.
● September 28, 1944	Final flight test of the Ju 287 V1.
● October 1944	Lippisch works intensively on his ramjet-powered P 13 rammer aircraft design.
● October 3, 1944	Heinkel's P 1073 is given the official RLM designation He 162.
● October 21, 1944	Junkers is given a contract to begin development of the Ju 248.
● October 25, 1944	Work begins on the first He 162 prototypes.
● November 1944	Willy Messerschmitt proposes a four-turbojet bomber design, sparking a new long distance bomber competition – TL-Grossbomber aka Langstreckenbomber.
● November 21-22, 1944	A meeting of the Entwicklungshauptkommission is told that the Ho 229 is to be developed in conjunction with Gotha and three prototypes of the H VII are to be completed. It is also stated that Lippisch's P 11 is to be developed in collaboration with Henschel. His P 13 is also briefly mentioned. It is also mentioned that the Henschel Hs 132 jet dive bomber "was to be subject to a decision

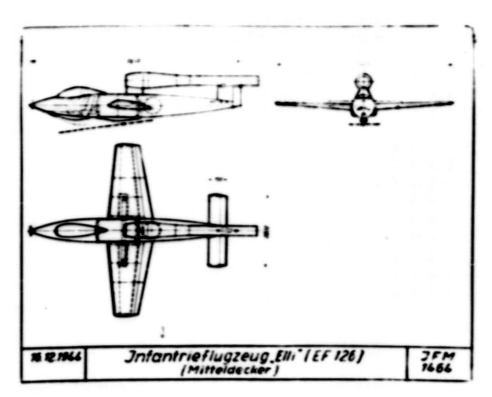

ABOVE: Junkers put forward the pulsejet-powered EF 126 Elli during December 1944 as a ground-attack aircraft. Like its rocket-engined 'Objektschützer' sibling, the EF 127 Walli, it was based on the V-1 flying bomb.

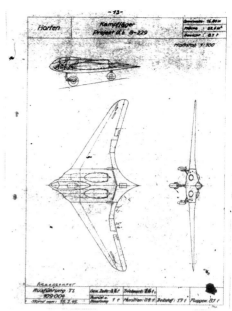

ABOVE: The final production version of the Horten 8-229 twin-jet flying-wing fighter was to be a two-seater, as shown in this drawing from February 15, 1945.

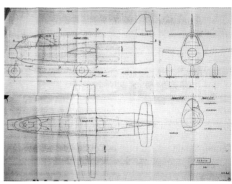

ABOVE: The last German aircraft design competition of the war was for a ramjet-powered fighter. Entries were produced by Heinkel – the P 1080 – and Skoda, which tendered this: the P 14. It is essentially an aircraft wrapped around a single enormous ramjet.

more Me 262s. There is also the view that German aircraft designers were merely making work for themselves to avoid being sent to the Eastern Front.

Both of these views are strongly coloured by hindsight. Even at the beginning of 1945, the Allies had yet to penetrate the borders of Germany itself – the final collapse came swiftly. And the overall state of the Reich's ground defences was largely unknown to the aircraft firms in 1944. They had no way of knowing when or even if Allied tanks were likely to

begin rolling up outside their factories.

Similarly, they had no way of knowing whether the V-1 and V-2 were having any effect on the Allies, whether some other branch of the military had some secret weapon in preparation that might just turn the tide of the war, even whether Hitler might somehow negotiate a peace settlement.

Many Germans believed that the Western Allies would, sooner rather than later, realise that the Soviet Union was the real threat and join forces with them to oppose the Red Tide sweeping in from the

GERMAN JET DEVELOPMENT TIMELINE

on the quantity to be produced". Submitted designs for the 'Objektschützer' requirement are reviewed. None of the four finalists are rejected but they are ranked in the following order: Messerschmitt's rocket-enhanced Me 262, Heinkel's 'Julia', the Junkers Ju 248/Messerschmitt 8-263 and Bachem's Natter.

• December 1, 1944	The He 162 M1 (V1) is finished and ready to fly.
• December 6, 1944	He 162 M1 flies for the first time.
• Early December, 1944	Junkers submits a new design for the 'Objektschützer' requirement, the EF 127 'Walli'.
• December 10, 1944	The He 162 M1 is destroyed during testing, killing its pilot.
• December 15, 1944	Discussions take place at the RLM in Berlin regarding the five companies' submissions to the '1-TL-Jäger' requirement. The companies present their updated designs – Junkers presents its EF 128 for the first time – but no agreement can be reached on the system of calculation that will be used to compare their projected performances.
• December 19-20, 1944	Meeting of the Entwicklungshauptkommission discusses the 'Objektschützer' competition.
• December 22, 1944	The He 162 M2 is flown for the first time. The EHK issues a statement following the December 19-20 meeting which indicates that the Ju 248/Me 263 is chosen for further development. Development of the rocket-enhanced Me 262 is to continue, work on Junkers' EF 127 'Walli' is to be suspended and both Bachem's Natter and Heinkel's 'Julia' are to be cancelled.
• January 11, 1945	The requirement for the new '1-TL-Jäger' is altered.
• January 12-15, 1945	Further discussions take place at the RLM in Berlin regarding the five companies' submissions to the '1-TL-Jäger' requirement. A mathematical formula for comparing the submitted designs has now been agreed but none of the submitted designs now comes close to meeting the amended requirements.
• January 26, 1945	Messerschmitt issues a brochure for the P 1107 jet bomber. The specification contained within is then assessed using data gathered from the Ju 287 test programme. A date is set for a full comparison between the two types and in the meantime the Horten XVIII is added to the comparison.
• January 27, 1945	Technical specifications are issued for the 'Schlechtwetter- und Nachtjäger' or 'Bad Weather Day- and Night-fighter' requirement.
• February 2, 1945	The Horten IX V2 makes its first flight.
• February 8, 1945	The Ju 248 V1 makes its first gliding test flight.

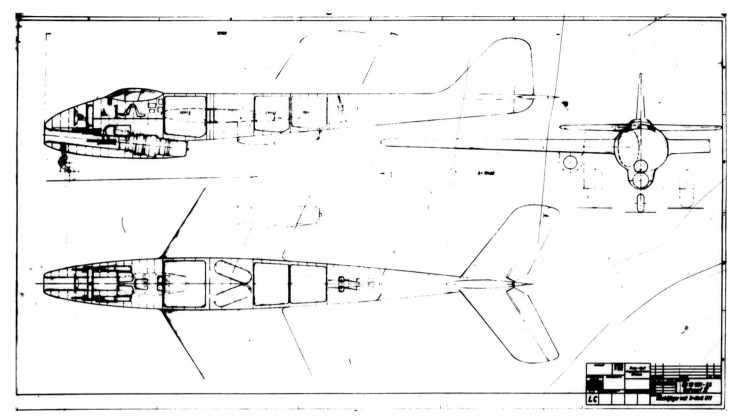

ABOVE: One of six advanced night fighter designs drafted by Focke-Wulf's designers during early spring 1945. This version, Entwurf IV, had three turbojets – one under the forward fuselage and one under each wing.

East. If some sort of deal to oppose Stalin was worked out, the Luftwaffe would need new aircraft to oppose the communists.

As for the designers' work, throughout 1943 and 1944 it was considered entirely possible that a breakthrough in engine design and production might finally deliver the powerplants necessary for reliable high performance jet aircraft. It always seemed as though such a breakthrough was imminent, and the fact that it wasn't could not have been guessed at the time.

In addition, although multiple advanced designs were worked on, very few actually reached the stage where any significant amount of manpower would be required to make them a fully functioning reality. Surviving documents suggest that a lot more time was spent working through complicated equations relating to aerodynamics and performance, and conducting tests on new construction processes, than was spent actually putting pen to paper and drawing pictures of potential aeroplanes.

After the war, it certainly seemed as though Germany had been working on a ridiculously large number of different projects – but had every British, American or Soviet aircraft manufacturer's vaults been emptied in 1945 and the contents piled up in a heap for examination, it seems unlikely that fewer 'secret projects' would be discovered. ●

• February 9, 1945	The first five production He 162s are completed.
• February 16, 1945	The Horten 8-229 and Gotha P 60 are compared at a DVL conference in Berlin.
• February 18, 1945	The Horten IX V2 is destroyed in a crash, killing test pilot Erwin Ziller.
• February 19, 1945	Final gliding flight of the Ju 248 V1.
• February 20-23, 1945	A conference is held at Dessau to compare the Langstreckenbomber designs.
• February 22, 1945	Hermann Göring rules that no further piston-engined fighters are to be developed.
• February 26, 1945	Further discussions take place regarding the Arado, Blohm & Voss, Dornier, Focke-Wulf and Gotha submissions to the 'Schlechtwetter- und Nachtjäger' requirement.
• February 27, 1945	Technical specifications for the 'Schlechtwetter- und Nachtjäger' requirement are altered, making the designs submitted so far inadequate. On the same day, the Luftwaffe pilots fly a He 162 for the first time – He 162 M19.
• February 27-28, 1945	Further discussions take place at the RLM in Berlin regarding the five companies' submissions to the '1-TL-Jäger' requirement.
• March 8-17, 1945	Arado drafts nine different configurations for its entries to the night and bad weather fighter requirement, seven of them tailless. One tailless and one conventional design are chosen to enter.
• March 20-21, 1945	Twin-jet night and bad weather fighter designs by Arado, Blohm & Voss, Dornier, Focke-Wulf and Gotha are compared but the only decision made is that the latest requirement is too severe and that it should be reverted back to the January 27 spec.
• March 22-23, 1945	A final discussion takes place at Focke-Wulf's Bad Eilsen facility regarding the five companies' submissions to the '1-TL-Jäger' requirement. Junkers receives a development contract for its EF 128 design.
• March 31, 1945	Heinkel's technical design department is evacuated from Vienna.
• April 8, 1945	British forces overrun Focke-Wulf's Bad Eilsen design facilities.
• April 24, 1945	American forces overrun Junkers' Dessau headquarters.
• April 29, 1945	American forces overrun Messerschmitt's Oberammergau design facilities.
• Early May 1945	Arado's Brandenburg facility is overrun by Soviet troops, ending work on all projects.
• May 3, 1945	British forces overrun Blohm & Voss's headquarters in Hamburg.

In the beginning

Heinkel and Messerschmitt were rivals in Germany's first jet fighter design competition but where nearly all of Heinkel's documents are lost, much remains to show how Messerschmitt approached the RLM's specifications.

G lider designer Alexander Lippisch created a series of successful sporting sailplanes at the DFS during the 1930s but his real passion was tailless aircraft – aircraft with fins but no tailplanes, rather than finless all-wing designs. When he felt himself at risk of being sidelined within the DFS in 1938, he quickly jumped ship and thanks to an earlier friendship with Theo Croneiss joined the Messerschmitt organisation, of which Croneiss was a director.

He brought an RLM work-in-progress design with him from the DFS, which the RLM was more than happy to see developed using Messerschmitt's considerable resources – Project X. This was essentially a redeveloped version of Lippisch's DFS 39 glider with the cockpit moved from a

central position to the nose and a rocket motor installed in the rear fuselage. It would eventually become the Me 163.

More than a dozen of Lippisch's co-workers decided to go with him and formed the nucleus of a new department within Messerschmitt AG's Augsburg-Haunstetten headquarters known as Abteilung L or 'Department L'.

According to Lippisch himself, writing in his autobiography Erinnerungen or 'Memories': "Now we were a sort of secret department, because we were supposed to build and test the

The Messerschmitt Me 262 with 'arrow wing' as it appears in AVA wind tunnel test reports in July 1942. Although it is recognisable as an Me 262, every aspect of the design at this stage differs from the final production model.

rocket-driven experimental aircraft, whose aerodynamics we had already worked on at DFS. Of course the rocket propulsion was strictly secret, so that the whole department had to be housed in a special part of the building and secured by appropriate positions at the doors. Since no other room was available at the moment, we moved into a large screening room on the top floor of the main building."

The arrival of a whole new team at Messerschmitt, dedicated to working on tailless aircraft designs, meant the company now had two separate project departments – the other being the company's existing projects team headed by Robert Lusser, who left the following month to be replaced by Waldemar Voigt.

Lippisch initially had three tasks: firstly to redesign Project X, which was now to have greater rocket thrust; secondly to convert another aircraft brought from the DFS, the DFS 194, into a Project X engine test-bed; and finally to begin design work on the RLM specification Messerschmitt received on January 4, 1939, for a single-seat fighter powered by a single turbojet engine.

It appears that Lippisch began by writing out a list of potential configurations, engine options and other features and allocating each one a different number from 111 to 119. Then, rather than having his department work through the different concepts in numerical order, he started work on the design designated P 01-116. Where many of the other ideas featured rocket engines in one way or another, the initial concept of P 01-116 was that of a single-seat fighter powered by a single turbojet

engine. The concept designated P 01-111 was also a single-seat, single turbojet fighter but work started with 116 – which might have been seen as the concept most closely matching the January 4 specification.

The P 01-116 of April 12 and April 13, 1939, was a remarkably small tailless aircraft – measuring just 5.48m long and with a wingspan of 6m. A large tailfin gave it a height of 2.715m. By way of comparison, the diminutive Me 163 B-1 was 5.98m long with a 9.33m wingspan and a height of 2.75m. The P 01-116's fuselage was cylindrical and its wings were broad and almost rectangular in shape, with only a slight sweepback to the leading edge. Take-off would have presumably involved a wheeled dolly and landing was to be accomplished on a long skid with a small additional skid at the extreme end of its tail.

Precisely which turbojet Lippisch had received data on for this project is unknown. While Lippisch got started on a single-jet design, so did Voigt's department under the designation P 65. Their first drawings evidently showed twin-boom layout similar to that of the de Havilland Vampire but by June 1939 it had been abandoned in favour of a twin engine design – what would eventually become the Me 262.

The first towed gliding flights of the DFS 194 took place on July 28, 1939, with further flights taking place in August. During the remainder of 1939, Abteilung L worked on a twin piston-engined tailless fighter-bomber/ bomber known as the P 04, and continued on with the P 01 sequence, going back to the start of Lippisch's list of concepts with the

ABOVE: During November 1939, Messerschmitt's Abteilung L significantly refined its approach to designing a single jet fighter with the P 01-111. The rudder is much enlarged, the cockpit is set back and the wings are swept.

P 01-111 being designed in November 1939.

This was a larger development of the P 01-116, being 6.6m long with a 7.5m wingspan. The pilot sat higher up in a larger cockpit with a nose intake for the single jet engine. The P 01-111's skid was improved and a pair of cannon were buried in its wing roots. The wings were more sharply swept, including a swept trailing edge, the tailfin was also more swept while the rudder was enlarged.

Elsewhere in Messerschmitt, the P 65 had reached the mock-up inspection stage by December 1939. It would seem that further data on the early jet engines was received around this time, since the next Abteilung L design, the P 01-112, featured a pair of turbojets within its fuselage. A full brochure on this design was issued in February 1940.

As the brochure foreword notes: "The drive is carried out by two jet engines (Jumo), which are arranged in the fuselage under the

BELOW: Messerschmitt's earliest known jet fighter design – the P 01-116 from April 1939.

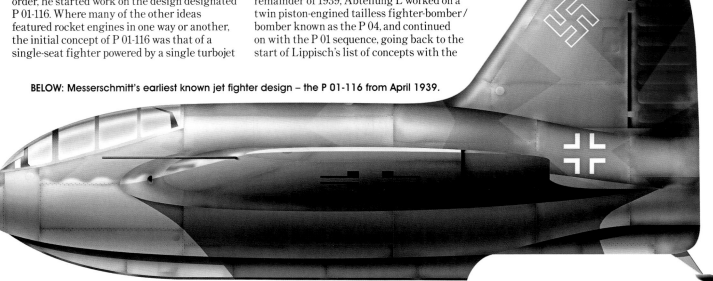

wing. This eliminates any negative influence of the engines on the flow on the wing. The pilot's seat, arranged in front of the wing and the engines, offers the best visibility and allows the formation of an armoured pressure booth which can be designed independently of the static structure of the fuselage.

"A central runner and spur, both retractable, are provided as the main landing gear. The take-off takes place on a jettisonable trolley. For the initial unarmed version without equipment, fuel is provided for half an hour's flight time. The space for armament and fuel tanks for one hour flight time will be available however."

Four weapons were to be fitted – two MG 151s under the pressure cabin and two MG 17s, one in each wing root.

The performance figures provided suggest a clear advantage over those provided in a late September 1939 report on the P 65 – albeit powered by Junkers engines rather than the BMW ones then being considered for that design. Maximum all-up weight of the P 01-112 was to be 3840kg, compared to

4325kg for the P 65. Top speed at 4000m was 1080km/h (671mph) compared to 975km/h (606mph) at 3000m. Landing speed was 125km/h compared to 150km/h.

While the first half of 1940 was spent working on the Me 163 and DFS 194, Abteilung L returned to the P 01 series in July – designing two more concepts which each featured rocket propulsion – the P 01-113 with a single turbojet plus a rocket engine, and the P 01-114 which had the same wings as the 113 but a new slender fuselage housing only a rocket engine.

In fact, according to the design brochure, the P 01-114 was intended simply as an experimental vehicle to assess the features of the P 01-112 and P 01-113 designs – rather than being a prototype for a production aircraft in its own right. The P 01 series was then shelved for 11 months before recommencing with a second P 01-116 in June 1941.

Despite all this effort, however, little came

of Abteilung L's work on turbojet designs – whereas the other team's P 65, re-designated the P 1065, then given the official RLM number Me 262, progressed rapidly towards prototype construction. The Me 262 V1 first flew on April 18, 1941, with a piston engine in its nose because its jet engines were not yet ready. Yet despite this somewhat inauspicious beginning, Messerschmitt had ambitious plans for the Me 262. In July 1942, a report was produced on wind tunnel tests of an Me 262 with a sharply swept 'arrow wing' and engine nacelles built into its wings rather than slung beneath them – and this was just the beginning. ●

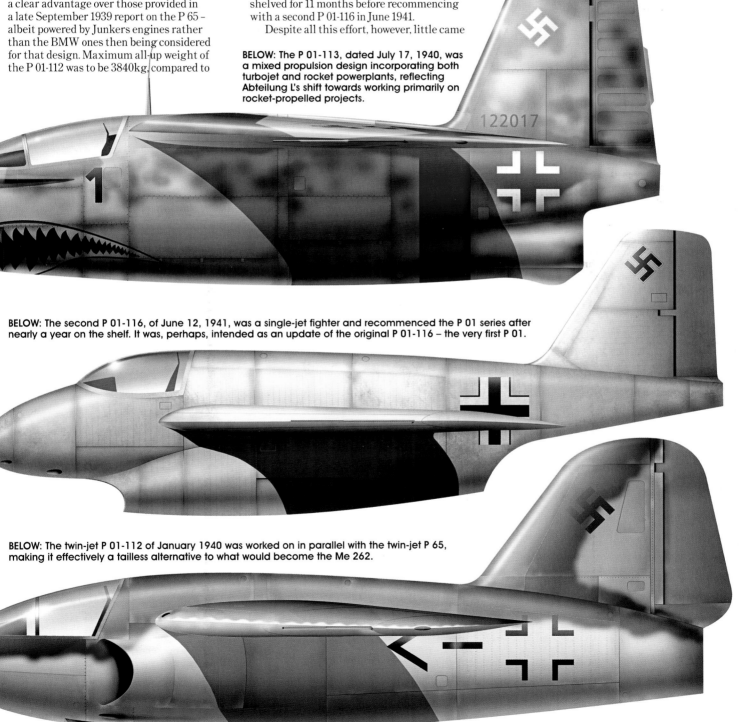

BELOW: The P 01-113, dated July 17, 1940, was a mixed propulsion design incorporating both turbojet and rocket powerplants, reflecting Abteilung L's shift towards working primarily on rocket-propelled projects.

BELOW: The second P 01-116, of June 12, 1941, was a single-jet fighter and recommenced the P 01 series after nearly a year on the shelf. It was, perhaps, intended as an update of the original P 01-116 – the very first P 01.

BELOW: The twin-jet P 01-112 of January 1940 was worked on in parallel with the twin-jet P 65, making it effectively a tailless alternative to what would become the Me 262.

Sustained success

Messerschmitt Me 262 versions

The basic Me 262 design underwent a huge number of revisions before finally entering series production. It reached a crossroads during the summer of 1943 when even the basic layout of the aircraft was reassessed...

A series of 20 BMW P 3302-powered prototypes of the P 1065 was proposed on March 1, 1940, though the production model was intended to get the much smaller and more advanced BMW P 3304. The first full project brochure, issued in March 1940, shows the aircraft as a tail sitter powered by a pair of P 3304s, each mounted mid-wing rather than slung underneath. Armament is a trio of MG 151s in the nose with 250 rounds each, and the whole nose tip could be swung upwards on hinges to allow access for reloading.

Unfortunately, BMW was struggling to get the P 3304 to a point where it could reliably power an aircraft in flight and by January 1941 the situation was becoming desperate. The rival He 280 had already begun flight

testing four months earlier – albeit under tow – whereas the P 1065, by now redesignated Me 262, did not even exist as a prototype.

Messerschmitt therefore proposed the use of a Jumo 210 G piston engine, fitted in the P 1065 V1's nose, bolstered by a pair of Walter R II 211 rocket engines. This plan, with four other prototypes to follow, was approved and the P 1065 V1 was built between February and March 1941.

The P 1065 received the official RLM designation Me 262 on April 8 and 10 days later the newly renamed Me 262 V1 flew for

Perhaps the most radical Me 262 variant was the high-speed HG III, with its two HeS 011 engines buried in its wing roots. Original drawings show it with a normal cockpit canopy and unswept tail surfaces.

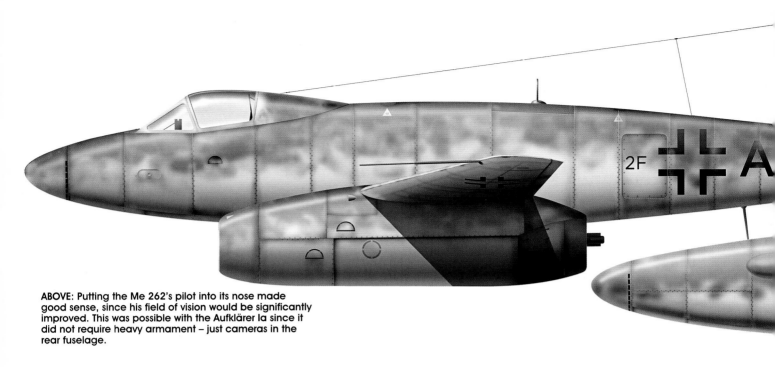

ABOVE: Putting the Me 262's pilot into its nose made good sense, since his field of vision would be significantly improved. This was possible with the Aufklärer Ia since it did not require heavy armament – just cameras in the rear fuselage.

BELOW: The deep forward fuselage of the Aufklärer II housed its cameras. Otherwise it was similar to the standard Me 262 fighter.

the first time – though only powered by its Jumo piston engine. The He 280 V2 had flown with jet engines nearly three weeks earlier.

The RLM confirmed the Me 262 V1-V5 series and also approved the building of 20 pre-production machines on July 21, 1941. Two BMW P 3302 prototype engines were delivered to Messerschmitt in September 1941 and it took until December to get them fitted. Having taken off 47 times on its piston engine alone, the V1 took off again on March 25, 1942, this time with the P 3302 prototypes under its wings. All eyes were on Messerschmitt test pilot Fritz Wendel as he lifted the aircraft off the runway at Augsberg – only for both jet engines to suffer compressor blade failure.

Wendel managed to get back on the ground safely with just the Jumo piston engine but the damage to the Me 262's reputation was already done. The RLM scrapped the order for 20 pre-production Me 262s on May 29, 1942, only keeping the initial order for five prototypes.

Just three days later, a pair of Jumo 004 engines were delivered to Messerschmitt and

over the next six weeks they were fitted to the Me 262 V3. On July 18, Wendel flew the aircraft for 12 minutes without problems in the morning, then flew it for another 13 minutes at around midday, managing to reach 342mph.

The Me 262 V3's sustained success with its Jumo 004s was the first real evidence that all the time, effort and money invested in jet fighters was going to pay off. The Me 262's series of pre-production aircraft was reinstated and it was decided that the Me 262 V2, which had been built for BMW P 3302 engines, should be converted to Jumo 004s by the end of September. The V3 was to be put back together and the V4 and V5, also on Jumos, would need to be ready by January and March of 1943.

On March 25, 1943, a new brochure for the Me 262 was produced – stating in its introduction that it supersedes the P 1065 brochure of March 1940. This appears to be

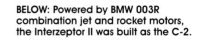

BELOW: Powered by BMW 003R combination jet and rocket motors, the Interzeptor II was built as the C-2.

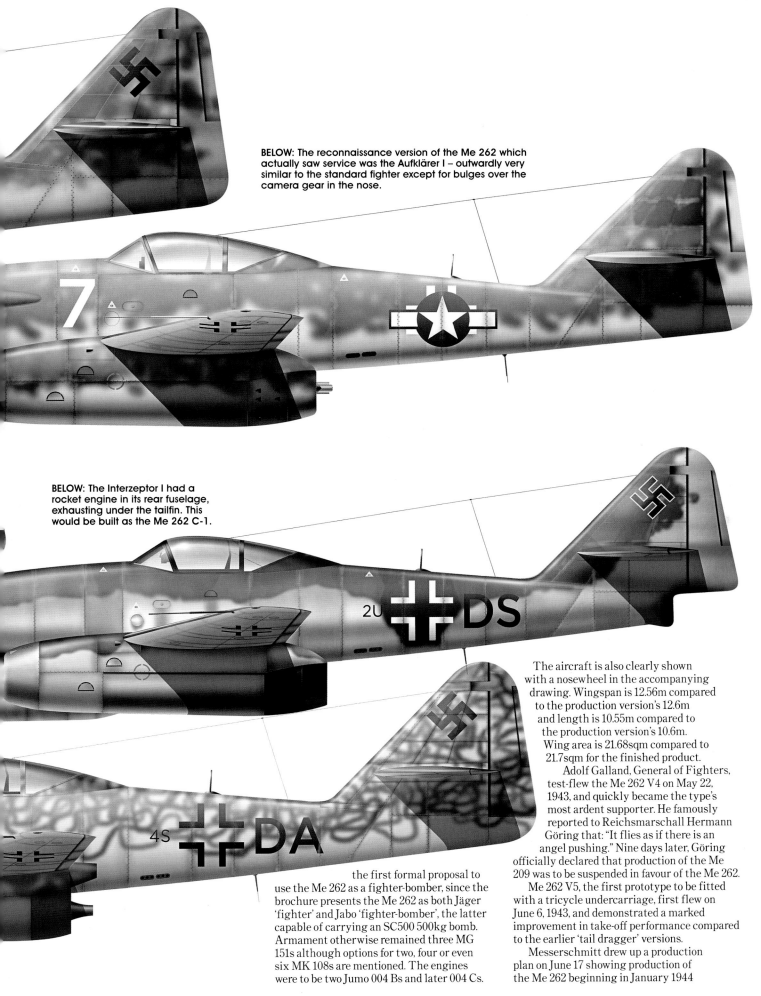

BELOW: The reconnaissance version of the Me 262 which actually saw service was the Aufklärer I – outwardly very similar to the standard fighter except for bulges over the camera gear in the nose.

BELOW: The Interzeptor I had a rocket engine in its rear fuselage, exhausting under the tailfin. This would be built as the Me 262 C-1.

The aircraft is also clearly shown with a nosewheel in the accompanying drawing. Wingspan is 12.56m compared to the production version's 12.6m and length is 10.55m compared to the production version's 10.6m. Wing area is 21.68sqm compared to 21.7sqm for the finished product.

Adolf Galland, General of Fighters, test-flew the Me 262 V4 on May 22, 1943, and quickly became the type's most ardent supporter. He famously reported to Reichsmarschall Hermann Göring that: "It flies as if there is an angel pushing." Nine days later, Göring officially declared that production of the Me 209 was to be suspended in favour of the Me 262.

Me 262 V5, the first prototype to be fitted with a tricycle undercarriage, first flew on June 6, 1943, and demonstrated a marked improvement in take-off performance compared to the earlier 'tail dragger' versions.

Messerschmitt drew up a production plan on June 17 showing production of the Me 262 beginning in January 1944

the first formal proposal to use the Me 262 as a fighter-bomber, since the brochure presents the Me 262 as both Jäger 'fighter' and Jabo 'fighter-bomber', the latter capable of carrying an SC500 500kg bomb. Armament otherwise remained three MG 151s although options for two, four or even six MK 108s are mentioned. The engines were to be two Jumo 004 Bs and later 004 Cs.

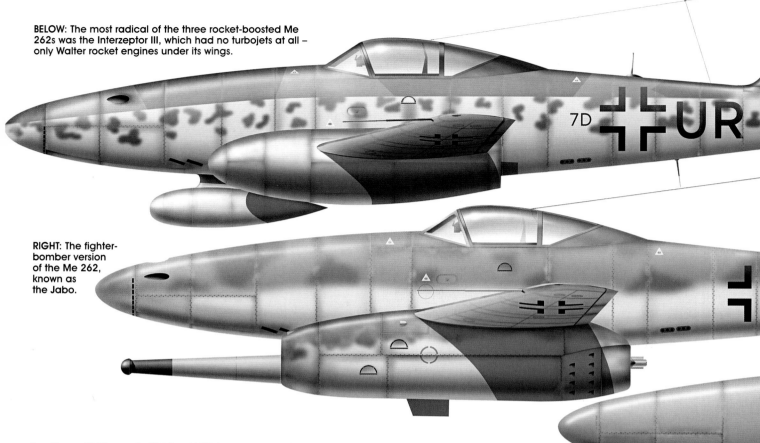

BELOW: The most radical of the three rocket-boosted Me 262s was the Interzeptor III, which had no turbojets at all – only Walter rocket engines under its wings.

7D +UR

RIGHT: The fighter-bomber version of the Me 262, known as the Jabo.

but Generalfeldmarschall Erhard Milch, desperate for the Me 262 to reach front line service, ordered that the first 100 aircraft should be ready by the end of 1943.

Even at this late stage, however, during July and August 1943, Messerschmitt's engineers and draftsmen worked on an array of designs showing how the basic Me 262 platform might be significantly altered to improve performance in a variety of different roles. The resulting report published on September 11, 1943, shows the standard Me 262 A-1 fighter compared against a fighter-bomber 'Jabo' version as before, but now with three additional 'Schnellbomber' fast bomber versions, three new 'Aufklärer' reconnaissance versions and three 'Interzeptor' interceptors plus a 'Schulflugzeug' trainer version.

The Schulflugzeug had an extended fuselage enabling the instructor and pupil to sit in tandem with dual controls. A ballast weight of 150kg was installed in the nose in place of armament. The Jäger u. Jabo 'fighter-bomber' version was similar to the normal fighter but with four MK 108s in the nose rather than six, an extra 750-litre fuel tank in the rear fuselage and the option to carry either a single SC500 bomb or two SC250 bombs under its forward fuselage.

The Schnellbomber I looked like the A-1 fighter but had no weapons other than its bomb load – one SC1000 bomb, two SC500s, or two SC250s. A fourth option was a single BT 700 torpedo bomb. In place of the fighter version's cannon its nose was fitted with a 1000-litre fuel tank. A second tank of equal capacity was installed in the rear fuselage. The Schnellbomber Ia had its cockpit in its nose and

fuel tanks filling the rest of the fuselage. A pair of MK 108s could be positioned beneath the pilot and bomb load possibilities were the same.

For the Schnellbomber II, the aircraft's forward fuselage was made deeper to create an aerodynamic fairing over the bomb load. Again, there was no provision for defensive armament and the same payload options were available. Each undercarriage mainwheel had a second wheel on it, giving the aircraft a total of five wheels on three legs.

The layouts of the three Aufklärer 'reconnaissance' versions followed the same pattern. The Aufklärer I was outwardly identical to an A-1 but had a 500-litre fuel tank inside its nose and a pair of cameras immediately behind that – either an Rb 75/30 and an Rb 20/30 or two Rb 75/30s. The Aufklärer Ia, like its Schnellbomber counterpart, had its pilot sitting in its nose with the option of two MK 108s. The cameras, two Rb 75/30s, would be housed in the rear fuselage.

The Aufklärer II had the same undercarriage arrangement and expanded fuselage as the Schnellbomber II, allowing it to carry a trio of cameras – an Rb 20/30 and two Rb 75/30s in the end of its nose. The underhanging section of the fuselage would be used to house a 1450-litre fuel tank.

None of the Interzeptor designs featured the radical layout alterations of the bomber and reconnaissance versions but each was subtly different to the A-1, being configured for maximum speed and rate of

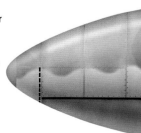

RIGHT: The deep fuselage made another appearance for the Schnellbomber II. This time, the extra metal formed an aerodynamic fairing over the bomb load – reducing aerodynamic drag. The type remained unbuilt, however.

climb with the inclusion of rocket engines. Each had four MK 108s in the nose.

Interzeptor I had the Me 262's usual Jumo 004s supplemented by a Walter R II/211/3 rocket motor mounted inside its tail. Interzeptor II had a pair of BMW 003R engines in place of the Jumo 004s in its wings. The BMW 003R was essentially a normal BMW 003 turbojet with a BMW P 3395 rocket engine attached to it, the latter running on concentrated nitric acid (SV-Stoff) and monoxylidene oxide/triethylamine (R-Stoff), rather than the methanol-hydrazine-water mixture (C-Stoff) and hydrogen peroxide (T-Stoff) used for Walter-type rockets. Lastly, the Interzeptor III was to be a pure rocketplane – powered by a Walter HWK 509 rocket engine under each wing.

In addition to the normal Me 262 A-1 fighter, the Jäger u. Jabo was built as the Me 262 A-2, the Schulflugzeug as the Me 262 B-1, the Interzeptor I as the Me 262 C-1 and the Interzeptor II as the Me 262 D-1, later redesignated Me 262 C-2. But this wasn't where development of the Me 262 ended.

The pfeilflügel or 'arrow wing' wind tunnel work of 1942 was continued into 1943 and then 1944 when a series of three experimental high-speed versions of the Me 262 was proposed. The first, HG I, was to have a swept tailplane, a low profile cockpit canopy and triangular sections inserted ahead of the wing on either side of the nose. HG II would have a fully swept wing and tailplane plus low canopy, and most radical of all the HG III would have its engines fitted into its wing roots. Drawings show this latter stage, however, without the swept tailplane or the low canopy – just the altered engine arrangement.

These designs were a work in progress when Messerschmitt was called upon to further expand the Me 262's CV with a night fighter version… ●

BELOW: Messerschmitt's Schnellbomber I was completely unarmed except for its bomb load. Once that was dropped, it would need to make a very quick exit.

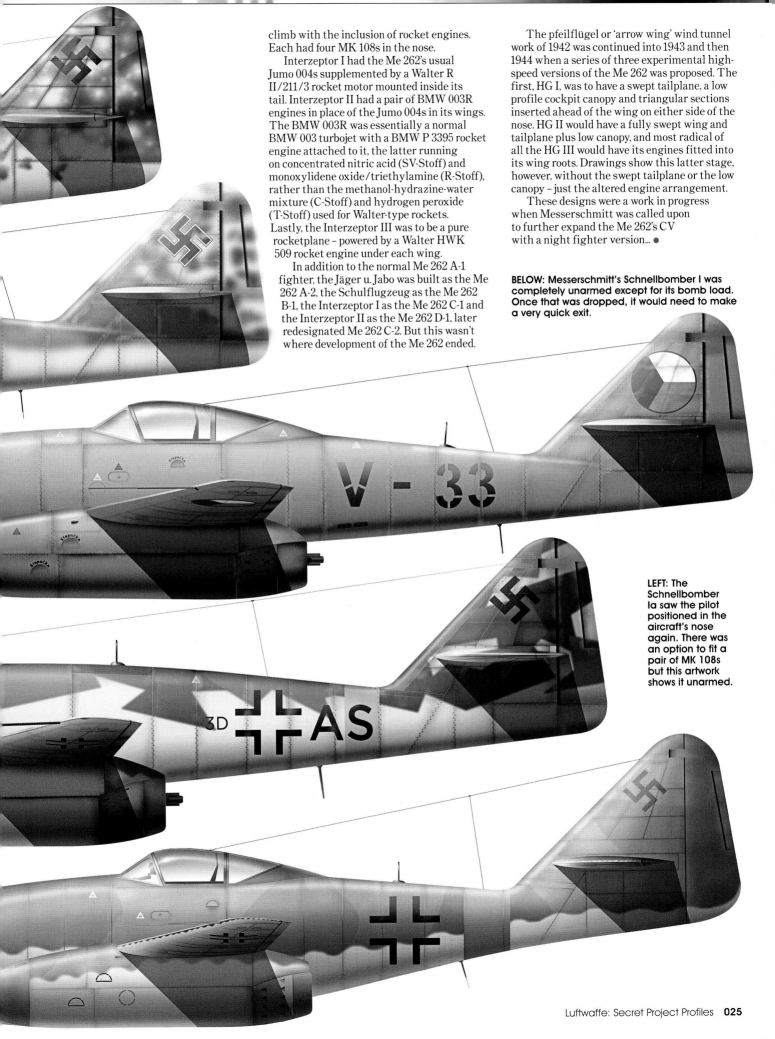

LEFT: The Schnellbomber Ia saw the pilot positioned in the aircraft's nose again. There was an option to fit a pair of MK 108s but this artwork shows it unarmed.

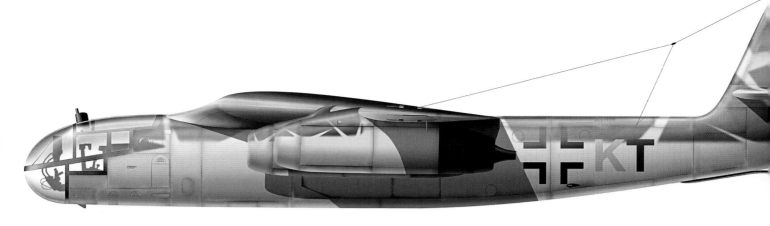

Complicating simplicity

Arado Ar 234 versions

Designed as a simple high-speed camera platform, the Ar 234 was such a success that Arado went on to propose bomber, day fighter, night fighter, multirole and even rocket-propelled versions of it...

While Heinkel and Messerschmitt were busy working on their competing designs for Germany's first jet fighter, a third company quietly got on with the business of designing and building a much less ambitious jet aircraft.

When Oberstleutnant Theodor Rowehl of the Aufklärungsgruppe Oberbefehlshaber der Luftwaffe – the reconnaissance wing of the commander-in-chief of the Luftwaffe – became aware of jet technology in 1940, he quickly realised that a jet-powered reconnaissance platform might be fast enough to easily evade interception by enemy fighters.

He therefore approached the RLM with a request for a jet that would have the range to overfly any part of Britain, up to and including Scapa Flow, and the ministry agreed to have one made for him. Giving the job to government-

controlled Arado meant there was no need for a lengthy tendering process with uncooperative private companies – design and development commenced immediately and a limited production run of just 50 aircraft was envisaged.

The company's project designation was E 370 and nine simple layouts with straight wings, cigar-shaped fuselages and conventional tails were studied before E 370/IVa was chosen in October 1941. According to the E 370 brochure of October 18: "Task: It is to design and investigate a reconnaissance aircraft capable of achieving the highest speeds and having a range of 2000km. The speed should be so great that this aircraft can no longer be attacked by the present or expected in the near future fighters. Accordingly, a maximum speed of about 750km/h must be achieved, the

The Arado design team became increasingly convinced that the next step in the Ar 234's evolution should be to fit it with swept wings and pioneered the new 'crescent' wing-form in the process.

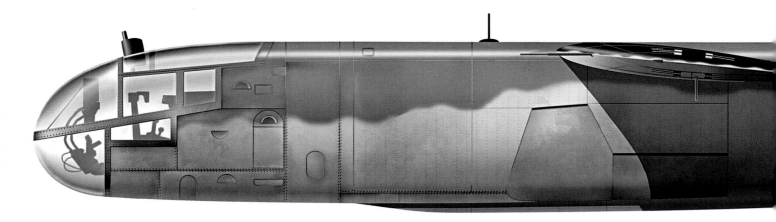

BELOW: During the spring of 1944, Arado worked on a version of the Ar 234 powered solely by rockets for short-range high-altitude reconnaissance.

cruising speed should not be below 700km/h.

"As engines, jet engines of the company Bramo BMW 600 TL V11-V14 are provided. According to its task, the aircraft should be equipped with two camera devices Rb 75-50/30. The equipment with radio devices is limited to the minimum permissible.

"The installation of defensive armament was omitted, however, an MG 131 can be temporarily installed. The restriction of the equipment is enforced by exceptionally high fuel volume in relation to the total aircraft volume. For the same reason, the arrangement of an undercarriage must be omitted."

The 'Bramo BMW 600 TL' was the BMW P 3302, which would later be renamed BMW 003, and the lack of undercarriage meant the aircraft had to land on a skid. It was to be 12.2m long and 3.1m tall, with a wingspan of 13m. There was no particular need for the aircraft to be manoeuvrable or capable of carrying a mission payload heavier than camera gear – it simply had to get airborne then fly as far and as fast as possible before returning to base.

When it became clear that BMW was struggling with the P 3302, Arado switched to the Jumo 004 and on February 3, 1942, shortly before it received the official RLM designation Ar 234, the E 370 was depicted with an undercarriage consisting of multiple small wheels, similar to that used by the Ar 232 transport. Its dimensions had grown to 12.5m long, 3.35m tall and with a wingspan of 14.2m.

With the project progressing smoothly, construction of six prototypes with metal skids was approved in April. For take-off, the aircraft sat on a basic three-wheeled trolley which remained attached until just after take-off, when it was detached and descended on parachutes.

Attachment points for rocket-assisted take-off units were also included in the design, just outboard of the aircraft's engines. Construction work on the Ar 234 V1 commenced in the autumn of 1942, during which time Arado's designers switched their attention to potential upgrades of the design. A key concern was the aircraft's straight wings – essential for getting the design completed and built quickly but unlikely to provide the best performance at high speed.

An increasing amount of data was becoming available from Germany's various research institutions on the advantages of swept wings in high-speed aircraft design, so Arado launched a new project under the designation E 560 in November 1942 to assess this data and work out whether swept wings would indeed result in improved performance.

The Ar 234 V1 was finally completed early the following year with the finished aircraft being larger in every dimension than the E 370: 12.64m long and 3.75m tall, with a wingspan of 14.41m. Difficulties getting the necessary engines, and further difficulties getting the aircraft off the ground resulted in delays, during which time the Arado design team continued to work on different potential modifications for their new aircraft.

The earliest proposal to use the Ar 234 as a bomber seems to have been drawn up in January 1943, along with a proposal to introduce a tricycle wheeled undercarriage arrangement. Only one bomb would be carried at a time though, an SC250, SC500 or an SC1000, which would be housed semi-recessed under the fuselage.

A fighter version with a solid armoured nose and stepped canopy was drawn up during May 1943. This aircraft was to be heavily armed, with three MK 108 30mm cannon fitted beneath its fuselage, an MG 151 under each engine and another two MG 151s firing rearwards. It would be powered by either a pair of HeS 011s or two Jumo 004 Cs and would have a conventional wheeled undercarriage.

The Ar 234 V1 finally made its first flight on July 30, 1943. Two days later, the aircraft managed to reach 404mph during 54 minutes of test manoeuvres and

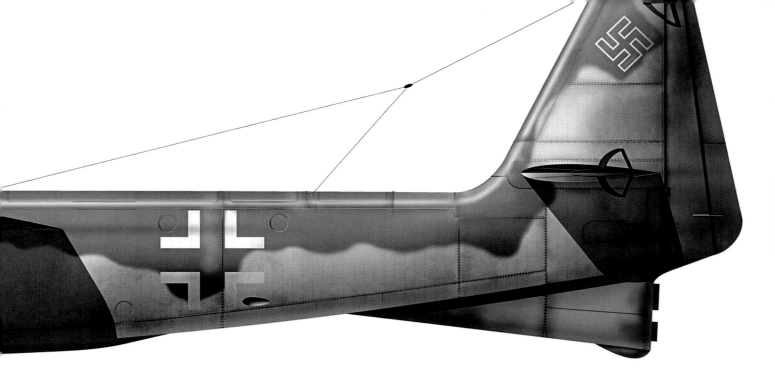

although the V1 was destroyed during a landing accident after its third flight, the V2 was soon ready and testing continued.

As the reconnaissance type Ar 234 took shape, the RLM's interest in the potential of the aircraft as a bomber increased. The former would become the Ar 234 A and the latter the Ar 234 B, while the Ar 234 C was to be another bomber but powered by a pair of BMW 003s under each wing. As time went on however, Ar 234 A came to denote simply the skid undercarriage version, Ar 234 B the wheeled undercarriage version whether used for reconnaissance or bombing, and Ar 234 C a multirole version that could be adapted on the production line to night fighter, fighter-bomber, bomber or reconnaissance duties as required.

With project E 560 having been under way for a year, it was decided in late 1943 to build an Ar 234 prototype with swept wings or 'pfeilflügel'. However, rather than featuring straight leading edges, the E 560 wing had a crescent shape with the innermost section being more sharply swept than the outer section. It was also proposed to raise the wings' mounting point, with contemporary drawings and photographs of wind tunnel models

showing them sitting atop a modified upper fuselage – resulting in a most unusual forward and side profile.

The first Ar 234 to feature the new wheeled undercarriage was V9 and this first flew on March 10, 1944. The following month another radical version of the type was proposed – the Ar 234 B mit R-Gerät, aka the Ar 234 R. This was to be a short-range high-altitude reconnaissance type but its only source of propulsion was to be a rocket motor fitted into the rear fuselage, with the wings entirely devoid of their usual bulky engine nacelles. Landing would be accomplished with the now-standard wheeled undercarriage.

The first pre-production Ar 234 B-0 was completed in early June and first flew on June 8, 1944. Serial production of the Ar 234 B-2, the first full production type, began in July 1944 – following the completion of the first 20 pre-production Ar 234 B-0s. Ar 234 B-1 reconnaissance versions were Ar 234 B-2s retrofitted with camera equipment.

The Arado design team's attention was now largely focused on the Ar 234 C series, with plans to fit the aircraft with a bulbous pressure cabin, an under-fuselage weapons gondola and under-nacelle drop tanks. Other ideas included using the Ar 234 as an airborne launcher for V-1 flying bombs, air-to-ground guided weapons and even the E 381 midget fighter. The final version of the Ar 234 was the P-series, detailed elsewhere in this publication. ●

BELOW: The heavily armed and armoured fighter version of the Ar 234 designed in May 1943.

Blazing a trail

Rocket fighters

The only role that the Me 163 could fulfil was that of point defence – and it wasn't particularly good at it. Designer Alexander Lippisch realised this early on and attempted to design something better. After this came to nothing, and as the bombing of Germany intensified, the Objektschützer competition was launched to create a new rocket-powered interceptor.

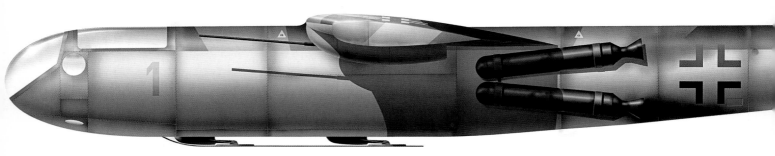

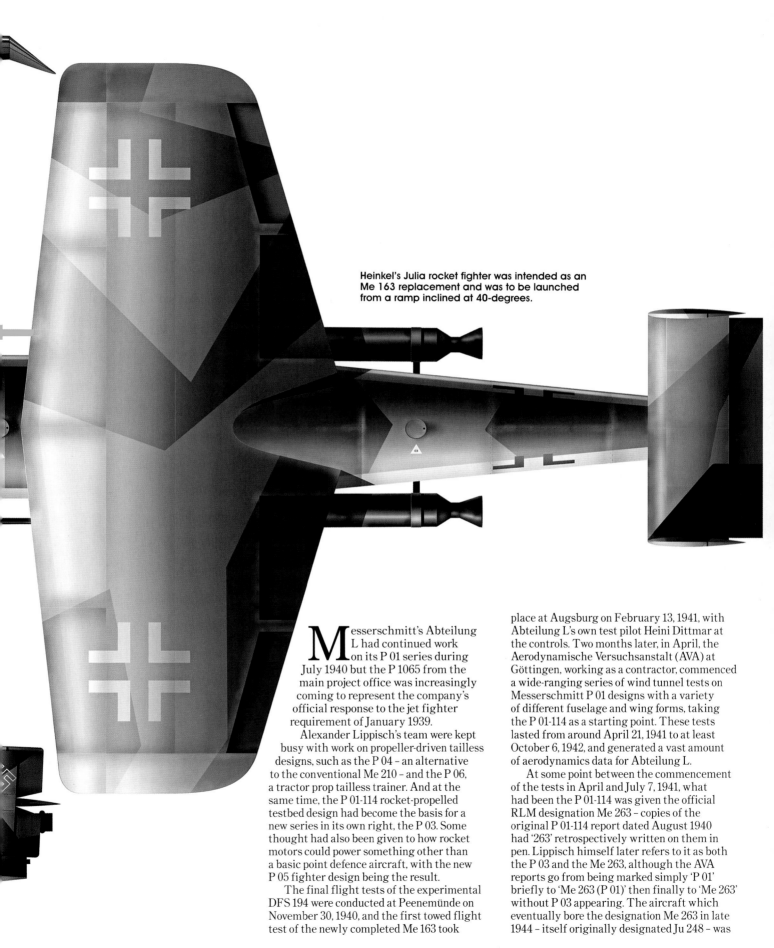

Heinkel's Julia rocket fighter was intended as an Me 163 replacement and was to be launched from a ramp inclined at 40-degrees.

Messerschmitt's Abteilung L had continued work on its P 01 series during July 1940 but the P 1065 from the main project office was increasingly coming to represent the company's official response to the jet fighter requirement of January 1939.

Alexander Lippisch's team were kept busy with work on propeller-driven tailless designs, such as the P 04 – an alternative to the conventional Me 210 – and the P 06, a tractor prop tailless trainer. And at the same time, the P 01-114 rocket-propelled testbed design had become the basis for a new series in its own right, the P 03. Some thought had also been given to how rocket motors could power something other than a basic point defence aircraft, with the new P 05 fighter design being the result.

The final flight tests of the experimental DFS 194 were conducted at Peenemünde on November 30, 1940, and the first towed flight test of the newly completed Me 163 took

place at Augsburg on February 13, 1941, with Abteilung L's own test pilot Heini Dittmar at the controls. Two months later, in April, the Aerodynamische Versuchsanstalt (AVA) at Göttingen, working as a contractor, commenced a wide-ranging series of wind tunnel tests on Messerschmitt P 01 designs with a variety of different fuselage and wing forms, taking the P 01-114 as a starting point. These tests lasted from around April 21, 1941 to at least October 6, 1942, and generated a vast amount of aerodynamics data for Abteilung L.

At some point between the commencement of the tests in April and July 7, 1941, what had been the P 01-114 was given the official RLM designation Me 263 – copies of the original P 01-114 report dated August 1940 had '263' retrospectively written on them in pen. Lippisch himself later refers to it as both the P 03 and the Me 263, although the AVA reports go from being marked simply 'P 01' briefly to 'Me 263 (P 01)' then finally to 'Me 263' without P 03 appearing. The aircraft which eventually bore the designation Me 263 in late 1944 – itself originally designated Ju 248 – was unrelated to the P 01-derived 1941 design.

Having previously been suspended, the P 01 series now recommenced with the first design drawing to emerge, on June 12, 1941, being given the designation P 01-116. Like its namesake of more than two years earlier, it was a single jet fighter. This out-of-numerical-sequence reboot of the series left a gap at P 01-115 which was filled on July 2 with the creation of a mixed propulsion single turbojet and rocket-propelled design – the same day that Dittmar made his last unpowered flight in the Me 163 V4 before it was moved to Peenemünde so that its Walter rocket engine could be fitted. On July 16, another new P 01-116 was drafted – another pure rocket-propelled design that is the only one of the three P 01-116s to fit correctly with the numerical sequence.

A final trio of P 01 designs were produced in the space of three weeks – the P 01-117 on July 22, the P 01-118 on August 3 and the P 01-119 on August 4. The first featured a cockpit where the pilot lay on a couch, chin up and head forward, the second boasted a novel tilting seat arrangement to improve the pilot's visibility during a steep near-vertical climb, and the third had a pressure cabin for high altitude operations. Each of them was to be powered by a Walter rocket engine but only the P 01-118 also had a second rocket engine to provide greater endurance for level flight. From this point on, all mention of the P 01 ceased and the project continued as the Me 263.

Then, on August 13, 1941, Dittmar made the first powered flight in Messerschmitt Me 163 V4. This demonstrated that the concept of a highly manoeuvrable rocket-powered interceptor was sound and also freed up Abteilung L's design staff for new projects.

Lippisch himself believed that a combination of the practical Me 163 tests and the theoretical and wind tunnel-tested P 01 series would produce the engineering data needed to design and build a single seat rocket-powered combat aircraft. However, it would not necessarily need to embody the features of the Me 163 or any of the P 01s up to that point.

With this in mind, on August 27, 1941, Lippisch finally unveiled his first proposal for a military design based on Me 163 flight experience – the P 05 Interceptor. The title page of the P 05 brochure, bearing Lippisch's signature, is revealing: "If, during the course of the further flight testing of the Li 163, comparative engine changes are necessary, the manufacturer reserves the right to carry them out. Messerschmitt AG, Augsburg."

Lippisch is now referring to 'his' creation as the Li 163. The brochure is even headed 'Projektbaubeschreibung Li P 05 Interceptor' though it is printed on a standard Messerschmitt-headed form.

The foreword states: "On the basis of the flight experiences and characteristics test of the Me 163 V4 the present project was developed as a massive enlargement of the tried and tested pattern. In accordance with the intended use, the rocket engine propulsion interceptor achieves the shortest climbing time at the application altitude and on the other hand ensures superior speed and climb performance compared to normal combat and fighter aircraft."

The P 05 was to be the ultimate point defence fighter. It had four engines – three of them, the 'climb engines', producing the same 1500kg thrust as that of the Me 163. The fourth 200kg-750kg thrust engine was for level flying and would give the P 05 much greater endurance than the Me 163. Armament was four MG 151/20s with 100 rounds each.

Lippisch's attempt to have his department's creations branded with his own name naturally caused some heated discussion about his future within Messerschmitt and the company's main project office seems to have taken a dim view of Abteilung L's efforts in general; its leader Woldemar Voigt attempted to have his team's P 1079 built in place of the P 05.

The latter was discussed during September 1941 and the project appears to have then been split in two – rather than have a large rocket fighter that could climb extremely rapidly and then retain sufficient endurance for dogfighting, it was decided to work on a small rocket fighter with the fast climb but little endurance and a large fighter that would climb slowly but have far greater endurance. The latter was to be powered by two turbojets.

In his book Ein Dreieck Fliegt, Lippisch wrote that the Li P 05 "was a true-to-scale enlargement of the Me 163 V4 to ensure the design of an aircraft of known characteristics, good weaponry (four machine guns), and

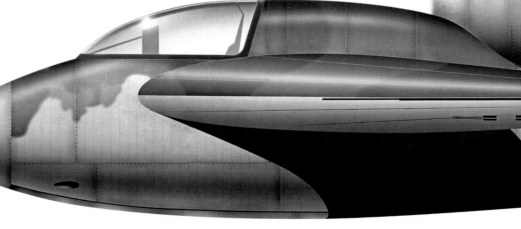

BELOW: Following on from the P 01-114 rocket-powered design was the P 01-115 mixed rocket and jet propulsion fighter, dated July 2, 1941.

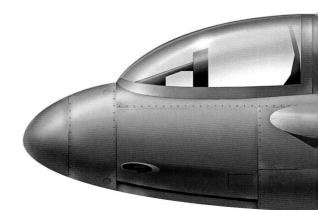

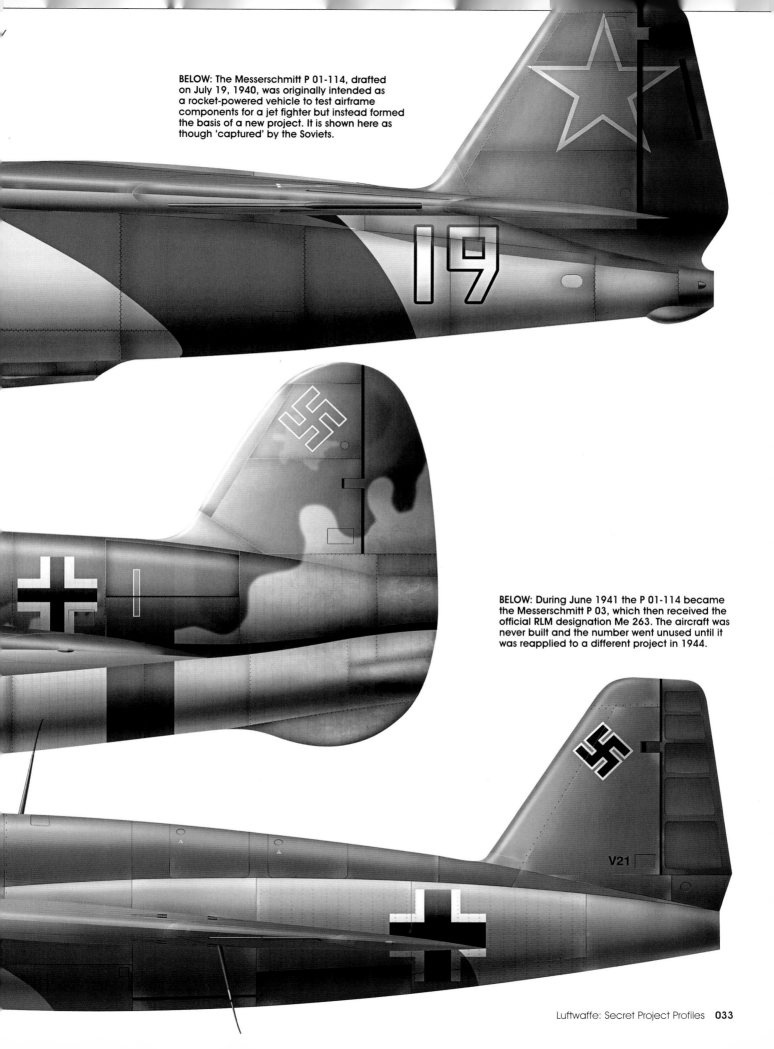

BELOW: The Messerschmitt P 01-114, drafted on July 19, 1940, was originally intended as a rocket-powered vehicle to test airframe components for a jet fighter but instead formed the basis of a new project. It is shown here as though 'captured' by the Soviets.

BELOW: During June 1941 the P 01-114 became the Messerschmitt P 03, which then received the official RLM designation Me 263. The aircraft was never built and the number went unused until it was reapplied to a different project in 1944.

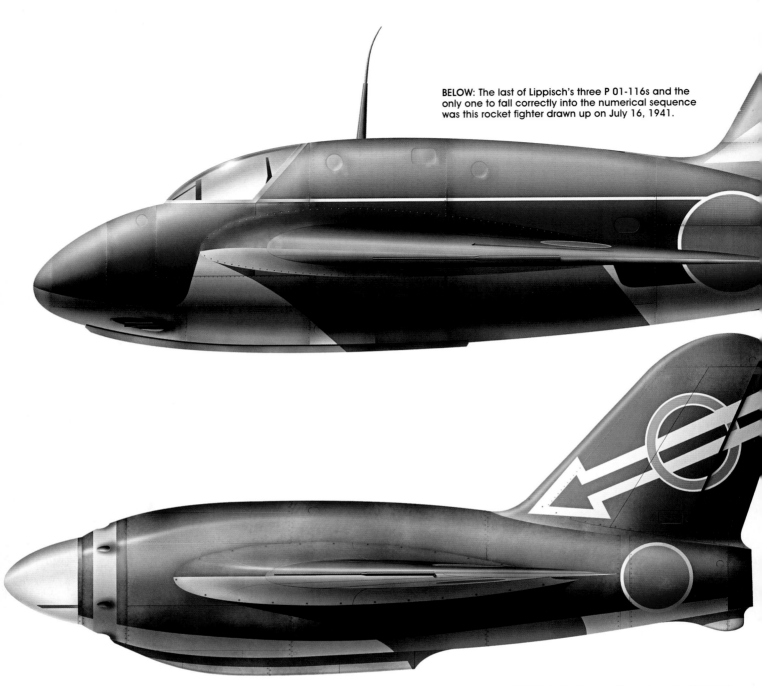

BELOW: The last of Lippisch's three P 01-116s and the only one to fall correctly into the numerical sequence was this rocket fighter drawn up on July 16, 1941.

ABOVE: Following quickly on from the P 01-116 was the new P 01-117, dated July 22, 1941. This rocket-powered fighter featured a prone position for the pilot, who looked out through a blister of bulletproof glass.

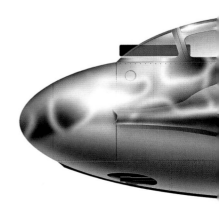

great range. However, since it was feared that in this aircraft of 12.8m wingspan the control forces would be too high, it was decided to return to the smaller size.

"On September 14, 1941, we produced a smaller design, the Li 163 S (S for series production) with a wingspan of 9.2m that was to be armed with four machine cannons".

As Abteilung L began working out how to produce a twin-jet fighter that would offer some appreciable advantage over the Me 262, on October 2, 1941, Dittmar became the first man to fly faster than 1000km/h in the Me 163.

The official first draft of the twin-jet fighter, designated P 09, was finally produced on October 28, 1941. It was 50cm shorter in length than the P 05 and its wingspan was 1.2m narrower. The Li 163 S, meanwhile, had evolved into a more rounded aerodynamic form and been given the designation

Me 163 B, retrospectively making all existing examples of the type Me 163 As.

BACHEM'S FI 166

In a report dated December 4, 1941, Erich Bachem, chief designer at Fieseler, put forward a proposal for two types of rocket-powered high-altitude fighter – a turbojet-powered fighter launched vertically on top of a rocket and a pure rocket fighter. The former was to have a flight time of 45 minutes thanks to its assisted take-off, although it could not be guaranteed that the launch rocket, once detached and hopefully floating back to earth on a built-in parachute, wouldn't land on somebody's house or on high-voltage power lines. The latter would have a flight time of only five minutes and would therefore only be able to make one attack before having to break off and land on a belly skid.

Neither concept seems to have gone any further but Bachem remained interested in the potential of a vertical-launch rocket-propelled interceptor.

Abteilung L spent the first four months of 1942 fully engaged in design work on the Me 163 B, now almost a completely different aircraft from its predecessor despite the name. Lippisch himself, who was increasingly being called upon to undertake management level activities, seems to have had little direct involvement in this work but he did begin to consider what the successor to the Me 163 B might look like. In a notebook bearing his signature and dated January to February 1942, he penned drawings of what he called the 'Super 163' – a low aspect ratio interceptor based on the Me 163 with a short and wide delta wing, a longer, flatter canopy and a sharply swept tail fin with substantial under-fin. Alongside this, he jotted down calculations on what he referred to as the Me 163 C.

It was the latter that became the subject of a full report on March 23, 1942 – the Super 163 evidently proceeding no further than a handful of calculations and sketches. The Me 163 C (Nahaufklärer) or 'Me 163 C (Close reconnaissance)' was a relatively simple modification of the new Me 163 B, with a pressure cabin being installed and the fuselage being lengthened to accommodate an FK 50/30 camera. A small second rocket motor was also fitted to provide a little more flight time at altitude. The aircraft's wings and tail remained the same.

Messerschmitt was thrown into turmoil when the Bf 110's successor, the Me 210, was cancelled on April 14, 1942. The aircraft's development had been a disaster and Willy Messerschmitt himself was forced to personally shoulder some of the responsibility for its failure, being removed from office as chairman of the company. However, his personal relationship with the firm's powerful financial backers made this little more than a temporary setback in his career.

In the short term, however, he went 'back to the floor' as Messerschmitt AG's chief designer and therefore Lippisch's line manager. Lippisch, who was used to operating independently, was suddenly forced to operate within the bounds of the firm's own rules and quickly fell out with Messerschmitt over the design of the P 10, a high-speed bomber. Messerschmitt was particularly annoyed that Lippisch had completely changed the project's

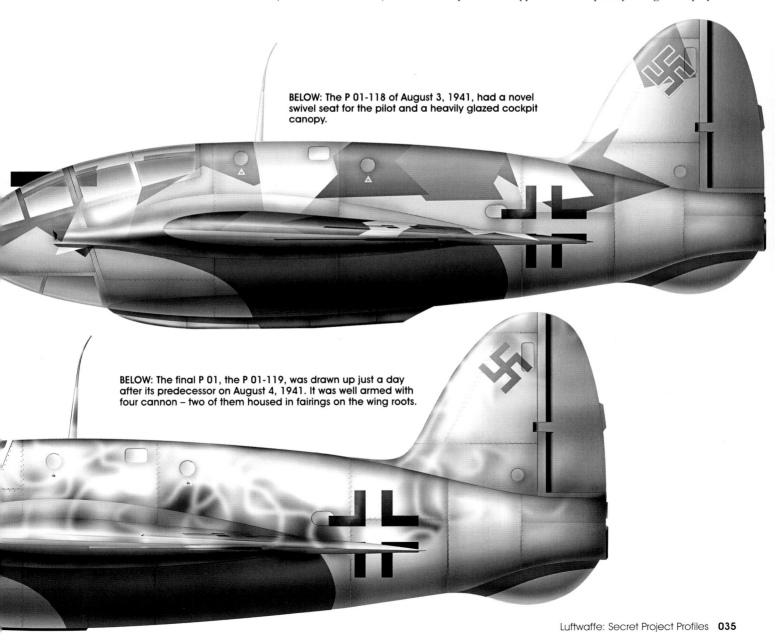

BELOW: The P 01-118 of August 3, 1941, had a novel swivel seat for the pilot and a heavily glazed cockpit canopy.

BELOW: The final P 01, the P 01-119, was drawn up just a day after its predecessor on August 4, 1941. It was well armed with four cannon – two of them housed in fairings on the wing roots.

design without consulting him – and lost an RLM development contract in the process.

While Abteilung L continued to work on predominantly turbojet-powered tailless projects, Messerschmitt and Lippisch engaged in a power struggle which could have only one outcome. In March 1943, it was agreed that Abteilung L would be dissolved and its remaining staff reincorporated into the rest of the company. Lippisch himself officially left Messerschmitt on April 28.

OBJEKTSCHÜTZER

Even as all this was going on, Arado was making its own efforts to design a potential successor to the Me 163 – even though the type was still more than a year away from entering service with the Luftwaffe. A report published by the company on August 11, 1943, entitled Vorschlag für die Weiterentwicklung schneller Zweisitzer or 'Proposal for the development of a fast two-seater' detailed three potential fighter types.

These were referred to as the TL-Jäger, R-Jäger and K-Jäger – the turbojet-powered TL-Jäger appearing in drawing TEW 16/43-23 of June 3, 1943, the rocket-powered R-Jäger in drawing TEW 16/43-13 of March 18, 1943, and the K-Jäger, powered by a 'Kombination' of rocket and jet propulsion, in TEW 16/43-15 of March 20, 1943.

The report suggested that while the turbojet lacked climbing speed, and the rocket lacked endurance, putting both together in a single Kombination-Jäger would offer the best of both worlds. The company's

designs went no further, but this would not be the last time Arado dabbled with rocket propulsion.

Meanwhile, back at Messerschmitt, there was a real reluctance to pursue any further work on tailless aircraft designs following the departure of Lippisch, which meant further development of the Me 163 beyond the Me 163 B was stalled. The company had decided on July 27, 1943, to conduct further work on the extended-fuselage Me 163 C with a second rocket engine for cruising at altitude, but this made little progress.

At the beginning of 1944, Messerschmitt began to consider a new concept – a tiny rocket fighter that could be towed aloft behind an Me 262. Work on the P 1104, a wooden machine with short straight wings and armed with a single 30mm MK 108 cannon, appears to have begun in April 1944. Four months later, a new competition was begun to

ABOVE: Erich Bachem at Fieseler put forward a report on December 4, 1941, suggesting two designs for a rocket-powered interceptor. They were both presented under the designation Fi 166 and this is the first – a pure rocket fighter.

BELOW: While the Me 163 B was taking shape largely without his input, Lippisch drew up what he called the Super 163 – an aerodynamically advanced version of the design.

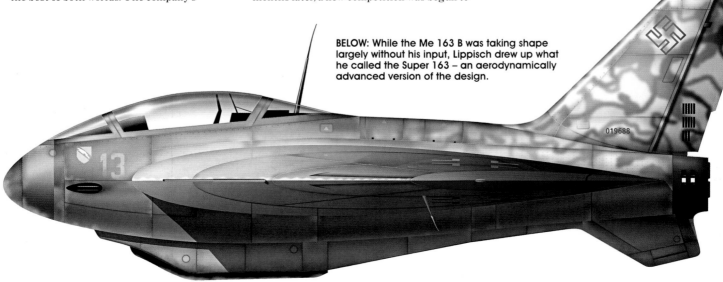

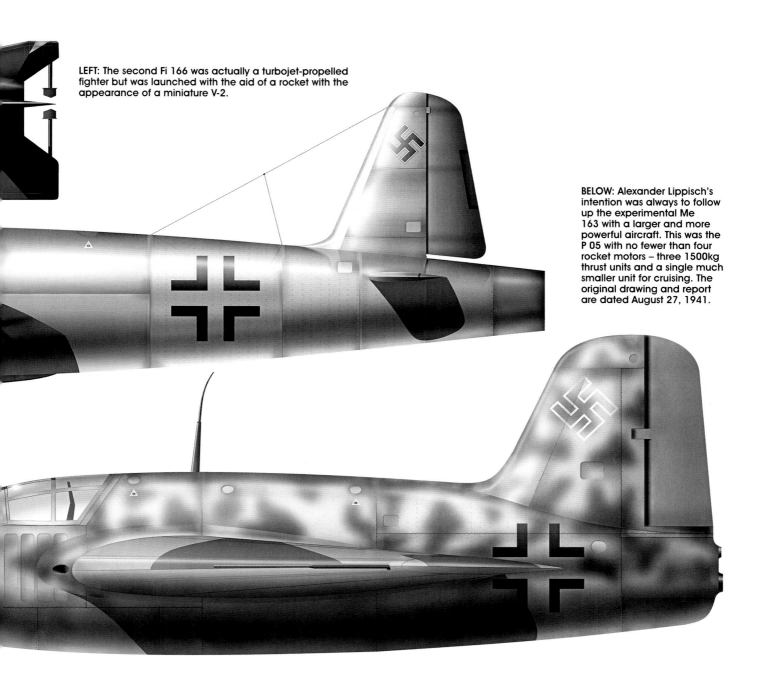

LEFT: The second Fi 166 was actually a turbojet-propelled fighter but was launched with the aid of a rocket with the appearance of a miniature V-2.

BELOW: Alexander Lippisch's intention was always to follow up the experimental Me 163 with a larger and more powerful aircraft. This was the P 05 with no fewer than four rocket motors – three 1500kg thrust units and a single much smaller unit for cruising. The original drawing and report are dated August 27, 1941.

design a direct replacement for the Me 163: an Objektschützer or 'target defence aircraft'.

STÖCKEL

This timing coincides neatly with the drafting of some unusual concepts by DVL employee Karl Stöckel. On August 23, 1944, he produced a drawing showing a 'Manuell gesteuerites Raketenprojektil' or 'MGRP'. Similar in concept to Bachem's Fi 166, this involved a large missile, nearly the size of a V-2, with a very small parasite aircraft attached at its base, barely large enough for one man. The missile would weigh five tonnes, the aircraft 0.5 tonnes and the remaining 4.5 tonnes of the combination's all-up weight would be rocket fuel. A diagram and notes on the same sheet indicate how the MGRP was intended to operate.

After a vertical launch, the rocket would reach a speed of 1789mph or a little over Mach 2 at an altitude of 164,000ft. It would then be steered downward for a descent on to the target 300km away, with the tiny aircraft breaking away at the last moment to enter a climbing turn before flying back to base under the power of its own small ramjet engine.

This would no doubt have been just about the most terrifying or perhaps thrilling ride of the pilot's life, assuming he survived it. A second design showed a smaller rocket attached to a somewhat larger fighter. Two days later, Stöckel drew up a pair of rocket fighters powered by a form of ramjet and the following month he came up with a 'Rammrakete' or ram rocket. This was another vertical launch one-man aircraft but this

time fitted with a heavily armoured front end shaped like a speartip. The idea, it would seem, was to crash through enemy aircraft and cause as much damage as possible before the aircraft was wrecked, whereupon a small explosive charge would separate the armoured cockpit from the rest of the fuselage and the pilot could parachute safely to the ground.

The Rammrakete measured 17ft from end to end and had a wingspan of just 13ft. It seems that the aircraft could be fitted with a pair of bombs too, although how it would have used these is uncertain.

THE CONTEST

Whether Stöckel's designs were produced very rapidly in response to the Objektschützer requirement, or even prompted it, is unclear.

However, during August and September Messerschmitt continued to refine its P 1104 with the option to equip it with a pair of solid powder rockets for extra speed. Erich Bachem, having left Fieseler and started his own company, now developed his earlier concept into what he called the BP-20 Natter – a small fighter not unlike the P 1104 but launched vertically using four external booster rockets as well as an internal rocket motor. Heinkel also worked on a near-vertical launch fighter under the designation P 1077 and later simply 'Julia'. The reason for Heinkel's choice of this particular name has never been adequately explained although it almost certainly comes from the German version of Romeo and Juliet – Romeo and Julia. Julia itself had even shorter

wings than its short-winged competitors, a prone pilot position and a twin tail.

Junkers took over responsibility for building and developing the Me 163 on September 1, 1944, and in doing so, implemented its own design changes to make production quicker and easier. By this point, Messerschmitt seems to have abandoned the P 1104. Willy Messerschmitt sent Erich Bachem a letter on October 4, 1944, advising him to make his project more like the P 1104 and appended a brief description of the project entitled "Kurzbaubeschreibung P 1104 II. Ausf. v. 25.9.44".

Bachem presumably ignored this, having already made significant progress towards finalising the design of his Natter. On October

11, 1944, Junkers produced a description of its own Objektschützer design, the Ju 248, which used many of the same components as the Me 163, particularly the wings, but also featured a lengthened fuselage incorporating a fully retractable tricycle undercarriage. Just 10 days later Junkers was awarded a contract to develop the Ju 248, though not for series production. The firm began by creating two development aircraft, dubbed Me 163 D, out of existing Me 163 Bs – the V13 and V18. These were given new fuselage sections in front of and behind the wing plus a fixed tricycle undercarriage that could be shifted to different positions on the airframe to determine which worked best. The Ju 248 designation was contentious, given the origin of most of its

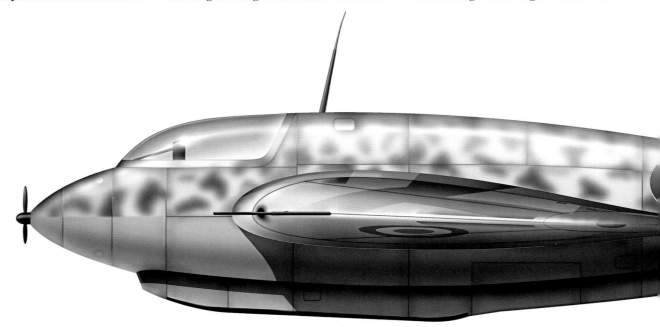

ABOVE: Another Lippisch design from early 1942 was the original Me 163 C – essentially an Me 163 B with a longer fuselage and, crucially, a small additional rocket motor for cruising.

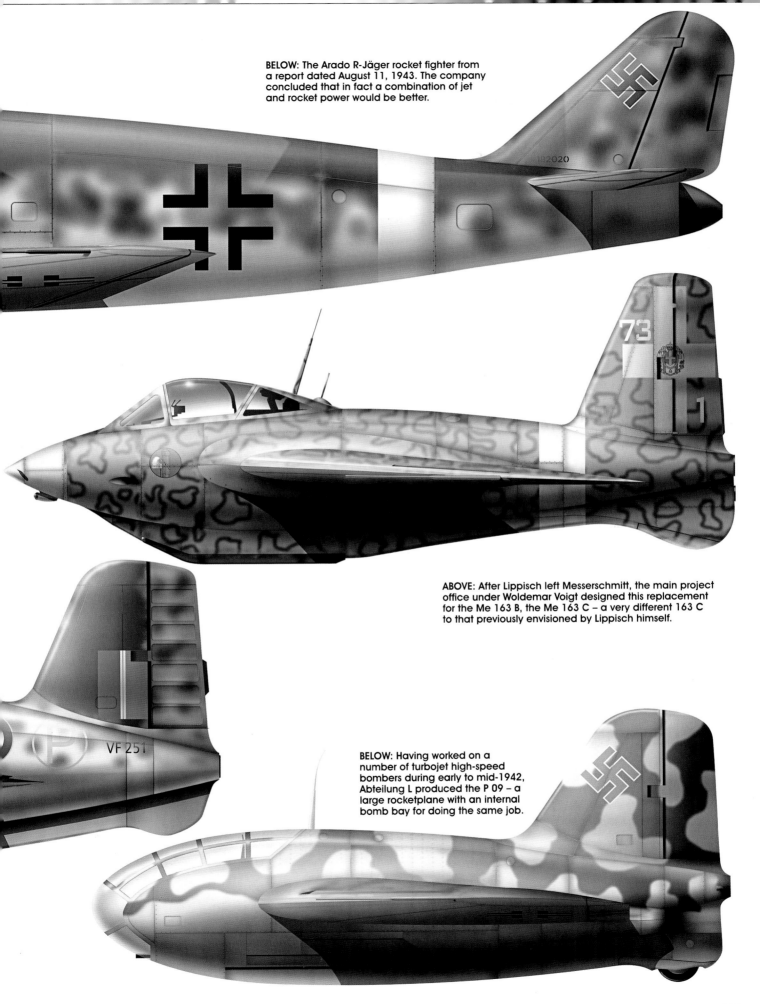

BELOW: The Arado R-Jäger rocket fighter from a report dated August 11, 1943. The company concluded that in fact a combination of jet and rocket power would be better.

ABOVE: After Lippisch left Messerschmitt, the main project office under Woldemar Voigt designed this replacement for the Me 163 B, the Me 163 C – a very different 163 C to that previously envisioned by Lippisch himself.

BELOW: Having worked on a number of turbojet high-speed bombers during early to mid-1942, Abteilung L produced the P 09 – a large rocketplane with an internal bomb bay for doing the same job.

components, and Messerschmitt appears to have successfully lobbied to have the old Me 263 designation reused for this new design.

Messerschmitt also offered a rocket-boosted version of the Me 262 itself, presumably the C-1 or C-2. According to the British report *German Aircraft: New and Projected Types*, discussing minutes of an EHK meeting on November 21-22, 1944, under the heading 'target defence aircraft': "The importance of target defence was emphasised and consideration was narrowed down to the 8-248 (8-263), a development of the Me 163 B; the Heinkel 'Julia'; Bachem 'Natter'; and the Me 262 interceptor with supplementary rocket propulsion.

"It was decided that since these developments were in an advanced state it was not expedient to abandon any of them. A proposal by the Special Commission for Jet Aircraft and Special Aircraft to defer or reject the 8-263 in favour of the He 162 was opposed on the ground that further development and series production of the 263 could be based on the work already undertaken in connection with the 163.

"The four types of target defence aircraft already enumerated were to be developed in the following priority: 1. Me 262 with supplementary rocket propulsion. 2. Heinkel 'Julia'. 3. 8-248. 4. Bachem 'Natter'."

It is interesting that "consideration was narrowed down" to those five designs – it is unknown which other designs were rejected at this stage. Perhaps

the P 1104 or Stöckel's designs?

In any case, Junkers put forward another design in December, which it called the EF 127 'Walli'. This would be simpler and cheaper to build than the Ju 248/Me 263, utilising the wings and tail planes of a Fi 103 flying bomb. During a meeting of the EHK at Arado's Brandenburg offices on December 19-20, 1944, the entries for the competition were discussed.

BLUME'S MIDGET
According to the minutes, signed off by Arado chief executive Walter Blume on December 22, the chairman of the commission, Roluf Lucht "discusses Natter, Julia, Walli; rejects Natter". He also "rejects prone pilot arrangement, since during acceleration head pressed on chin rest and no longer rotatable".

General discussion followed, during which it was stated that both range and flight duration were too short. Then Willy Messerschmitt "suddenly says that he had considered that it would be possible to quickly bring the jet fighter up to scratch with cheap means and to throw in additional material, so that the task would already be solved". General Ulrich Diesing said he "welcomes this and expects further details".

RIGHT: Karl Stöckel's 'Manuell gesteuerites Raketenprojektil' (MGRP) from a drawing dated August 23, 1944.

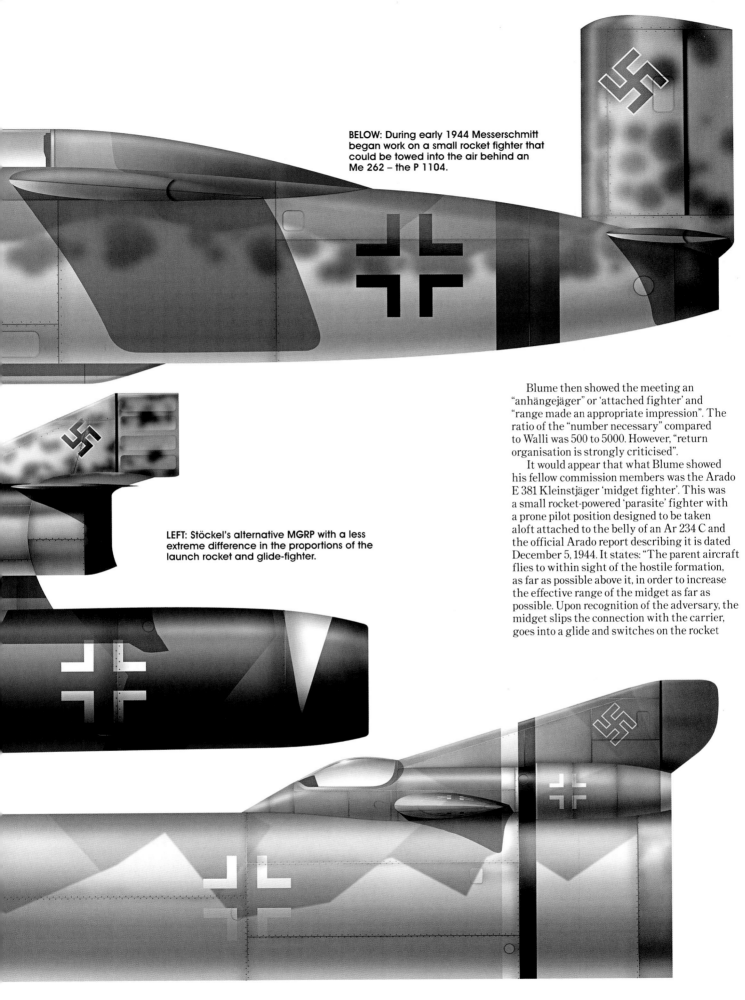

BELOW: During early 1944 Messerschmitt began work on a small rocket fighter that could be towed into the air behind an Me 262 – the P 1104.

LEFT: Stöckel's alternative MGRP with a less extreme difference in the proportions of the launch rocket and glide-fighter.

Blume then showed the meeting an "anhängejäger" or 'attached fighter' and "range made an appropriate impression". The ratio of the "number necessary" compared to Walli was 500 to 5000. However, "return organisation is strongly criticised".

It would appear that what Blume showed his fellow commission members was the Arado E 381 Kleinstjäger 'midget fighter'. This was a small rocket-powered 'parasite' fighter with a prone pilot position designed to be taken aloft attached to the belly of an Ar 234 C and the official Arado report describing it is dated December 5, 1944. It states: "The parent aircraft flies to within sight of the hostile formation, as far as possible above it, in order to increase the effective range of the midget as far as possible. Upon recognition of the adversary, the midget slips the connection with the carrier, goes into a glide and switches on the rocket unit, which, when developing its mean thrust, gives the fighter a speed about 200km/h in excess of the speed of the enemy formation.

"It is so protected by armour, that it has every chance of penetrating the enemy fire barrage without serious damage, and opening fire at closest range from its MK 108 guns."

However, regarding landing and recovery ('return organisation') – it is little wonder that the other members of the EHK raised concerns. The Arado report goes on: "When the ammunition is expended, the rocket unit is stopped, to have an available reserve of fuel on landing, and the fighter glides down. A landing parachute brake is provided to enable a belly landing on a relatively confined space, a carefully designed shock-absorber skid and springing of the pilot's support mitigating the landing shock.

"To facilitate towing-off after landing, the midget should be brought down near some main road, airfield, or the like, which should easily be possible in view of the considerable gliding range of the aircraft. Meanwhile, the parent aircraft will be in a position to attack the enemy in the capacity of an escort fighter. If the operational situation permits, it will endeavour to spot the landing place of its midget before returning to base, where one or more further midgets should be available for operational use.

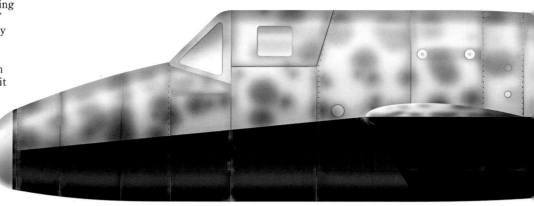

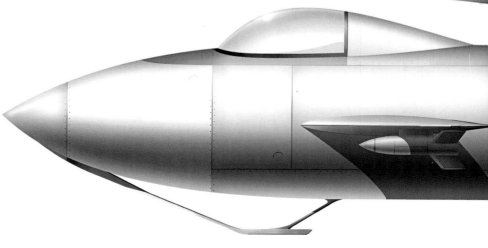

RIGHT: The fourth Stöckel fighter with rocket and ramjet propulsion.

RIGHT: A small rocket fighter designed by Karl Stöckel on August 25, 1944.

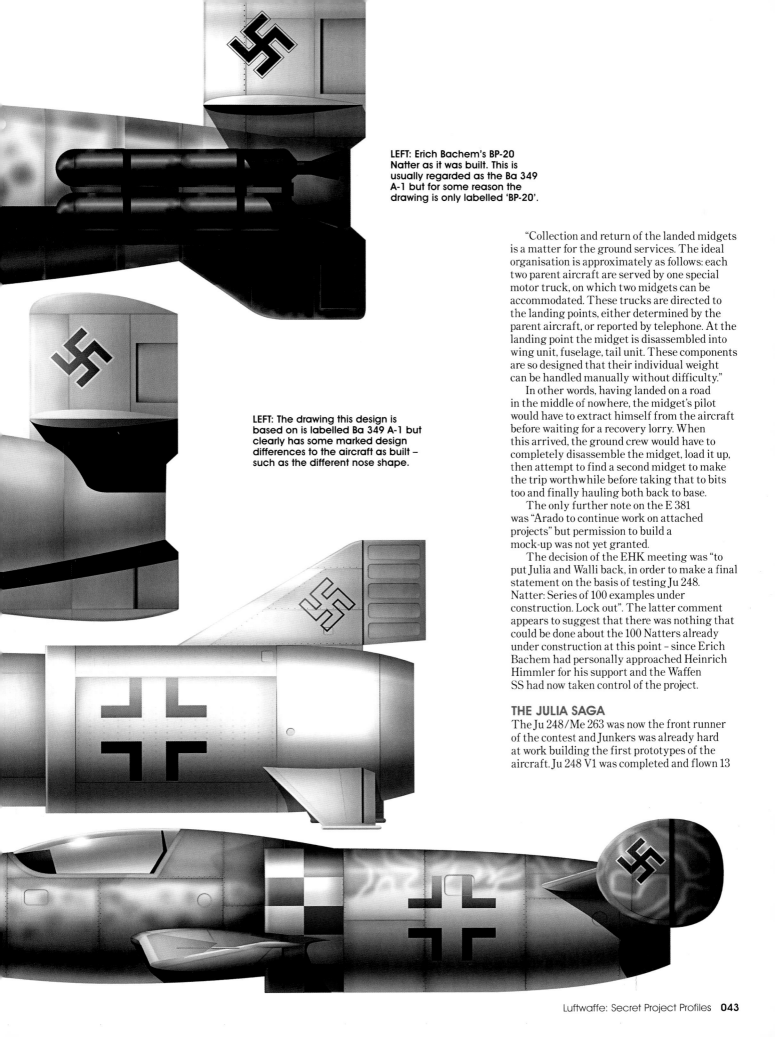

LEFT: Erich Bachem's BP-20 Natter as it was built. This is usually regarded as the Ba 349 A-1 but for some reason the drawing is only labelled 'BP-20'.

LEFT: The drawing this design is based on is labelled Ba 349 A-1 but clearly has some marked design differences to the aircraft as built – such as the different nose shape.

"Collection and return of the landed midgets is a matter for the ground services. The ideal organisation is approximately as follows: each two parent aircraft are served by one special motor truck, on which two midgets can be accommodated. These trucks are directed to the landing points, either determined by the parent aircraft, or reported by telephone. At the landing point the midget is disassembled into wing unit, fuselage, tail unit. These components are so designed that their individual weight can be handled manually without difficulty."

In other words, having landed on a road in the middle of nowhere, the midget's pilot would have to extract himself from the aircraft before waiting for a recovery lorry. When this arrived, the ground crew would have to completely disassemble the midget, load it up, then attempt to find a second midget to make the trip worthwhile before taking that to bits too and finally hauling both back to base.

The only further note on the E 381 was "Arado to continue work on attached projects" but permission to build a mock-up was not yet granted.

The decision of the EHK meeting was "to put Julia and Walli back, in order to make a final statement on the basis of testing Ju 248. Natter: Series of 100 examples under construction. Lock out". The latter comment appears to suggest that there was nothing that could be done about the 100 Natters already under construction at this point – since Erich Bachem had personally approached Heinrich Himmler for his support and the Waffen SS had now taken control of the project.

THE JULIA SAGA
The Ju 248/Me 263 was now the front runner of the contest and Junkers was already hard at work building the first prototypes of the aircraft. Ju 248 V1 was completed and flown 13

times before the war's end. Fourteen production model Ba 349 A-1 Natters were completed, four of them for tests, though none of them flew. Walli appears to have been quickly abandoned, as does the E 381. However, Heinkel persisted with Julia almost until the end of the war.

Lucht believed that he had cancelled Julia in December 1944 but a Heinkel document dated February 14, 1945, shows he was astonished to discover that the company had disobeyed this instruction. Heinkel argued that it had contacted another member of the EHK, Robert Lusser, to clarify the position

on Julia after the December meeting and been told that Julia was not cancelled.

On February 15, Heinkel technical director Carl Francke contacted Hans-Martin Antz at the RLM about Julia and Antz advised him to continue with development. Another Heinkel director, Karl Frydag, had also decided that day that work on Julia should continue in order to safeguard the Heinkel employees working on the project. On February 21, in another document, Francke admits that work on Julia has actually stopped and that the workshop tasked with building

the mock-up has been closed down.

Finally, a document dated March 6, states that Frydag had received a phone call the previous day on behalf of the EHK ordering that work on Julia be continued. Whether any further work actually took place is not known but it seems doubtful. ●

BELOW: Arado chief executive Walter Blume offered the E 381 midget fighter as an Objektschützer at the EHK meeting in late December 1944. Concerns about recovering the aircraft after a flight seem to have killed the project.

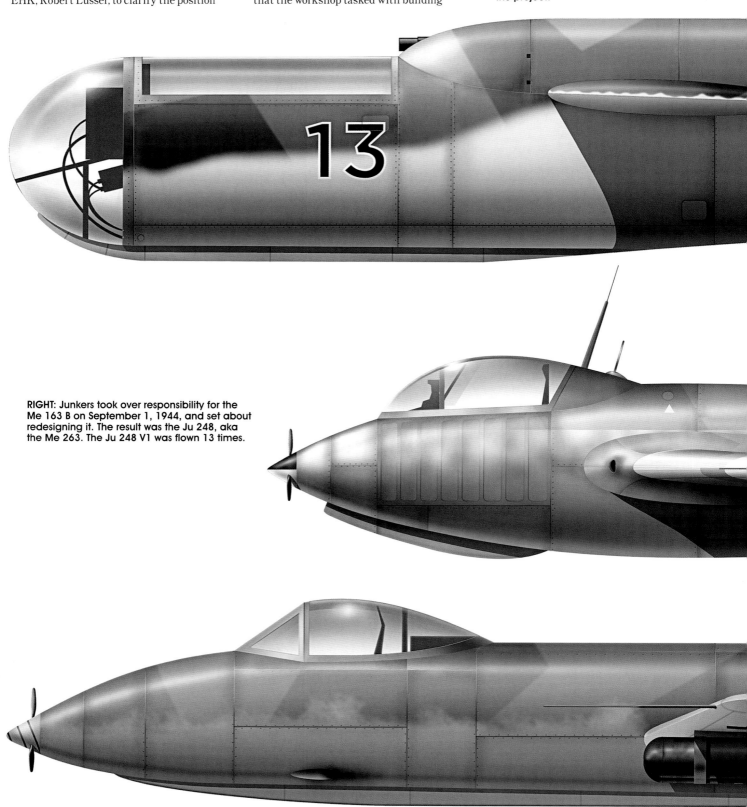

RIGHT: Junkers took over responsibility for the Me 163 B on September 1, 1944, and set about redesigning it. The result was the Ju 248, aka the Me 263. The Ju 248 V1 was flown 13 times.

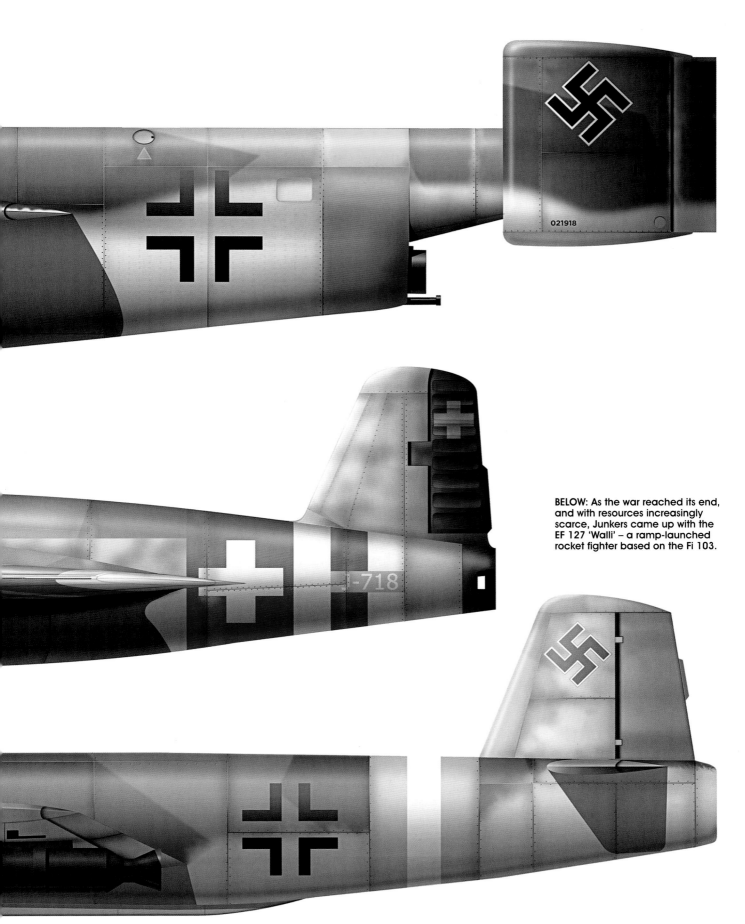

021918

BELOW: As the war reached its end, and with resources increasingly scarce, Junkers came up with the EF 127 'Walli' – a ramp-launched rocket fighter based on the Fi 103.

-718

Make do and mend

The Luftwaffe urgently needed modern night fighters in 1944 and set about developing them from existing advanced designs...

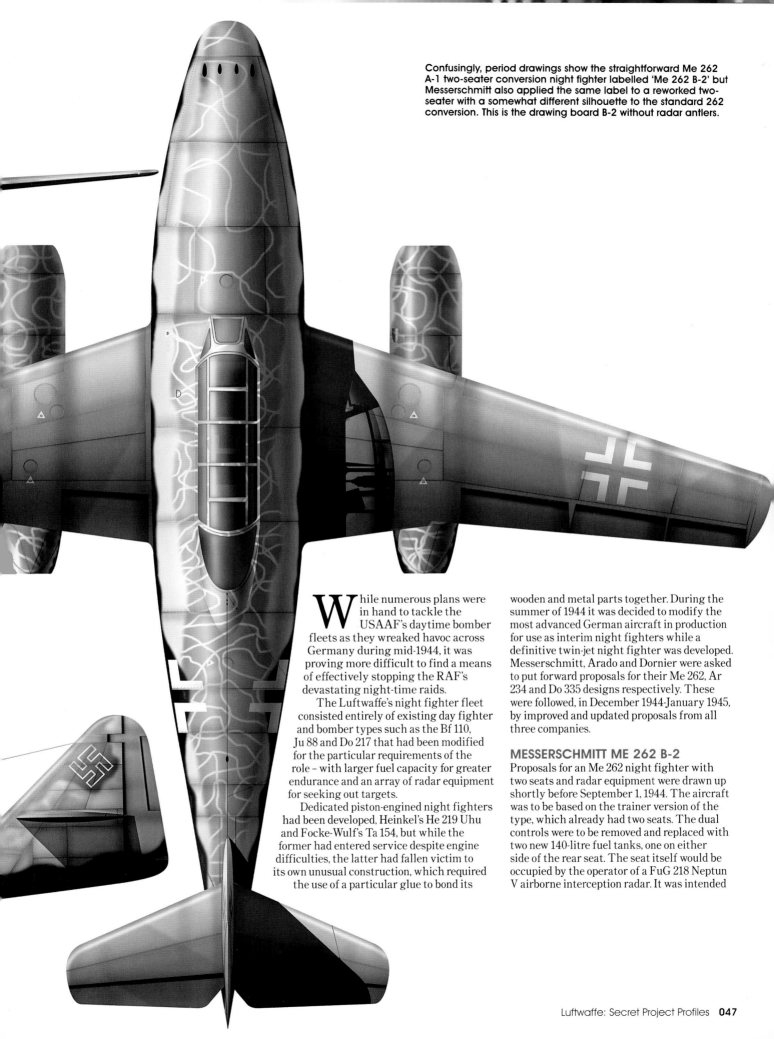

Confusingly, period drawings show the straightforward Me 262 A-1 two-seater conversion night fighter labelled 'Me 262 B-2' but Messerschmitt also applied the same label to a reworked two-seater with a somewhat different silhouette to the standard 262 conversion. This is the drawing board B-2 without radar antlers.

While numerous plans were in hand to tackle the USAAF's daytime bomber fleets as they wreaked havoc across Germany during mid-1944, it was proving more difficult to find a means of effectively stopping the RAF's devastating night-time raids.

The Luftwaffe's night fighter fleet consisted entirely of existing day fighter and bomber types such as the Bf 110, Ju 88 and Do 217 that had been modified for the particular requirements of the role – with larger fuel capacity for greater endurance and an array of radar equipment for seeking out targets.

Dedicated piston-engined night fighters had been developed, Heinkel's He 219 Uhu and Focke-Wulf's Ta 154, but while the former had entered service despite engine difficulties, the latter had fallen victim to its own unusual construction, which required the use of a particular glue to bond its

wooden and metal parts together. During the summer of 1944 it was decided to modify the most advanced German aircraft in production for use as interim night fighters while a definitive twin-jet night fighter was developed. Messerschmitt, Arado and Dornier were asked to put forward proposals for their Me 262, Ar 234 and Do 335 designs respectively. These were followed, in December 1944-January 1945, by improved and updated proposals from all three companies.

MESSERSCHMITT ME 262 B-2
Proposals for an Me 262 night fighter with two seats and radar equipment were drawn up shortly before September 1, 1944. The aircraft was to be based on the trainer version of the type, which already had two seats. The dual controls were to be removed and replaced with two new 140-litre fuel tanks, one on either side of the rear seat. The seat itself would be occupied by the operator of a FuG 218 Neptun V airborne interception radar. It was intended

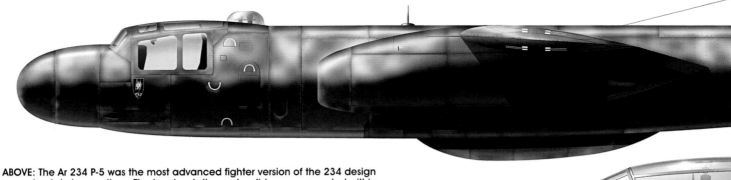

ABOVE: The Ar 234 P-5 was the most advanced fighter version of the 234 design conceived during wartime. The type's rotating radar dish was concealed within its armoured nose and with two crew seated side-by-side up front, the third crewman sat in the rear fuselage under a small Perspex canopy.

that a FuG 350 Zc Naxos homing device should also be fitted.

By late January or early February 1945 work began on creating the first examples of the Me 262 B-2 at the Berlin-Staaken workshops of Deutsche Lufthansa. A number of Lechfeld-built Me 262 A-1as were delivered to the facility and underwent significant modifications. The radar operator's position was put together using roughly finished sheets of plywood to house the equipment and instruments and it is likely that the Naxos device was never fitted to any of the small number of examples built – most likely between six and 12.

ARADO AR 234 B-2/N

The first proposal for Arado's interim night fighter is dated September 12, 1944. It was decided that 30 Ar 234 B-2 bomber airframes should be modified under the designation Ar 234 B-2/N. Like the Me 262 B-2, the Arado aircraft was fitted with a compartment for a second crew member who operated a FuG 218 Neptun V radar. Unlike the Messerschmitt design, the Arado's radar man had to sit in a very cramped compartment built into the rear fuselage with a small window above his head. Armament was two MG 151 20mm cannon. It is believed that just two of these interim machines were produced but it was quickly found that the Ar 234 B-2's extensively glazed cockpit did not suit night-time operations.

DORNIER DO 335 A-6 AND P 254

The Do 335 production process had suffered horrendous delays as a result of Allied bombing – particularly an American raid in March 1944 which destroyed all the tooling and carefully prepared jigs needed for its manufacture. Yet Dornier's designers nevertheless drew up a new interim night fighter version, the A-6, in September 1944.

As with the Messerschmitt and Arado designs, a rear compartment was to be created for a radar operator. This was to be positioned

facing forwards directly behind the pilot, with the fuselage fuel tank accordingly reduced in size to accommodate it. Like the Arado 'back-seater', the Do 335's radar man benefited from a small glazed panel above his head that was flush against the line of the fuselage. The standard aircraft's armament of one 30mm MK 103 and two 20mm MG 151s was kept but additional fuel tanks were to be fitted into the aircraft's wings to make up for the capacity lost in allowing for the radar operator's position.

At around the same time, Dornier also worked on another night fighter based on the Do 335 airframe but with mixed piston engine and jet propulsion under the designation P 254. This was to have either a Daimler-Benz DB 603 IA or a Jumo 213J engine in its nose, with a HeS 011 turbojet mounted in the rear engine position, with large intakes on either side of the rear fuselage to feed it. In addition to a pair of fixed forward-firing MG 151s, the P 254/1 also had at least one MK 108 positioned to fire upwards at an oblique angle for attacking enemy bombers from below.

MESSERSCHMITT THREE-SEATER NIGHT FIGHTER

With work either under way or about to commence on the serial production of its Me 262 B-2 interim night fighter design, Messerschmitt put forward several proposals for a more complete development of the Me 262 to fulfil this role.

The first of these, published on January 18, 1945, involved relatively small modifications to the design. The fuselage was to be lengthened by 1.5m to provide room for the radar operator behind the pilot without reducing internal fuel tank capacity.

The canopy over the men's heads was to be made taller to accommodate the FuG 350

Naxos Zc homing device scanner and the radar operator was even to be given blackout curtains so that it could be read more easily. Radar aerials would naturally be fitted to the aircraft's nose unit too.

Another, far more radical, design of February 1945 featured the possible inclusion of a third crewman – a navigator – within the stretched fuselage and a pair of HeS 011 engines but buried in the aircraft's wingroots. The wings themselves would also have a 45-degree sweepback, compared to the standard Me 262's sweep of just 18.5 degrees. In March, more two- and three-seater designs followed, one with less swept back but more thickly corded wings and with the engines underslung, and another with a similar layout but with the engines once more buried in the wingroots.

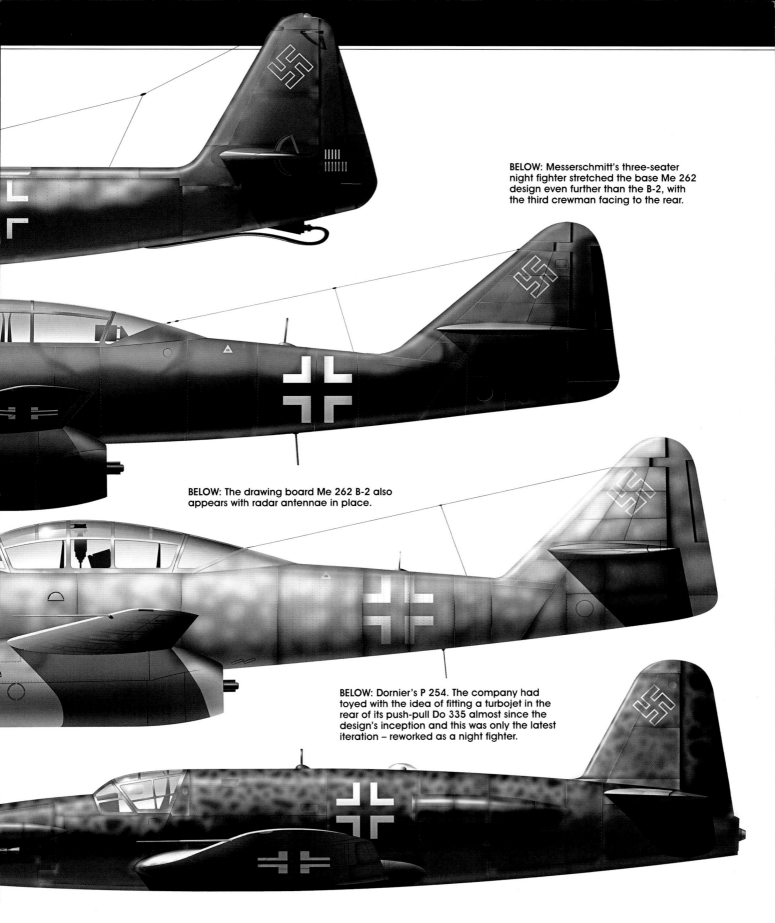

BELOW: Messerschmitt's three-seater night fighter stretched the base Me 262 design even further than the B-2, with the third crewman facing to the rear.

BELOW: The drawing board Me 262 B-2 also appears with radar antennae in place.

BELOW: Dornier's P 254. The company had toyed with the idea of fitting a turbojet in the rear of its push-pull Do 335 almost since the design's inception and this was only the latest iteration – reworked as a night fighter.

ARADO AR 234 P-5

With the Arado Ar 234 B-2/N night fighter being found, at best, to be of lesser value than the Me 262 B-2 and at worst to be completely unsuited to night fighting, the company set about rapidly amending the design.

The still-in-development Ar 234 C series was used as the basis for a new sub-type, the P-series, of which the P-5 was the most

promising as a night fighter. This design featured a lengthened nose, providing room for the pilot and a second crewman to sit side by side. The full vision cockpit was no longer a feature, with an unglazed armoured nose and a more fighter-like canopy above the crew – not dissimilar to that seen on the much earlier Ar 234 fighter design.

The P-5 had two HeS 011 engines and a third

crew member too, the radar operator, who still had to sit in a small compartment at the rear of the aircraft. Armament was three fixed, forward-firing guns – an MG 151 and two MK 108s – and two MK 108s positioned to fire upwards at an oblique angle.

Beyond the P-5, Arado was to design a whole series of dedicated advanced twin-jet night fighters. ●

Hundreds thousands

1000 x 1000 x 1000 bomber

Presented with two separate designs for a twin-jet bomber supposedly capable of carrying 1000kg of bombs for 1000km at 1000km/h, Reichsmarschall Hermann Göring gave each designer RM 500,000 and told them to get on with prototype construction...

The Schnellbomber requirement of spring 1942, which ultimately resulted in the Dornier Do 335 defeating the twin-fuselage Messerschmitt Me 109 Zw to become the Luftwaffe's new fast bomber, gave rise to a multitude of different projects and design proposals.

A key feature of the competition was a complete lack of restrictions on airframe design or even engine choice. The aircraft manufacturers were free to decide how they wanted to meet the necessary specification. During the early stages of the competition Blohm & Voss, for example, had come up with the highly unorthodox triple-engined P 170 while both Heinkel and Junkers had each come up with numerous different designs, some of them powered by turbojets.

This unrestrained approach invited innovation and among the most promising projects - though they would take too long to develop to meet the requirement in time - were the jet Schnellbombers.

At Messerschmitt, Alexander Lippisch's Abteilung L had considered creating a large tailless twin-jet heavy fighter as early as October 28, 1941, in the form of the P 09, drafted by Rudolf Rentel. Nearly a month later, on November 26, 1941, Rentel created a similarly configured twin-jet ground-attack aircraft designated the P 010 but this brief twin-jet series was then shelved.

When the Schnellbomber requirement came along, Abteilung L came up with a new piston engine design - the P 10. This was nominally designed by Dr Hermann Wurster on May 20, 1942, but a sketch exists dated May 17, 1942, in Lippisch's own hand, suggesting that the idea originated with him. The P 10 was to be unarmoured and unarmed except for its payload, sacrificing defensive capability for pure speed, and was powered by a single DB 606.

Lippisch appears to have taken this design directly to Hermann Göring in June 1942 and received a contract to build an experimental version of the aircraft as a result. However, Lippisch later decided to scrap this design and apply the P 10 designation to a completely different aircraft instead - a tailless version of the Me 210/410. This change resulted in the development contract for the original design being lost and incurring the wrath of Willy Messerschmitt, who had to explain to his board of directors how this contract had been squandered.

The friction generated by this episode, combined with the death of Messerschmitt

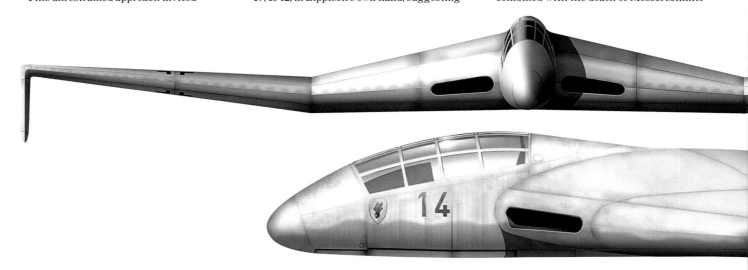

and

director Theo Croneiss, Lippisch's strongest advocate at the firm, on November 7, 1942, would result in Lippisch leaving the company the following year as previously related. However, in the meantime, Lippisch's mercurial approach to drawing board projects saw him shift his attention to another completely different Schnellbomber – the P 11 tailless twin-jet two-seater of September 13, 1942, which amounted to a return to the previous P 09/P 010 layout.

While the company's main project office focused its attention on the Me 109 Zw, which used as many parts of existing aircraft as possible, Abteilung L continued to rapidly evolve its entirely new design. A second P 11 drawing, of December 2, 1942, shows an aerodynamically cleaner arrangement, with the aircraft becoming a larger single-seater.

When the final design meeting for the Schnellbomber competition took place on January 19, 1943, Willy Messerschmitt declined to offer any of Lippisch's work, and presented the Me 109 Zw instead. There then followed Lippisch's departure from Messerschmitt at the end of April and his subsequent move to the Luftfahrtforschungsanstalt Wien (LFW) or 'Aeronautical Research Institute Vienna', where he was put in charge of a 100-strong workforce.

Having taken four trusted colleagues with him from Messerschmitt – Dr Friedrich Ringleb, Handrick, Sanders and Dr Volker – he set about continuing his work on the P 11. Less than a month after leaving Messerschmitt, in May 1943, he produced a 13-page report entitled Projektbaubeschreibung Versuchsflugzeug für Hochgeschwindigkeit or 'Project construction description of an experimental aircraft for high-speed'.

The aircraft it outlined, powered by two Jumo 004 jet engines, was intended to fly at 1000km/h while carrying a bomb load of 1000kg for a range of 1000km – the original 1000 x 1000 x 1000 aircraft. The drawings showed the aircraft equipped with a single SC1000 bomb but other loads were possible.

Unlike the earlier P 11 designs, the single-seater May 1943 design had almost no fuselage to speak of. The pilot sat in a tiny cockpit which protruded from the leading edge of an enormous flying wing. There was a single tail fin to the rear and both turbojets were positioned close together in the central part of the wing behind the cockpit and above the huge faired-over bomb bay. Their intakes were positioned either side of the cockpit in the leading edge of the 10.6m span wing. The aircraft's length was 6.8m.

The undercarriage was a tricycle arrangement, with the nosewheel withdrawing to a position between the pilot's feet. The mainwheels went almost directly upwards into the wing. And within the wing itself were a pair of 1200kg fuel tanks, one on either side.

While the report may have been ready in May, it took Lippisch until September 28, 1943, to get another audience with Göring to present it personally.

THE HORTENS

Meanwhile, tailless aircraft enthusiast siblings Walter and Reimar Horten had been working on their own tailless twin-jet aircraft. Without official sanction, using only their contacts, personal charm and creativity with paperwork, the pair had managed to set up their own tiny 'off the books' organisation within the labyrinthine bureaucracy of the Luftwaffe, Sonderkommando LIn 3, for the sole purpose of designing and building their own flying-wing type aircraft.

During the winter of 1941-42, Walter had presented his brother Reimar with rough copies he had made of documents showing the projected performance and physical dimensions of the Junkers Jumo 004 turbojet being developed by Dr Anselm Franz at Dessau. And what was more, Walter believed he might be able to lay his hands on some of these engines.

The pair considered what sort of aircraft might be propelled by these engines and

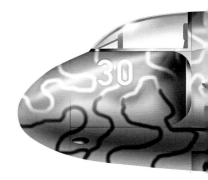

RIGHT: Abteilung L's P 09 fighter of October 28, 1941, marks the first appearance of what was to become Alexander Lippisch's distinctive tailless twin-jet layout.

BELOW: The P 09 and 010 may have established the form, but the two-seater P 11 of September 13, 1942, began the series that would become the original '1000 x 1000 x 1000' bomber.

RIGHT: The P 11 of December 2, 1942, considerably refined the design – with the cockpit now projecting ahead of the aircraft rather than being mounted within it.

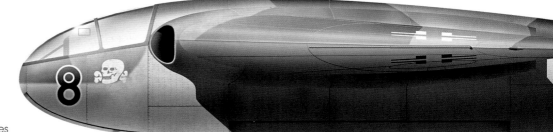

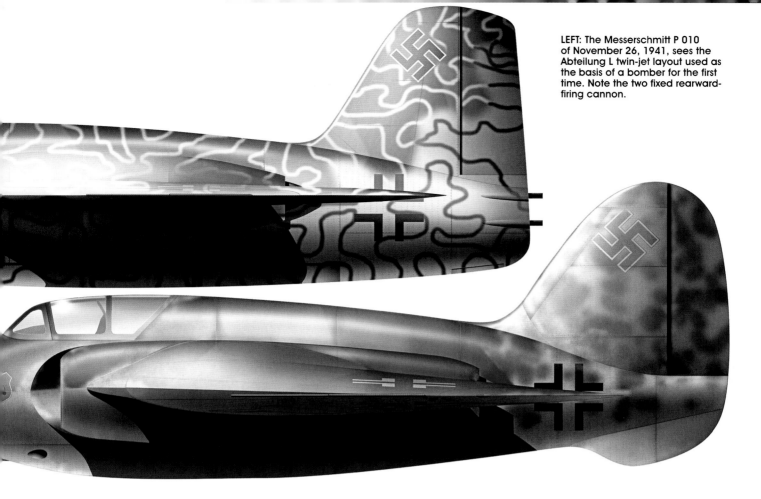

LEFT: The Messerschmitt P 010 of November 26, 1941, sees the Abteilung L twin-jet layout used as the basis of a bomber for the first time. Note the two fixed rearward-firing cannon.

initially thought about putting a single turbojet into their piston-engined H VII flying wing design. However, it soon became clear that an entirely new aircraft was needed. The brothers therefore began work on what they designated the H IX. This would be a flying wing, like most of the brothers' other designs, but the question remained – where to put the engines? Eventually it was decided that they should be entirely buried within the wing, with their intakes on the leading edge and exhausting over the trailing edge.

The H IX design evolved during the course of 1942 and into 1943 but disaster struck in spring 1943 when the RLM evidently realised something fishy was going on and ordered that Sonderkommando LIn 3 be disbanded.

Thinking quickly, the brothers managed to give the impression that the order had been obeyed by 'dispersing' rather than actually disbanding Sonderkommando LIn 3.

In March 1943, Walter attended a speech made to aviation industry leaders by Hermann Göring where he called for an aircraft that could carry 1000kg of bombs 1000km with a maximum speed of 1000km/h. This appeared to be the opportunity that the brothers had been hoping for. If they could massage the H IX design a little to meet this specification, at least in part, they might have an opportunity to secure a development contract.

Unable to meet the 1000/1000/1000 spec, they managed to come up with calculations showing a speed of 950km/h, a range of 700km and a payload of 2000kg. Walter worked his contacts once again and managed to get a 20-page design proposal to General Diesing. Diesing apparently passed this on to Göring and a meeting was arranged for September 28, 1943.

THE BIG MEETINGS

TLR documentation shows that Göring met Lippisch concerning the P 11 from 3.45pm to 4pm on the 28th, then met the Hortens about their H IX from 4pm to 4.20pm on the same day.

During the first meeting, according to the minutes, "Prof Lippisch reports that he left the Messerschmitt company and that he is currently working on a new project on behalf of the research leadership of the Luftwaffe in the Vienna Research Institute. Task: Lippisch fast-attack aircraft, shell construction, two Jumo jet engines. Project capabilities: 1000kg bombs, 1000km/h speed, 3000km flight

distance [1000km to the target, 1000km back, with a 1000km margin for manoeuvring and safety]. V1 should fly in June 1944. Apart from normal teething troubles Lippisch does not expect major difficulties despite the three fundamental innovations (jet engine, all-wing design, plastic-wood construction). If the level of urgency, which is currently set at RM 30,000, is increased to approximately RM 500,000, Lippisch believes that the test pattern can fly as early as February. Apart from the increased extent of urgency, Prof Lippisch has no wishes at the moment.

"When questioned by Herr Reichsmarschall why his project did not come to fruition earlier, Lippisch reports that in earlier times there was strong resistance to all-wing projects, especially by General-Ing. Reidenbach and Stabs-Ing. Friebel. Lippisch traces these resistances ideologically back partly to the old rivalry of the Akaflieg against the Rhönflieger. Herr Reichsmarschall shows an extraordinary interest in the project of Prof Lippisch and gives his full support to Prof Lippisch for the construction of his test samples. He wishes that the urgent request of Prof Lippisch be met by the Generalluftzeugmeister [Erhard Milch] after a factual examination as soon as possible."

It is unknown whether Lippisch crossed paths with the Hortens on the way out but the next meeting then started. The minutes state: "Herr Reichsmarschall has Hauptmann [Walter] Horten present his work on the basis of photographic material and asks about the new projects. Hauptmann Horten reports that he has an arrangement with the Peschke company, where there are currently three twin-engine propeller-driven trainer

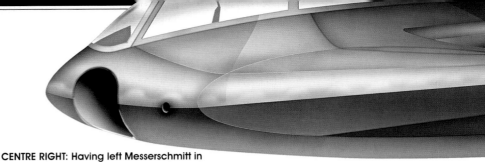

aircraft of all-wing construction running. Awia and the local designer Kaupa has been included on the orders of the general.

"In the opinion of Hauptmann Horten, however, neither this company nor the designer Kaupa is suitable for cooperation, since the construction system Kaupa (crosswise welded tubular spar) is not suitable for a shell construction of a high-speed aircraft."

Horten told Göring that he would rather have the construction work done at Peschke. Then "at the request of Herr Reichsmarschall, as to whether a fighter or combat aircraft in all-wing construction was being worked on, Hauptmann Horten reports that at present he is running a project for a fighter jet (fighter-bomber), which he builds in a road maintenance centre near Göttingen. It is to have two Jumo jets, 1000kg bombs, 950km/h speed with a flight distance of 1500km. The first V-pattern will be finished without engines in February as a towed glider, be equipped with an engine in June and from August 1944 also have full equipment.

"An order from the RLM for this aircraft has not yet been issued. The aircraft is well suited for a large series in the opinion of Hauptmann Horten because of its simple mixed construction method, which requires only small tooling capacity. At the request of the Reichsmarschall, Hauptmann Horten reports that his work has received little support from the Technical Office [of the RLM], that in between the work was interrupted by order of the Office, and that in the past especially General-Ing. Reidenbach and Stabs-Ing. Friebel have pronounced against the all-wing construction.

"Hauptmann Horten, in his opinion, could also considerably speed up his work if he receives a corresponding urgency to procure the necessary material. In addition, Hauptmann Horten asks for the assignment of his designated soldiers who are currently referred to by the military as indispensable. Hauptmann Horten also asks for his command to be issued with a budget and clear referrals to ensure that soldiers who have made a valuable contribution to his service are not left behind in promotions and awards.

"Herr Reichsmarschall thanks the Horten brothers for their research and development work and assures them of full support for their further work. In conclusion, Herr Reichsmarschall states that, in his view, there has not been sufficient attention in the past in the direction of the development of all-wing aircraft, in particular the swept-wing, and that this area must be more closely respected by the Generalluftzeugmeister."

It is not recorded in the minutes, but speaking years later Reimar said Erhard Milch had given Walter the order for the construction of the H IX, although it had come from Göring: "Milch drew up all the paperwork for the transfer of the RM 500,000 grant from Göring. Milch asked us who should this contract be made out to? Hauptmann Horten or what? Walter paused and told Milch that he was not sure, however he would return in a day or two with the correct information. Before going back to Milch, we incorporated ourselves and called our new company the Horten Company for Aircraft Design or the Horten Flugzeugbau."

CENTRE RIGHT: Having left Messerschmitt in April 1943, Lippisch produced this design in May 1943 – a new P 11 with an enormous aerodynamic belly fairing to cover a single 1000kg bomb.

THE H IX AND 8-229

With a million Reichsmarks between them, Lippisch and the Hortens set about building their prototypes. The unpowered H IX V1 was ready on March 1, 1944 – albeit with a Heinkel He 177 tail wheel assembly as its nosewheel, main landing gear wheels from a Messerschmitt Bf 109 G, components from a captured B-24 Liberator and other assorted bits and pieces from a damaged Me 210. Bad weather delayed its first flight but on March 5, 1944, it was towed up to 3600m by an He 111 before gliding back down to the runway. On touching down the pilot found he was unable to brake effectively on the icy runway. In order to avoid collision with a hangar, he deliberately retracted the nosewheel, putting the skidding aircraft's nose on to the ground.

More tests followed on March 23 and April 5. During the latter, the nosewheel failed and repairs led to further delays.

When it came to building the powered H IX V2, Reimar discovered that with all the necessary accessories added to their exterior, the engines were actually 20cm greater in diameter than he had planned for, necessitating a redesign. The original plan had called for the V2 to be flown for the first time on June 1, 1944, but work was still ongoing as this deadline passed. The RLM placed an order with Horten Flugzeugbau for a number of further prototype H IXs on June 15 with the new type designation 8-229.

Horten Flugzeugbau, however, did not have the facilities or the manpower to build more than the one airframe it was then working on so Gotha was engaged as a subcontractor to build the 8-229 V3 to V6. During this work, Gotha's aerodynamics specialist Rudolf Göthert decided that the original Horten design was irredeemably flawed and designed his own alternative – the Gotha P-60, which had its two crew in prone positions in a glazed cockpit built into the leading edge of the aircraft's wing. The two turbojets were positioned one above and one below the wing/fuselage.

Horten Flugzeugbau was still struggling to complete the H IX V2 by November 1944 but on December 17, 1944, it was declared ready to fly and was transported by rail from Göttingen to Oranienburg, just north of Berlin, for flight testing.

The designated pilot, Erwin Ziller, received twin-engine jet flight training in a two-seat Me 262 B-1 on December 29-31 but apparently was not shown the proper procedure for starting the Jumo 004 engines. Testing was halted while the Horten brothers travelled back to Bonn to spend Christmas with their parents and during January Gotha

ABOVE: The later P 11/Delta – now fitted with a huge underslung cannon. The precise specification of this weapon is not made clear on the original drawing, dated October 21, 1944.

appears to have slowed or even halted its programme of work on the V3, V4, V5 and V6. Göthert was certainly working on his P-60 designs and it is possible that the rest of the company was fully occupied with gearing up for and then commencing mass production of wings for the Heinkel He 162.

Ziller finally took the 8-229 V2 up for its first powered flight on February 2, 1945, having had the aircraft's engines started for him by another member of the Horten

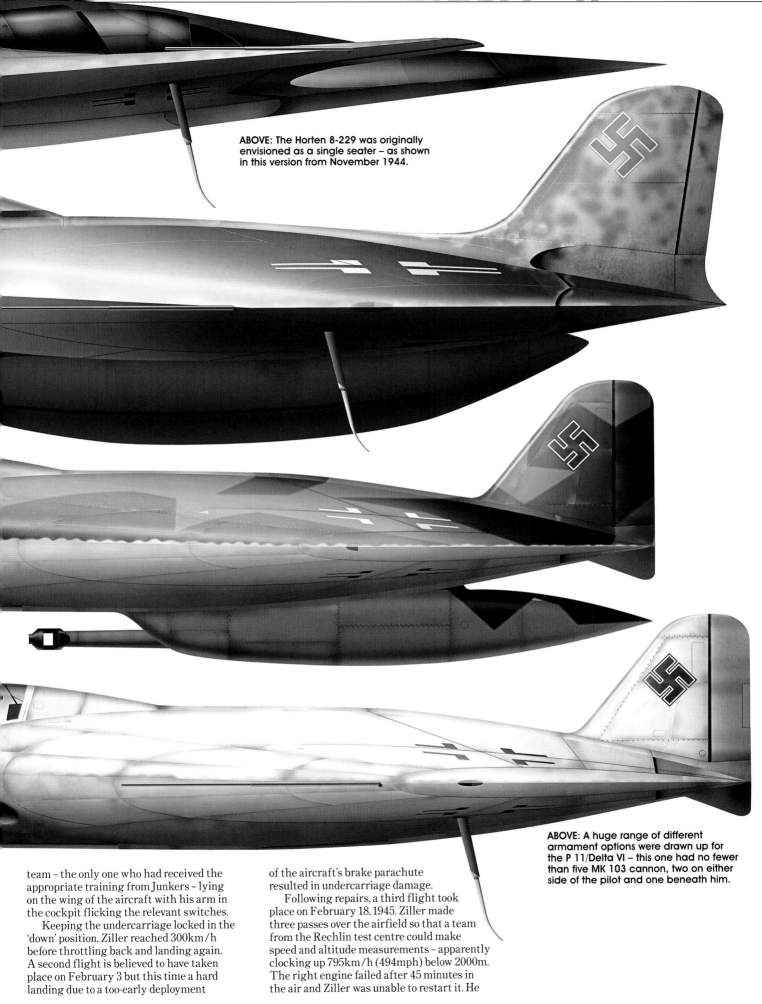

ABOVE: The Horten 8-229 was originally envisioned as a single seater – as shown in this version from November 1944.

ABOVE: A huge range of different armament options were drawn up for the P 11/Delta VI – this one had no fewer than five MK 103 cannon, two on either side of the pilot and one beneath him.

team – the only one who had received the appropriate training from Junkers – lying on the wing of the aircraft with his arm in the cockpit flicking the relevant switches.

Keeping the undercarriage locked in the 'down' position, Ziller reached 300km/h before throttling back and landing again. A second flight is believed to have taken place on February 3 but this time a hard landing due to a too-early deployment

of the aircraft's brake parachute resulted in undercarriage damage.

Following repairs, a third flight took place on February 18, 1945. Ziller made three passes over the airfield so that a team from the Rechlin test centre could make speed and altitude measurements – apparently clocking up 795km/h (494mph) below 2000m. The right engine failed after 45 minutes in the air and Ziller was unable to restart it. He tried to bring the aircraft in to land but put the gear down too soon – 400m from the landing strip. The landing gear hydraulic system, powered by the right engine, was inoperative so Ziller had to use the contents of a compressed air bottle, his emergency backup, to lower the gear. This meant that once it was down, it could not be retracted.

The increased drag slowed the aircraft and Ziller realised he wasn't going to make the strip. He powered up the remaining engine but the drag produced by the gear was too great and its airspeed could not be increased. The aircraft then entered a broad turn to the right which it maintained until it hit the ground. The impact was so great both engines and Ziller himself were thrown from the aircraft. He hit a tree and was killed instantly.

It has been suggested that Ziller was rendered unconscious by engine fumes entering the cockpit during these final moments, which would explain why he made no further efforts to recover the aircraft after it entered its wide turn. It was found that his harness, though torn open by the force of the impact, had not been unfastened, and he had made no attempt to activate the ejection seat either.

On March 1, Reimar produced a new report outlining the design and calling for Gotha to be given additional resources in order to complete its work on the 8-229 prototype. It states: "The company Gothaer Waggonfabrik 20 V samples have been ordered with DE-urgency starting from November 1944. The output begins with V3. From V3-incl. V5 is the single-seater. As of V6, the aircraft will be built as a double-seater. The standard processing can be carried out by the company GWF.

"In order to achieve the lowest possible risk during a series run, it is necessary that the test aircraft are manufactured as quickly as possible. The current deadline, which provides for the production of 1 piece per month, is sufficient to ensure a satisfactory trial during the course of the year 1945.

"The prerequisite for this is that the specified dates are kept. For example, the first aircraft to be deployed by the company GWF has a deadline of three months, a larger support of the company is necessary."

Evidently work on the V3 to V5 8-229 prototypes had been taking place on Gotha's behalf at the Ortlepp Möbel Fabrik at Friedrichroda – which is where the incomplete airframes were captured by elements of the American 3rd Army's VII Corps on April 14, 1945. Both the V3 and V4 had their engines fitted, the V3 being near completion. The V5 existed only as a steel frame. By now both Horten brothers had also been captured and taken into custody as prisoners of war.

LIPPISCH P 11/DELTA VI

Not long after his meeting with Göring, Lippisch's tailless P 11 was renamed the Delta VI. His small workforce at the LFW in Vienna diligently laboured over his designs, even as he constantly changed and altered them. Before long, the Delta VI bore little more than a passing resemblance to the P 11 endorsed by the Reichsmarschall.

Work on building the glider itself had begun by June 1944 when disaster befell the

project. According to Technical Intelligence report no. A.424: "The construction of this aeroplane was started in a factory in Vienna which was bombed out in June 1944 by the American Air Force.

"By this event Dr Lippisch lost 43 of his collaborators. The factory was then rebuilt in the Wiener Wald but the first experimental aircraft of this all-wing type, Li P 11, was never finished as the Russians invaded the region of Vienna."

Vienna was bombed twice in June 1944 by the USAAF – on the 16th and 24th. The former seems more likely to have hit the LFW.

Writing about the attack in his book Erinnerungen some 30 years later, Lippisch put the number of dead slightly higher: "At the time of the highest activity an air attack on aeronautics research in Vienna (LFW) occurred in June 1944, during which severe damage and, above all, 45 deaths were to be lamented; including some of my most valuable employees."

Now work on the Delta VI slowed to a crawl as Lippisch became increasingly focused on a new project – the ramjet-powered P 12, P 13a and P 13b designs. Yet work did not stop completely. At one point Henschel appears to have become involved, perhaps as a construction partner to help with the construction of the Delta VI. The minutes from a meeting of the EHK on November 21-22 state "the Lippisch P 11, a parallel development with the Ho 229, was to be developed in collaboration with Henschel" and a report from Henschel chief designer Friedrich Nicolaus suggests that this did happen, although to what extent is currently unknown.

Even as late as December 2, 1944, Junkers' special engines division OMW-Kobü Sondertriebwerke was struggling to get a pair of Jumo 004s to fit inside the Delta VI V2 – the powered version that was to follow the unpowered glider V1.

When the Russians reached Vienna at the beginning of April 1945, Lippisch found it necessary to abandon all the partially completed work already carried out on the Delta VI. The unfinished V1 was abandoned on the edge of a motorway.

FOCKE-WULF

During the month after Göring's meeting with Lippisch and the Hortens, October 1943, Focke-Wulf's design office began studying the possibilities of a fast bomber based on the use of two Jumo 004 Cs. After several months of work, including a rough sketch of a snub-

RIGHT: Perhaps one of the ugliest German project designs, Focke-Wulf's first attempt at a 1000 x 1000 x 1000 bomber was considerably improved over time.

BELOW: The conventional layout counterpart of Focke-Wulf's tailless 1000 x 1000 x 1000 was an elegant refinement of the lumpen early design.

nosed conventional-layout aircraft with long narrow strongly swept wings and tail planes and a podded turbojet on either side, a draft report entitled "Kurzbeschreibung 1000-1000-1000" was produced. However the document, dated March 8, 1944, was not published and remained in note form. The introduction says: "It is to be investigated whether, with a normal jet aircraft, i.e. non-tailless design, an SB 1000 bomb can be taken over a penetration depth of 1000km, the aircraft being able to reach a top speed of 1000km/h."

The whole typed report is covered in annotations and crossings-out but it appears

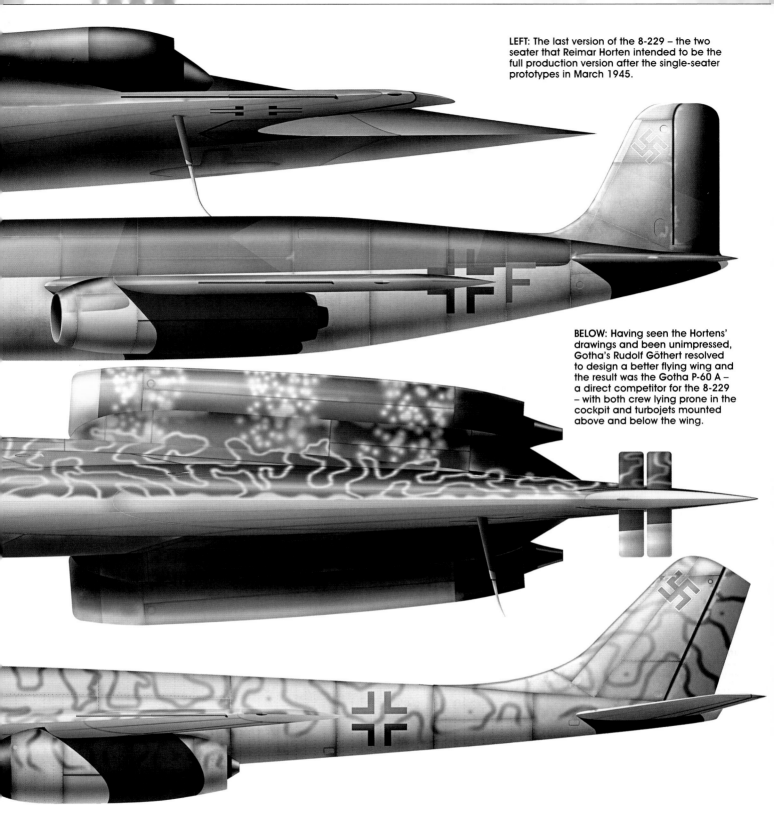

LEFT: The last version of the 8-229 – the two seater that Reimar Horten intended to be the full production version after the single-seater prototypes in March 1945.

BELOW: Having seen the Hortens' drawings and been unimpressed, Gotha's Rudolf Göthert resolved to design a better flying wing and the result was the Gotha P-60 A – a direct competitor for the 8-229 – with both crew lying prone in the cockpit and turbojets mounted above and below the wing.

that the best possible performance with a pair of HeS 011s was a "best travel speed" of 960km/h, a range of 2500km – 1000km there, 1000km back and sufficient fuel for manoeuvring – and a bomb load of 1000kg. However, this bomber would need to be entirely stripped of armour and defensive weaponry and the author of the report, probably the leader of Focke-Wulf's Flugmechanik L department, Herbert Wolff, does not appear convinced by the findings he is presenting.

Finally, a complete report was published on August 14, 1944, entitled Vergleich zweier Strahlbomber in normaler und schwanzloser Bauart or 'Comparison of two jet bombers in normal and tailless design'. March to August had apparently been spent studying a tailless version of the Focke-Wulf two-jet bomber so that it could be compared against the original conventional layout design.

The introduction begins: "Based on the Lippisch projects 1000/1000/1000, a test is carried out to determine whether a fast bomber with an SB 1000 bomb and penetration depth of 1000km can reach a top speed of 1000km/h. Two special engines, HeS 109-011, are selected. With respect to the high fuel consumption, the penetration depth of 1000km is equated to a range of 2500km; this condition is justified by the special use and by the low drifts resulting from the high flight speed."

The advantages of the normal layout were better visibility, ease of maintenance and replacement for the engines and no intake losses thanks to the engines being in underwing nacelles. The tailless design offered greater climbing capabilities and would be easier to land but would have poorer flying characteristics, particularly at high Mach numbers. Focke-Wulf appears to have abandoned its twin-jet bomber project at this point after some 10 months of work. ●

Down
the tubes

The Argus As 014 pulsejet presented a dilemma – it was cheap and could provide enough thrust to propel something small to high speeds but it also produced vibrations severe enough to damage a pilot's health. Nevertheless, the aircraft companies continued to view it as a possible engine for manned fighters...

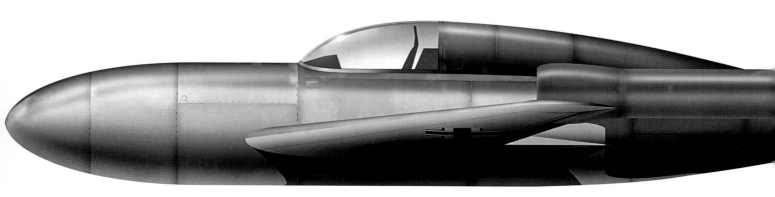

Messerschmitt commissioned tests of a sleek swept-wing version of its pulsejet-powered Me 328 in 1943. The AVA, which carried out the tests, produced a report on the results on July 14, 1943.

When Alexander Lippisch produced his P 05 as the evolution of the Me 163 at Messerschmitt in 1941, the leader of the company's main project office, Woldemar Voigt, countered with a proposal for a fighter powered by two pulsejets – the P 1079.

There had originally been plans to power the Me 262 with pulsejets and at this point the vibrations they caused were not viewed as a serious problem. There were initially more than 17 different designs for the P 1079 and these were whittled down to just one contender – the P 1079/13c. After a substantial redesign this received the RLM type number Me 328. Three versions were initially proposed: an unpowered glider, a turbojet-powered fighter and a fighter powered by one or more Argus As 014 pulsejets.

The pulsejet itself was patented by engineer Paul Schmidt in 1931 and consisted of a simple tube of mild steel with a set of shutters over the intake at the front and a fuel inlet valve and igniter inside. Engine company Argus built the As 014 and a larger version with a square-shaped intake, the As 044.

From a standing start, it was run up using blasts of compressed air to the intake. It was then allowed to build up to a minimum operating temperature before this was removed. A single pulse would start with the shutters open. Fuel was injected into the tube and ignited, which caused a rapid expansion of gases – snapping the spring-loaded shutters closed forced the gases to blast free from the other end of the tube, creating thrust.

Once the pressure from this blast had subsided, there was nothing to hold the shutters closed and they snapped open again – allowing air to be sucked in and the cycle to repeat. This happened 45-55 times per second.

While the Me 163 B went forward to full series production, Voigt's alternative remained a work in progress. It was decided that with extendable wings the Me 328 might make a good Bordjäger – a parasite aircraft carried by large long-range bombers for defence. Another plan was to launch it from a trolley down railway tracks or from the back of a Dornier Do 217 E and still another saw it developed into an expendable anti-shipping suicide attack bomber. In 1943, Messerschmitt commissioned wind tunnel tests of a swept-wing version of the Me 328 at the AVA.

The Me 328 V1 was constructed and gliding flight tests took place in 1944 but the project

BELOW: The only pulsejet aircraft from late 1944 which seemed to attract official interest was the Junkers EF 126 'Elli' ground-attack aircraft. Like its sibling, the rocket-powered EF 127 'Walli', it would have used several components borrowed from the Fi 103 flying bomb.

was shelved indefinitely after the As 014-powered Fieseler Fi 103 V-1 entered service.

Towards the end of 1944, however, interest in the pulsejet as a fighter engine was rekindled in the wake of the Volksjäger contest. It has been suggested that the RLM issued a requirement for a 'miniature fighter' powered by the As 014 at this stage, but there is only circumstantial evidence to support this idea – the fact that they all appear to have been designed in November 1944.

Blohm & Voss produced a brochure on November 10, 1944, for the P 213 – a "miniature fighter with As 014". The aircraft was to carry just one MK 108 cannon and 350kg of fuel with a minimum of equipment, resulting in a take-off weight of just 1280kg. Vibrations from the single pulsejet would be mitigated with a "sufficiently wide rubber sleeve" between the inlet pipe running through the fuselage and the intake of the engine unit itself.

Junkers was working on its own single As 014-powered fighter at around the same time – the EF 126 'Elli'. Like its Objektschützer sibling the EF 127 'Walli', 'Elli' made use of components borrowed from the Fi 103, but it was specified as being a ground-attack aircraft, rather than a fighter. It was to be

BELOW: The more familiar straight-wing Me 328 B. Messerschmitt drew up plans for a huge number of Me 328 variants.

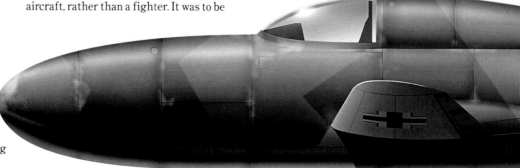

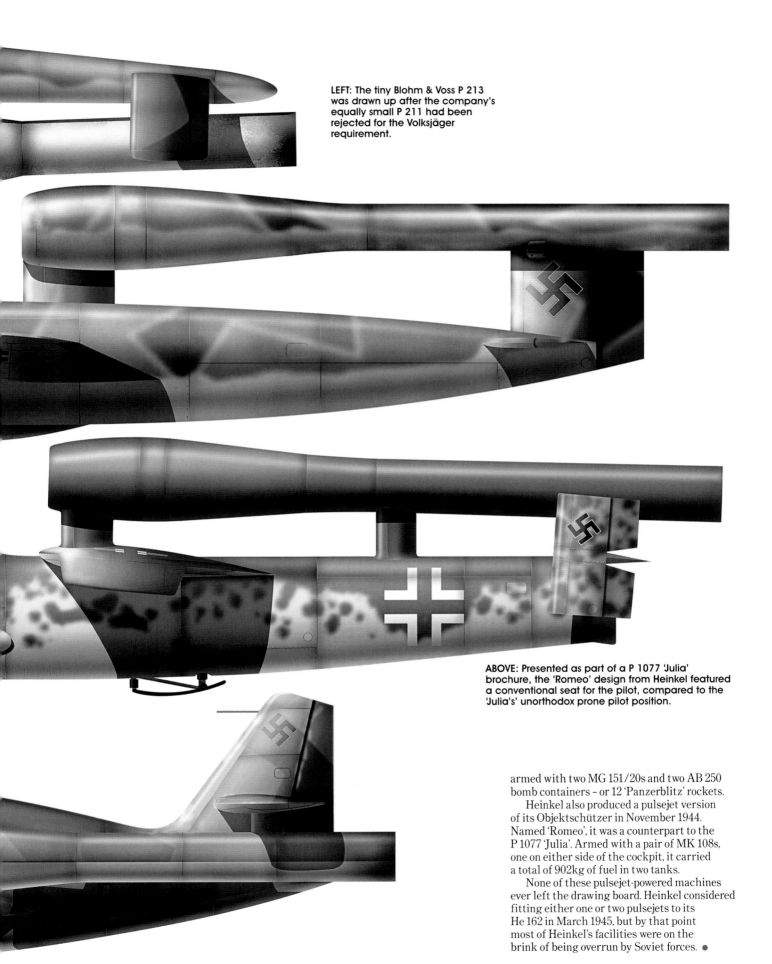

LEFT: The tiny Blohm & Voss P 213 was drawn up after the company's equally small P 211 had been rejected for the Volksjäger requirement.

ABOVE: Presented as part of a P 1077 'Julia' brochure, the 'Romeo' design from Heinkel featured a conventional seat for the pilot, compared to the 'Julia's' unorthodox prone pilot position.

armed with two MG 151/20s and two AB 250 bomb containers – or 12 'Panzerblitz' rockets.

Heinkel also produced a pulsejet version of its Objektschützer in November 1944. Named 'Romeo', it was a counterpart to the P 1077 'Julia'. Armed with a pair of MK 108s, one on either side of the cockpit, it carried a total of 902kg of fuel in two tanks.

None of these pulsejet-powered machines ever left the drawing board. Heinkel considered fitting either one or two pulsejets to its He 162 in March 1945, but by that point most of Heinkel's facilities were on the brink of being overrun by Soviet forces. •

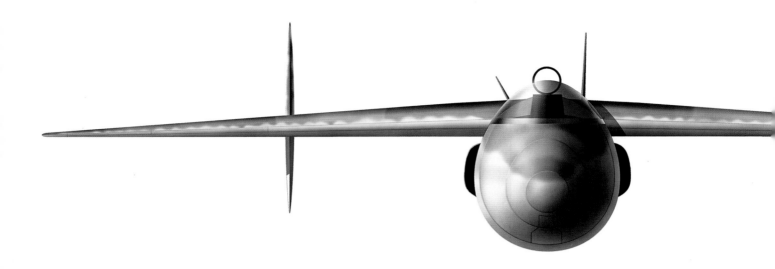

Me 262
replacement

The most important of the late-war German design competitions was 1-TL-Jäger – the idea being to replace the twin-jet Me 262 with something that only needed one precious turbojet but could do the same or better in combat.

The earliest version of the
Junkers EF 128 – as it appeared
at the December 19-21, 1944,
comparison meeting.

Attempts to design a high-performance fighter powered by a single jet engine had been made ever since the RLM first became aware of turbojet technology. However, the earliest working examples of the two most promising designs – the BMW 003 and Jumo 004 – simply weren't up to the job so the He 280, Me 262 and Ar 234 were each designed to take a pair of engines.

The situation changed when Heinkel's new HeS 011 turbojet, with a projected static thrust of 1300kg, became a viable proposition in 1943. The Me 262's Jumo 004 B-1s could manage 900kg each and the BMW 003 A-2 production version just 800kg.

Messerschmitt, Heinkel and Focke-Wulf had each been working on single-jet fighter designs based around the less powerful engines and had already begun to consider using the HeS 011 when, in July 1944, they were presented with the task of designing just such a fighter by the RLM.

On July 11, 1944, Rodde, the member of Focke-Wulf's Technischer Aussendienst or 'Technical Field Service' responsible for the Ta 154 and Ta 254 under Oberingenieur Ernst Lammel, wrote a memo headed 'Development Communication – TL-Jäger'. This began: "Subject: General definition for the start-up jet fighter. Task: It is extremely urgent to tackle the design of the jet fighter and to carry out both prototyping and serial production in such a way that a first prototype aircraft is ready to fly on 1.3.45."

The note was based on a technical direction meeting with the RLM. It is unclear exactly when the meeting took place, but presumably not long before the note was written. It goes on: "Implementation: The design work for the prototype aircraft shall be carried out in such a way that a first aircraft is ready for flight at 1.3.45, taking into account the fact that a series of prototype aircraft will be prepared with a maximum output of 30 aircraft per month. Parallel to this, the completion of the series drawings, where as far as possible steel is to be used."

Rated weight was to be 3700kg, take-off weight 3500kg. The engine was to be a single HeS 011 or a single Jumo 004 C (although this part of Rodde's note is crossed out on the original document).

A wooden dummy HeS 011 was to be "available in a few weeks" and all documents on the Jumo 004 C were being made available through the RLM. Fuel tanks in the fuselage were to be protected against 13mm bullets and "the outer wings are to be tightly riveted from the first machine, also the tail unit is required as container". It was to be clarified which corrosion protection was to be used for the tail containers since these might be required to hold rocket fuel.

Further clarification was needed on the points of heating for the cockpit and weapons. The aircraft was to be made using "mainly

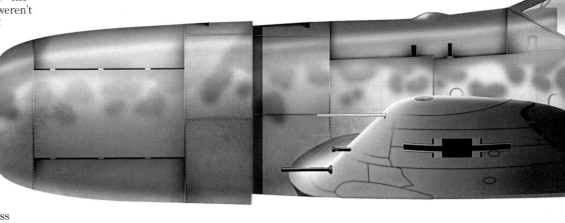

BELOW: Focke-Wulf's earliest known jet fighter design, from November 1942, involved simply attaching a very basic turbojet unit to the nose of an Fw 190.

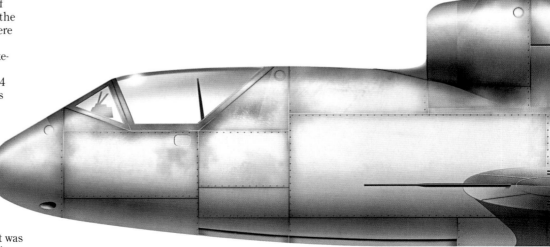

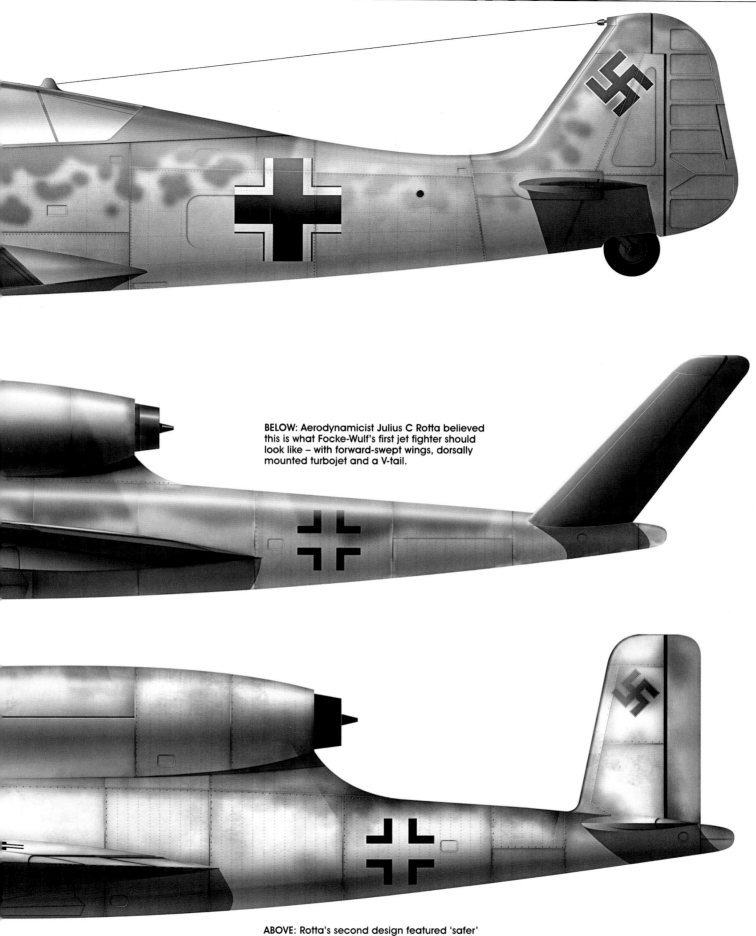

BELOW: Aerodynamicist Julius C Rotta believed this is what Focke-Wulf's first jet fighter should look like – with forward-swept wings, dorsally mounted turbojet and a V-tail.

ABOVE: Rotta's second design featured 'safer' design elements such as straight wings and an unswept V-tail.

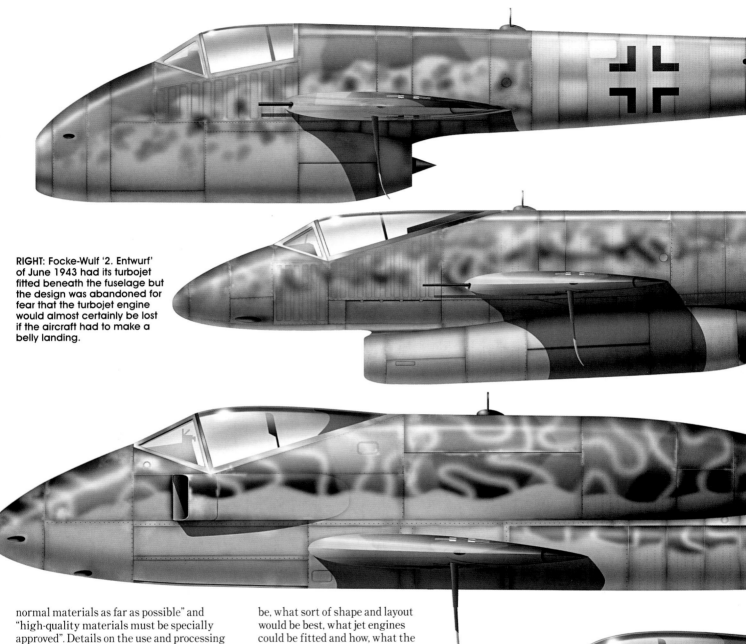

BELOW: This design from March 1943 was labelled '1. Entwurf' in an August 1944 report explaining the lineage of Focke-Wulf's single-jet fighter programme.

RIGHT: Focke-Wulf '2. Entwurf' of June 1943 had its turbojet fitted beneath the fuselage but the design was abandoned for fear that the turbojet engine would almost certainly be lost if the aircraft had to make a belly landing.

normal materials as far as possible" and "high-quality materials must be specially approved". Details on the use and processing of steel for series production of the new fighter were to be provided by the RLM during a follow-up meeting on July 19.

Focke-Wulf, Messerschmitt and Heinkel were all invited to participate in 1-TL-Jäger and a fourth company, Blohm & Voss, was also offered the opportunity to pitch a design but evidently not until the end of August or early September.

FOCKE-WULF
The earliest known Focke-Wulf attempt at a single-jet fighter, shown in a drawing dated November 5, 1942, had involved simply bolting a very basic in-house designed turbojet to the front of an Fw 190. Then on January 4, 1943, company aerodynamicist Julius C Rotta produced a report entitled 'Fundamentals For The Design of a Jet Fighter' which looked at how large a jet fighter ought to

be, what sort of shape and layout would be best, what jet engines could be fitted and how, what the advantages and disadvantages of piston engines and jet engines were and what the aerodynamic issues were.

To illustrate his points, Rotta came up with a trio of remarkably foresighted designs: Jäger mit Turbinentriebwerk BMW P 3302 Design 1, Jäger mit Turbinentriebwerk BMW P 3302 Design 2, and Jäger mit Turbinentriebwerk Junkers 109 004.

Each of the three had its jet engine mounted on its back, just as the Heinkel He 162 would be configured 20 months later. The first and third designs also had forward-swept wings and backward-swept V-tails. The second BMW P 3302 design had unswept wings and an unswept V-tail.

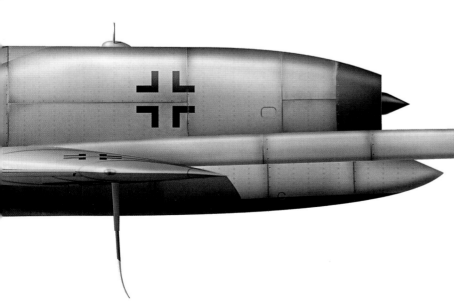

Suggested armament was two MK 108 30mm cannon with 200 rounds and two MG 151s with 300 rounds. Fuel load was 850 litres.

However, Focke-Wulf's design team seem to have completely ignored Rotta's ideas when they actually started work on a series of single-seat, single-engine jet fighters. A report produced on August 15, 1944, entitled Considerations for Designing a Single-Engine Fighter Aircraft with Turbojet charts the team's progress through seven different designs.

The first of these, dated March 1943, was a tail-sitter based on the Fw 190 but with the cockpit relocated to the nose in place of the familiar BMW 801 piston engine, and with the turbojet positioned directly below. According to the report: "With this arrangement, no satisfactory rolling properties were to be expected and there was also the risk of burning the airfield surface. This design was abandoned."

The second design, of June 1943, seems to have been more highly regarded and had its own separate Baubeschreibung or 'Construction description' number, the closest thing Focke-Wulf had to a 'P' designation. It was Baubeschreibung Nr. 264 Jäger mit Junkers-Turbinentriebwerk and had a tricycle undercarriage with the turbojet positioned more centrally under the fuselage. The report notes that Nr. 264 was "rejected because of the risk of engine damage during belly landings".

A different approach was taken for the third design, with the engine mounted in the upper part of the fuselage with its intakes on either side of the cockpit. A twin-rudder tail was used to prevent interference from the jet exhaust. According to the report: "The third draft satisfied in terms of rolling characteristics and behaviour in belly landings.

BELOW: The '3. Entwurf' Focke-Wulf design of November 1943 had twin rudders but there were concerns about the shape and positioning of its intakes.

The calculated flight performance was inadequate due to the lateral intakes."

There was another shift in layout for the fourth design of December 1943, with a twin-boom tail like that of the Fw 189, but again: "The horizontal velocity remained unsatisfactory."

The fifth and sixth designs were apparently worked on at the same time, though they are dated January 1944 and February 1944 respectively. The former was a swept-wing, T-tail, tricycle undercarriage fighter with a nose intake for its centrally positioned turbojet and the report explains: "In the fifth draft an attempt was made to raise the critical Mach number by particularly strong wing sweep.

"Extreme restriction in size made it possible to keep the entire surface approximately equal to that of '4. Design'. Experiments with a free-flying model raised concerns about the expected flight characteristics."

The sixth design also got a Baubeschreibung to itself – Nr. 280. It was another twin-boom layout but with a rocket engine to boost performance during a climb. This is the type that the whole document was written in support of, the report stating that "the intakes of the jet unit are positioned in the inner wing leading edge. Objections to this intake port design can be refuted by test measurements and wind tunnel tests".

It was this design that Focke-Wulf would pitch to meet the 1-TL-Jäger spec.

MESSERSCHMITT

Up to the end of June 1944, Messerschmitt had been working on a series of designs for jet aircraft using two, three or four HeS 011 engines under the designation P 1101. Each of these three layouts had been compared against the Me 262 and although each was substantially heavier, they were each much better armed. Where the Me 262 could carry six MK 108s, the P 1101/2TL could carry one BK 7.5 cannon or three MK 112s, the P 1101/3TL could carry one BK 7.5 or four MK 112s and the P 1101/4TL could manage one MK 7.5 or five MK 112s.

However, when the company was informed of the 1-TL-Jäger specification, it scaled back to a single HeS 011 and began a new line of designs

ABOVE: Featuring twin tailbooms and reshaped intakes, Focke-Wulf's '4. Entwurf' of December 1943 had a pair of rocket motors exhausting either side of its turbojet but without them it would have been too slow.

FIRST CONFERENCE

Each company produced performance figures for its design but these varied wildly even though the designs themselves were not that dissimilar – it was clear that each firm was using quite different calculations.

Therefore, a conference was scheduled for September 8-10, 1944, at Messerschmitt's Oberammergau facility where, according to the post-conference summary, "the task was to create comparable fundamentals for the performance calculation and, as far as possible, to carry out a comparison of the present jet aircraft designs".

A brief description of each firm's design was then given – it being noted that Blohm & Voss's Hans Amtmann had attended but opted not to present a design.

The Focke-Wulf design was presented in three slightly different forms – outwardly identical but with differing quantities of fuel for the supplementary rocket engine depending on mission. It was armed with two MK 103s in the fuselage and one MG 151 in each wing. Wing area was 17sqm, span was 8m and length was 10.5m. A pressure cabin was an option.

The P 1073 was a "pure jet" with two MG 213s in the fuselage, or two MK 108s or one MK 103 and one "20mm weapon". It had a wingspan of 14sqm, wingspan of 8m, wing sweepback of 35 degrees and length of 9.3m. It also offered a pressure cabin as an option.

And the P 1101 was also offered in three forms as a seemingly modular concept similar to the company's piston-engined P 1090, dating from February 1943. The summary notes: "Mtt AG. 1) Smallest jet single-seater with maximum flight performance. 2) Jet and rocket fighter with rocket fuel for fast climbing or as a combat aid. Extending possibility by inserting a fuselage intersection. 3) Possibility of expansion to two men by inserting a fuselage intermediate section, whereby the space for second man can also be used for additional weapons, additional fuel or additional drive."

In order to compare the weights of the different designs, a basic armament of two MK 108s each with 60 rounds and a fuel load of 830kg was assumed – no matter what the

under the P 1101 designation. The earliest known example is dated July 24, 1944, and the drawing shows a stubby economical fighter with its engine positioned centrally within the fuselage. Its wings, while sharply swept close to the fuselage, are less sharply swept closer to their tips. The aircraft is just 6.85m long with a V-tail and a wingspan of 7.15m. Armament is just two MK 108s. It is similar in some ways to Focke-Wulf's third design, with large intakes on either side of the cockpit, but the engine exhausts below the tail rather than above it.

The second known single-jet P 1101 is dated August 30, 1944, and is a considerable refinement of the earlier layout. The wings have a straight leading edge all the way to the tip, the intakes are smaller and the aircraft has a long nose for housing both the nosewheel and armament.

It would be this latter design which Messerschmitt entered for 1-TL-Jäger.

HEINKEL

Like Messerschmitt, Heinkel's new series of jet fighter designs, P 1073, started out with more than one turbojet. The first three examples are all dated July 6, 1944. One had an engine towards the front of the fuselage, underneath the cockpit, and a second mounted on its back, exhausting through a V-tail, and swept wings; the second had two engines side-by-side under the front fuselage and a conventional tail but with forward-swept wings; and the third had two engines side-by-side on its back, also with a conventional tail and backward-swept wings.

The fourth design, of July 10, 1944, reverted to the first configuration. However, the next design was not produced until July 22 and was the first since the 1-TL-Jäger spec had been issued. It was similar to the first and fourth designs but had only one turbojet – under the forward fuselage. The following day another twin-jet version was drafted, similar to the first and fourth designs.

A trio of new designs was produced on August 3 – one with a single engine, this time positioned on its back – and two more of the familiar twin-jet layout. Heinkel may have been attempting to demonstrate that it thought two HeS 011s was a better option.

More designs followed, with the one presented for 1-TL-Jäger being the 14th, dated August 19, 1944. This had a V-tail, swept wings, and a dorsally mounted turbojet.

ABOVE: In August 1944, Focke-Wulf firmly believed that this should be the Luftwaffe's first single-jet fighter. Labelled '6. Entwurf' in the chronology report, it was known formally as the Baubeschreibung Nr. 280 aircraft and informally as the 'Flitzer' or 'whizzer'. It was the company's first 1-TL-Jäger entry.

BELOW: This development of the early P 1101, still labelled P 1101, was drafted in August 1944 and was submitted for the first 1-TL-Jäger design comparison meeting in September 1944.

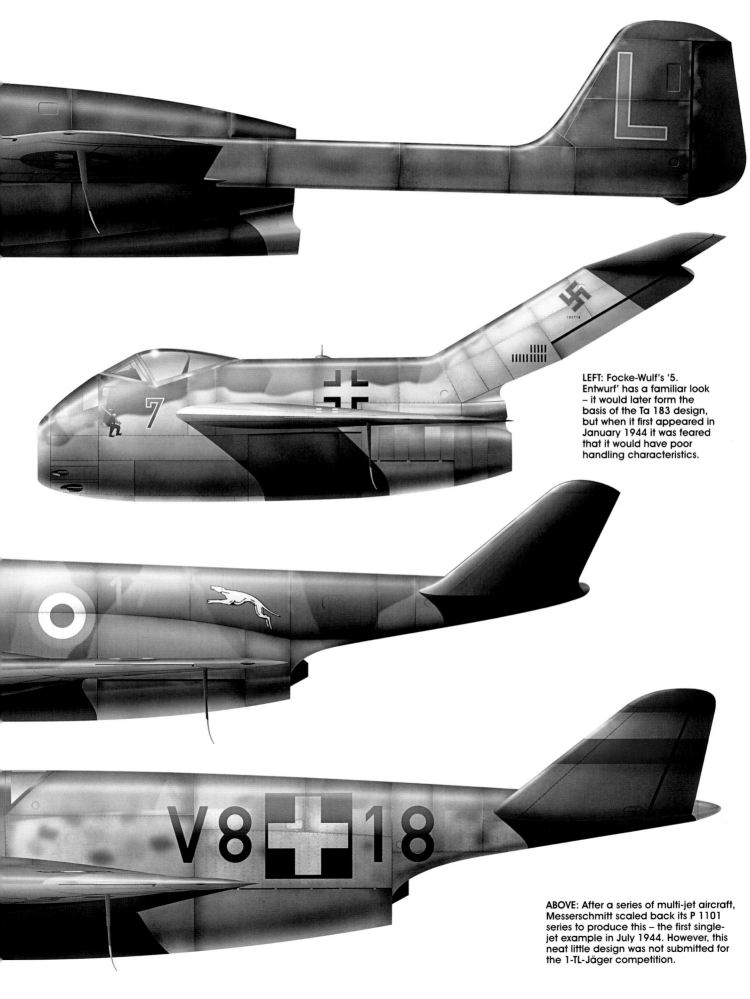

LEFT: Focke-Wulf's '5. Entwurf' has a familiar look – it would later form the basis of the Ta 183 design, but when it first appeared in January 1944 it was feared that it would have poor handling characteristics.

ABOVE: After a series of multi-jet aircraft, Messerschmitt scaled back its P 1101 series to produce this – the first single-jet example in July 1944. However, this neat little design was not submitted for the 1-TL-Jäger competition.

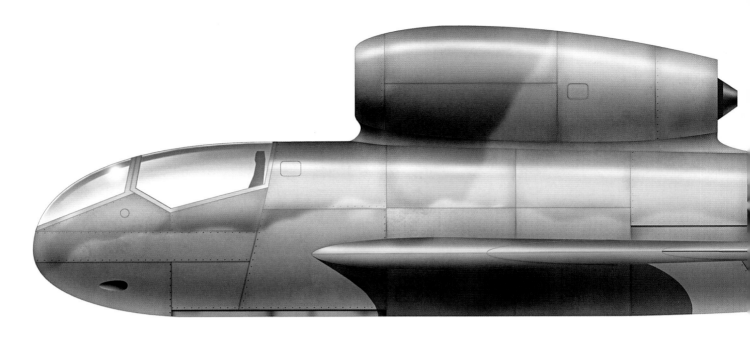

ABOVE: Heinkel's P 1073 sequence shows the company's designers shifting back and forth between fitting turbojets to the back of the aircraft and its underside. The P 1073.11 had its engine in the dorsal position but also featured a cockpit canopy design somewhat reminiscent of the He 219.

firms had put in their brochures. Then the companies' stats were played around with to try and find some common ground. The Heinkel and Messerschmitt designs were found to be heavier than the figures given, while the Focke-Wulf was deemed to be 70kg lighter – the difference corresponding to swapping steel components for ones made of duraluminium.

In terms of performance, Heinkel and Messerschmitt claimed similar top speeds but it was considered that the Heinkel design would suffer a loss of thrust due to the design of its jet inlet and unfortunately for Focke-Wulf, "the FW design should be less than 50-100km/h slower compared to the designs of Heinkel and Messerschmitt".

There was disagreement from the outset over the calculations used to determine top speed: "In the opinion of Heinkel and Focke-Wulf, the determined speed level is too high, whereas Messerschmitt, on the basis of the experience with the Me 262 and the Do 335, is in the opposite opinion and hopes to achieve even higher speeds with further improvements. For the calculation performed by Messerschmitt, the flight measurements of the Me 262, which has a relatively poor series state, are used as the basis."

At the end of the conference "a broad exchange of experience has been agreed upon in order to clarify these questions with a view to forthcoming designs. It is urgently necessary that, by the disposal of the RLM, all the development companies and the experimental stations are asked to provide flight results, together with the necessary documentation, for the evaluation".

It was the first attempt to come up with a standard basis on which the new single jet designs could be compared. However, on the last day of the meeting, September 10, a new requirement was issued for a single-jet fighter or 1-TL-Jäger with reduced performance compared to the designs just discussed, to be powered by a single BMW 003 engine. This is what would become known as the Volksjäger

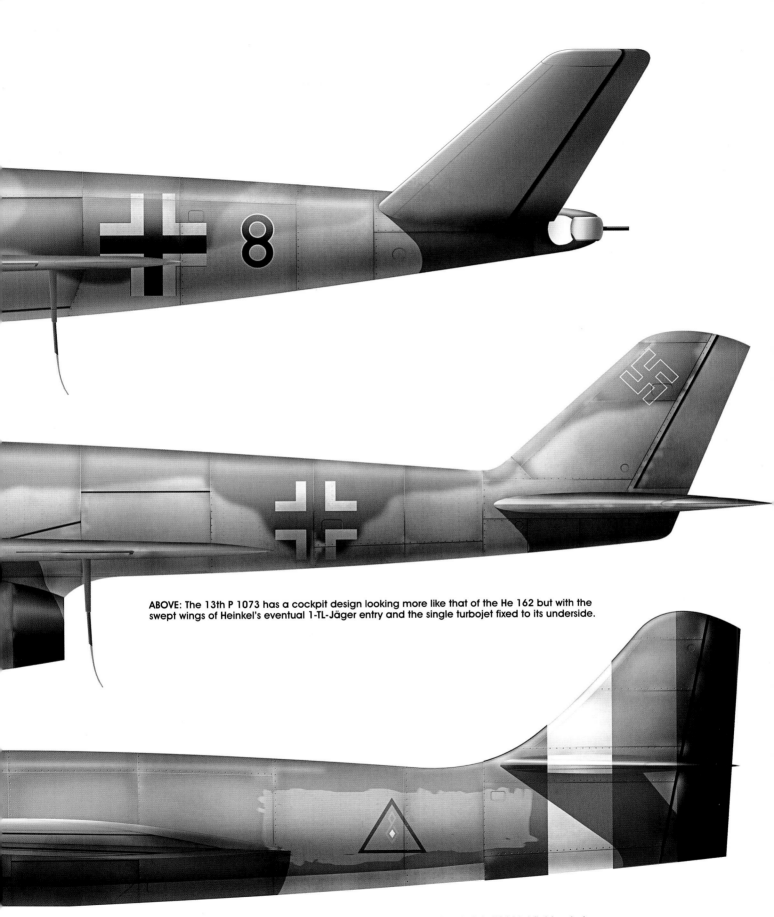

ABOVE: The 13th P 1073 has a cockpit design looking more like that of the He 162 but with the swept wings of Heinkel's eventual 1-TL-Jäger entry and the single turbojet fixed to its underside.

ABOVE: The second of Heinkel's trio of early July 1944 jet fighter designs – with two turbojets rather than one – and forward-swept wings.

competition and prospective participants had just five days to prepare their entries.

ROUNDS 2 AND 3

The sudden demand for Volksjäger designs seems to have temporarily stalled the primary 1-TL-Jäger competition, with the next conference for comparison of designs being delayed until December 19-21. This time Heinkel retained its P 1073, now referred to as 'He 162 development' but this seems to have been withdrawn since the comparison charts drawn up by the DVL following the meeting, while they list the Heinkel design, have blanks where its details should be.

Having initially had no project to show for the contest, Blohm & Voss now had two and both were highly unconventional in design – the P 209.02-03 and P 212.02-01. In terms of layout, the P 209.02-03 was similar to the early P 1101 designs in having a centrally mounted turbojet exhausting under the tail – but rather than side intakes it had a more straightforward nose intake and its wings were swept forwards rather than back. The P 212.02-01 was different again, being tailless. It had a nose intake like the P 209 but rather than having control surfaces on a conventional tail, these were moved to the wingtips instead. The turbojet was in the rear part of the stubby fuselage and the pilot sat right at the front above the intake opening.

A fifth company had also joined the contest by this point – Junkers. The company's design, the EF 128, was tailless like the P 212 but slimmer in profile and with side intakes for its turbojet. The wing control surfaces took the form of a pair of rudder plates positioned just over halfway along its sharply swept wings.

Messerschmitt's only entry at this point was another radical design – the P 1106. The turbojet was back in the nose position once more, with the tricycle undercarriage retracting into its housing, but the cockpit was shifted to the extreme rear of the aircraft's fuselage, just in front of the V-tail. The advantage of this, presumably, was elimination of any form of intake for the engine and a sizeable area of fuselage free for weaponry. The major disadvantage was visibility for the pilot.

Focke-Wulf's long-cherished twin-boom 'Flitzer' design had finally been dropped in favour of an evolution of the earlier '5. Entwurf' or 'fifth design'. This was Baubeschreibung Nr. 279 but was nicknamed 'Huckebein' within the company. As before, the design had a relatively conventional layout with nose intake, swept wings and swept T-tail.

At a third meeting, on January 12-15, 1945, the DVL put forward a new mathematical formula by which the expected performance of all designs could be calculated and this was agreed. Now Heinkel's P 1073, presumably thanks to the experience gained while building a downgraded version as the He 162, had been replaced with a new tailless design, the P 1078. However, the DVL assessors commented in their report afterwards that

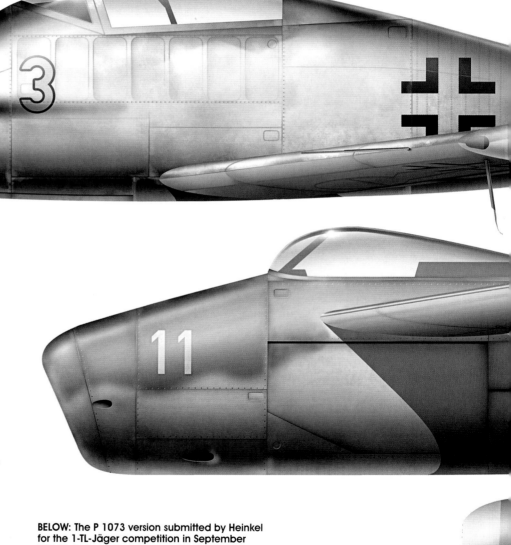

RIGHT: One of Blohm & Voss's two original 1-TL-Jäger entries – the P 209.02-03 – was very different from the earlier tailless P 209. It had a conventional tail but with sharply forward-swept wings.

BELOW: The P 1073 version submitted by Heinkel for the 1-TL-Jäger competition in September 1944 is believed to be this – effectively a large version of what would become the He 162 but with swept wings and a V-tail.

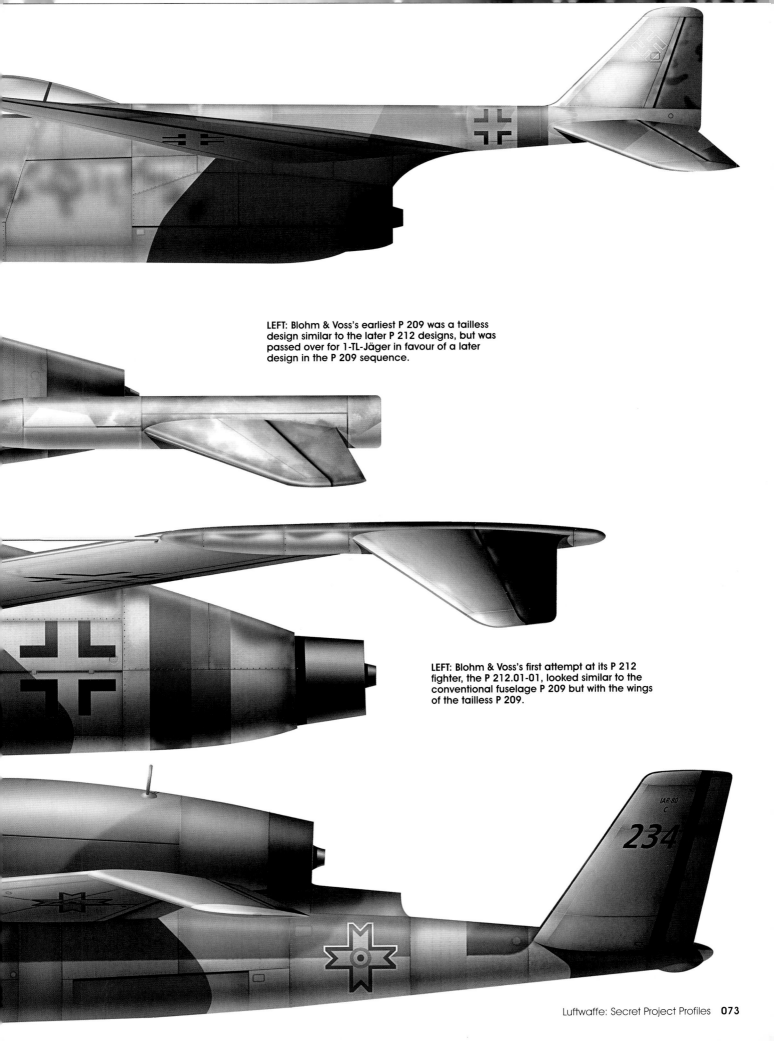

LEFT: Blohm & Voss's earliest P 209 was a tailless design similar to the later P 212 designs, but was passed over for 1-TL-Jäger in favour of a later design in the P 209 sequence.

LEFT: Blohm & Voss's first attempt at its P 212 fighter, the P 212.01-01, looked similar to the conventional fuselage P 209 but with the wings of the tailless P 209.

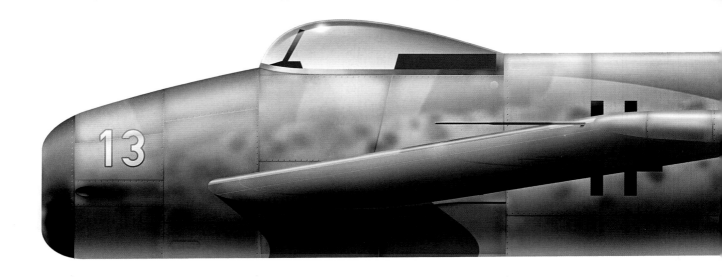

Heinkel had "brought a tailless project, which was still so little worked through, that the comparison was not used with it".

The first iteration of the P 1078 had a very short fuselage that was egg-shaped in cross section. A short flat section of wing protruded on either side before rising and then falling into a gullwing form. The undercarriage mainwheels were attached to the flat section but folded up into the sides of the crowded fuselage.

The cockpit was positioned as far forwards as Heinkel's designers might feasibly have been able to put it, with the rectangular nose intake almost under the pilot's feet. The canopy blended smoothly into the fuselage to the rear, which appears to have housed the generator and starter for the engine. The only known drawing – marked P 1078.01 – is too degraded for dimensions to be made out but the design is clearly very different from what had been offered up previously. The date of the drawing appears to be January 10, 1945 – two days before the design comparison conference.

Messerschmitt had retained the P 1106 as 'Messerschmitt I' and offered a new layout design – the P 1110 – as 'Messerschmitt II'. This latter design was somewhat similar in appearance to the original P 1101 design, with a long streamlined nose and V-tail, but rather than having the jet exhausting under the rear fuselage, the exhaust passed directly through the rear fuselage to the nozzle at the extreme rear end of the aircraft. And rather than side intakes, the aircraft had an unusual annular intake arrangement.

Focke-Wulf put forward its Nr. 279 aircraft again, now as 'Focke-Wulf I' plus a new but similar design, described in Kurzbaubeschreibung Nr. 30, as 'Focke-Wulf II'. The latter was effectively a less radical or 'safer' version of the other – with a conventional tail and with the cockpit located more centrally. Behind the scenes, Focke-Wulf had set up two separate teams to work on and assess the designs, now known as 'Projekt Multhopp' and 'Projekt Mittelhuber' after the two project leaders Oberingenieur Hans Multhopp and Chefingenieur Ludwig Mittelhuber.

Blohm & Voss put forward an updated version of P 212, the P 212.03, having withdrawn the P 209, and Junkers retained and refined the EF 128.

A date was then set for a fourth and, it was hoped, final round of comparison and assessment of the 1-TL-Jäger design submissions – February 27-28, 1945.

FINAL ROUND

The pre-conference report was prepared by Messerschmitt on February 26 and detailed the eight designs due to be discussed. These were the Blohm & Voss P 212.03, the same Focke-Wulf 'I' and Focke-Wulf 'II' as before, an updated Heinkel P 1078, the Junkers EF 128 as before, a revived Messerschmitt P 1101, a revised Messerschmitt P 1110 and a radical new tailless Messerschmitt design, the P 1111. The Messerschmitt designs were now referred to by their project numbers, presumably because the Messerschmitt offering had changed so much since the January conference.

The February report states: "At the request of the Entwicklungs Hauptkommission and the head of the Technische Luft Rustung, designs for single jet fighters were tendered by the following firms: Blohm & Voss, Focke-Wulf, Ernst Heinkel, Junkers, Messerschmitt. At the meeting of the Entwicklungs Hauptkommission on February 27-28, 1945, a decision concerning the completion of these designs is to be made.

"The purpose of this report, after careful work on the material in question, is to present a comparison between the designs tendered, and, thus, is to serve the EHK as the basis for decision.

"A considerable interruption of the work necessary for this report was brought about by war conditions. On account of the bad traffic and communication facilities, it was not possible to obtain in written form the report of the DVL on general performance and criticism of the characteristics of the aircraft.

"For the same reasons it was not possible to compare in the general discussion with DVL the additional designs tendered (design from Heinkel and designs P 1101 and P 1111 from Messerschmitt).

"In order to ensure the fairest possible comparison, reference was made to the performance and weights of all the designs submitted with regard to equipment and armament.

RIGHT: When the original long-nose P 1101 failed to make much of an impression, Messerschmitt switched to this design for 1-TL-Jäger – the radical P 1106. It may look too bizarre to be a genuine design, but this is really how its shape appears in the original drawing.

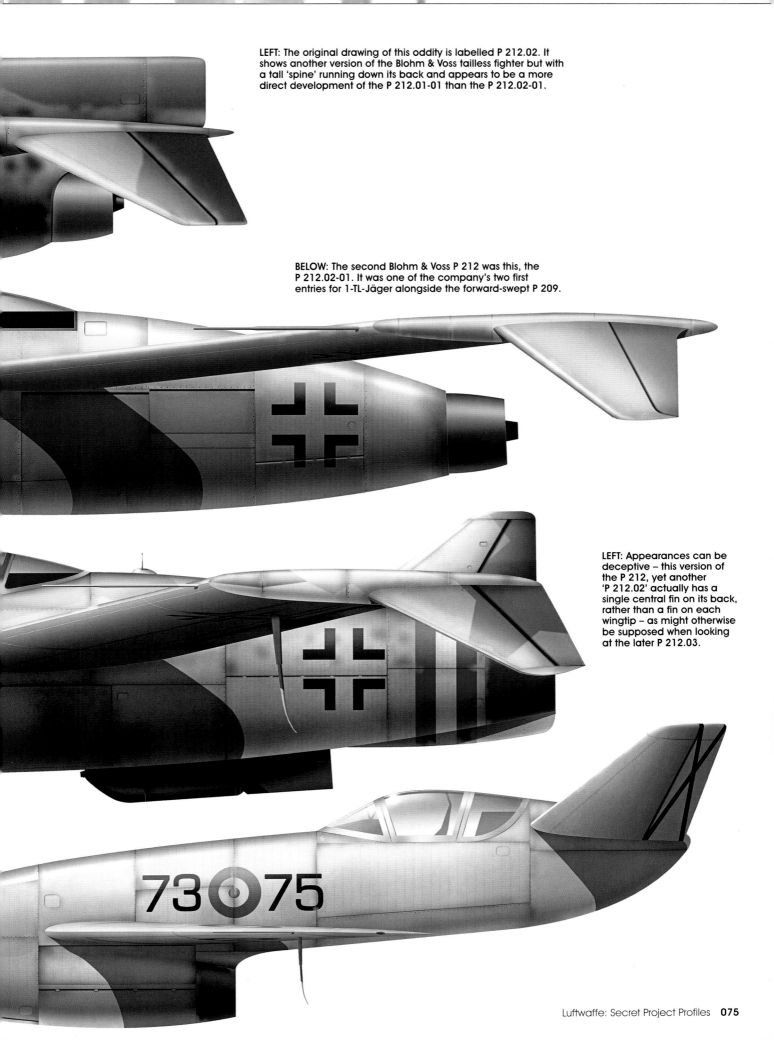

LEFT: The original drawing of this oddity is labelled P 212.02. It shows another version of the Blohm & Voss tailless fighter but with a tall 'spine' running down its back and appears to be a more direct development of the P 212.01-01 than the P 212.02-01.

BELOW: The second Blohm & Voss P 212 was this, the P 212.02-01. It was one of the company's two first entries for 1-TL-Jäger alongside the forward-swept P 209.

LEFT: Appearances can be deceptive – this version of the P 212, yet another 'P 212.02' actually has a single central fin on its back, rather than a fin on each wingtip – as might otherwise be supposed when looking at the later P 212.03.

73 75

"The aircraft weights were determined against each other at the beginning of the performance comparison. The bullet-proofing was not assumed to be of equal weight for the individual designs, but the bullet-proofing for each plane was set out so that an equal extent of protection was obtained wherever possible.

"Exceptions can be made for designs P 1101 and P 1111 from Messerschmitt, as these have to be considered with a view to their stronger armament (3 x MK 108 and 4 x MK 108 respectively, instead of 2 x MK 108). This happened on account of the fact that the arrangement of the supplementary armament at the extreme front of the aircraft presented great difficulties on both models in regard to the centre of gravity, and thus the firm provided additional armament as a fundamental.

"The design of EHF (Heinkel) was not included in the comparison of performance and weight, as it was not ready at the time. The comparison was finished, but the result has not yet been submitted at this time to Special Commission for Day Fighters. The estimated performances are thus the firm's specifications.

"The estimated performance for the designs P 1110, P 1101 and P 1111 from Messerschmitt do not correspond entirely to the values which were ascertained at the comparison of performance. For the design P 1110, an increase of wing and fuselage surface is contemplated and considered according to the fundamental process of calculating the performance comparison.

"The designs P 1101 and P 1111, which were not submitted for the performance comparison by Messerschmitt, were calculated by the firm according to an agreed process and were submitted for decision in place of the project P 1106.

"The estimated performances are comparative figures, which will serve as the deciding factor for the value of the designs submitted. They are not to be considered as absolute estimates of the velocities.

"The report consists of a short description, in concise form, of the separate projects, with the most important technical points such as the main dimension weights and important performances in comprehensive tables. These served the Special Commission for Day Fighters on January 12, 1945, as a basis. In the meantime, alterations proposed by the firms have not been considered."

From a competition that had begun with just three entries from three companies, in the space of five months the contest had expanded to eight entries from five companies.

DVL director Günther Bock noted on March 12, 1945, that at a meeting of the Entwicklungshauptkommission on March 1, 1945, "the direction of the development work was discussed. In this case, the following picture emerged according to the intended use of the aircraft types: a) Day fighter. Development work for day fighters with the HeS 109.011 A jet engine, the companies Focke-Wulf and Messerschmitt are expected to have one development contract each. Whether the companies Junkers or Blohm & Voss are also activated for development is still undetermined".

It would appear that Focke-Wulf was

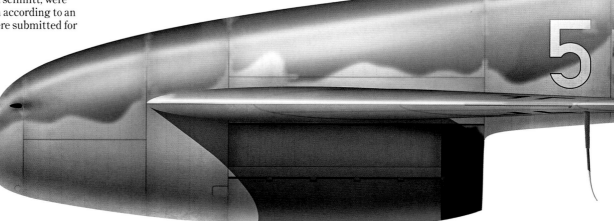

ABOVE: By January 1944, Messerschmitt had significantly amended the P 1106 design to this version. The V-tail has been replaced with a T-tail and the cockpit has been built into the fin – making the aircraft look even stranger, if that is possible.

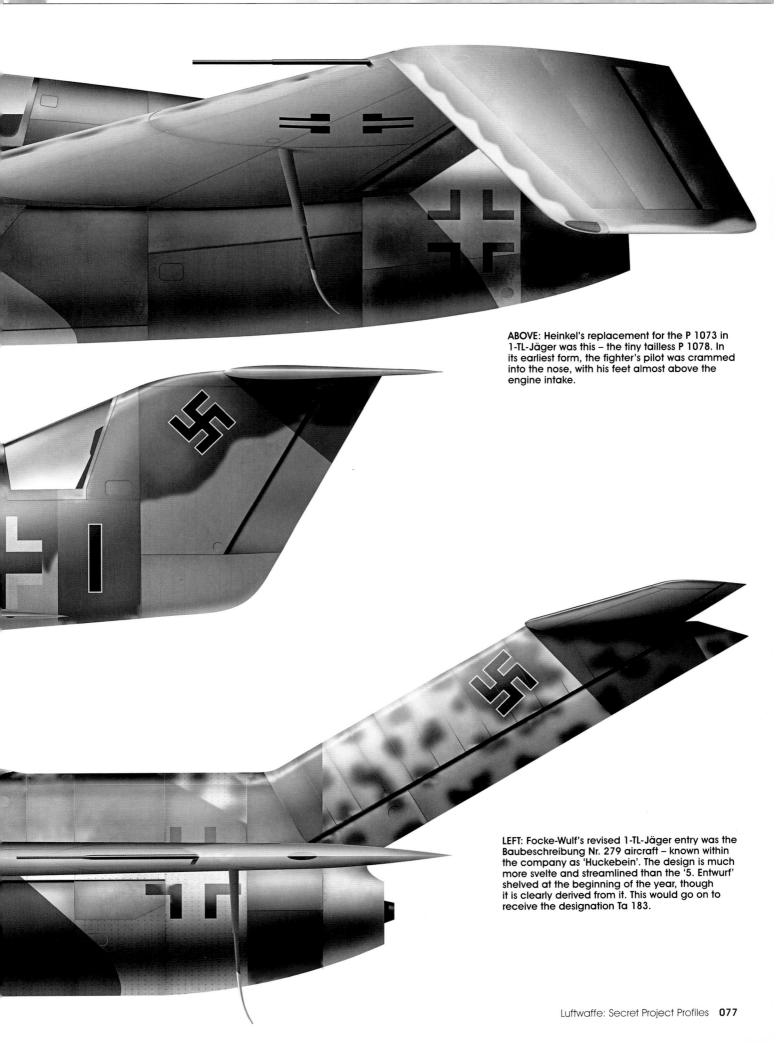

ABOVE: Heinkel's replacement for the P 1073 in 1-TL-Jäger was this – the tiny tailless P 1078. In its earliest form, the fighter's pilot was crammed into the nose, with his feet almost above the engine intake.

LEFT: Focke-Wulf's revised 1-TL-Jäger entry was the Baubeschreibung Nr. 279 aircraft – known within the company as 'Huckebein'. The design is much more svelte and streamlined than the '5. Entwurf' shelved at the beginning of the year, though it is clearly derived from it. This would go on to receive the designation Ta 183.

ABOVE: The last known form of the Blohm & Voss P 212 – the P 212.03. The aerodynamic shape is noticeably cleaner than that of earlier designs and rather than a single central fin, it has a fin on each wingtip for control.

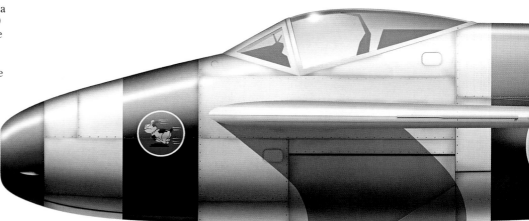

It would appear that Focke-Wulf was expecting a development contract for the Nr. 279 aircraft, what was designated the Ta 183, and Messerschmitt was expecting a development contract for either the P 1110 or the P 1111. It is unlikely to have been the P 1101, since the company seems to have largely abandoned work on the prototype of this model that it had already built. The EF 128 and P 212 had not been ruled out.

A further meeting of the EHK took place on March 20-24 at Focke-Wulf's Bad Eilsen facility, two days of which, the 22nd and 23rd, were devoted to a fifth comparison of the 1-TL-Jäger designs. It is unknown whether the companies chose to revise their entries or whether they remained the same. A brief summary of the meeting is given in the war diary of the chief of the TLR, Ulrich Diesing: "No final decision on the proposals, since the chairman of the Special Commission for Fighter Aircraft – Prof Messerschmitt – was absent. Fl-E-Chef has, with the approval of the plenipotentiary for jet aircraft, SS-Obergruppenführer Kammler, commissioned the Junkers firm with the development of design EF 128."

It would appear as though, with Germany on the very brink of collapse, the tailless Junkers EF 128 was approved for development. With Germany now being invaded on both eastern and western fronts and defensive positions being hastily prepared around Berlin in anticipation of the imminent arrival of Soviet forces, it seems unlikely that this development got very far. ●

RIGHT: The second and last known version of the Junkers EF 128. This design was actually approved for production in March 1945 – but by then it was far too late.

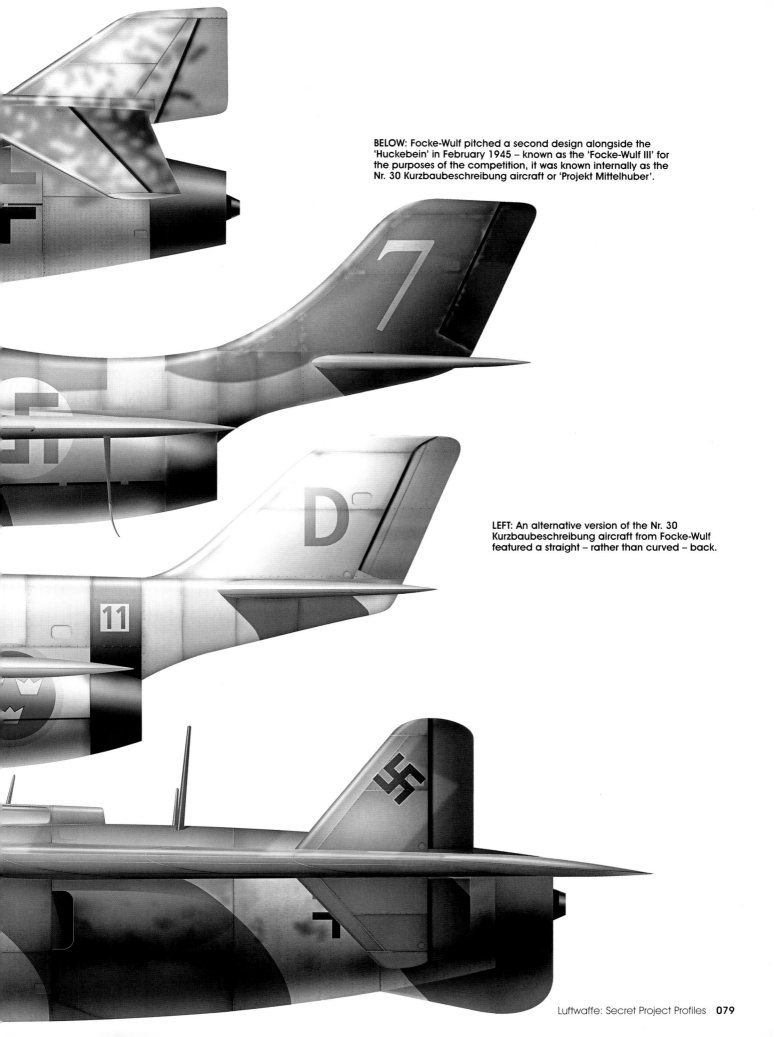

BELOW: Focke-Wulf pitched a second design alongside the 'Huckebein' in February 1945 – known as the 'Focke-Wulf III' for the purposes of the competition, it was known internally as the Nr. 30 Kurzbaubeschreibung aircraft or 'Projekt Mittelhuber'.

LEFT: An alternative version of the Nr. 30 Kurzbaubeschreibung aircraft from Focke-Wulf featured a straight – rather than curved – back.

RIGHT: The last Messerschmitt 1-TL-Jäger design was the P 1111. This tailless design had a sharply swept form but shortly after the war company project office chief Woldemar Voigt told Allied interrogators that its extreme design was regarded as too 'risky'.

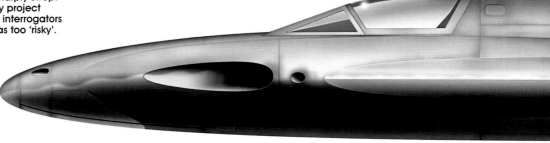

RIGHT: The final form of Messerschmitt's P 1101. A prototype of an earlier P 1101 design had actually been built but this version features a differently shaped canopy and fuselage.

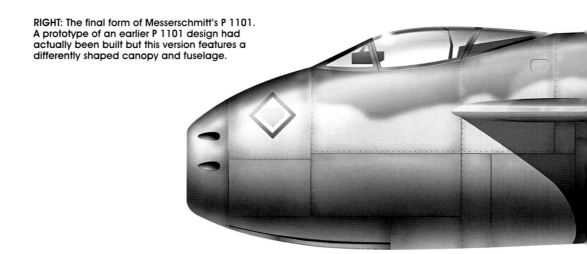

LEFT: Heinkel persisted with its little P 1078 into this new, slightly less cramped design. But the competition judges continued to take a dim view of it.

LEFT: Messerschmitt's remarkable P 1110 design looks strikingly modern. It is depicted here in Swedish colours to draw attention to its similarity to the later Saab 32 Lansen – which first flew in 1952.

Back to basics

Just as the search for a single-jet Me 262 replacement was getting into gear, a new single-jet fighter competition was launched. It was hoped that the result would be a 'people's fighter' that even untrained pilots could successfully fly into combat...

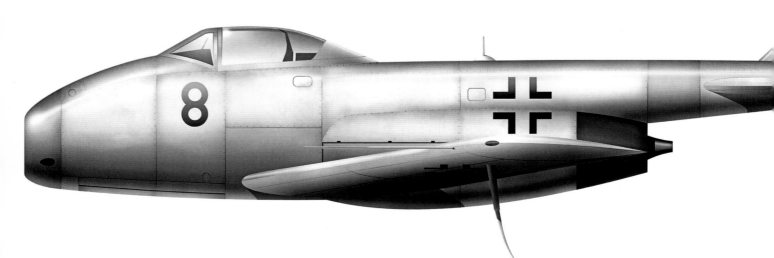

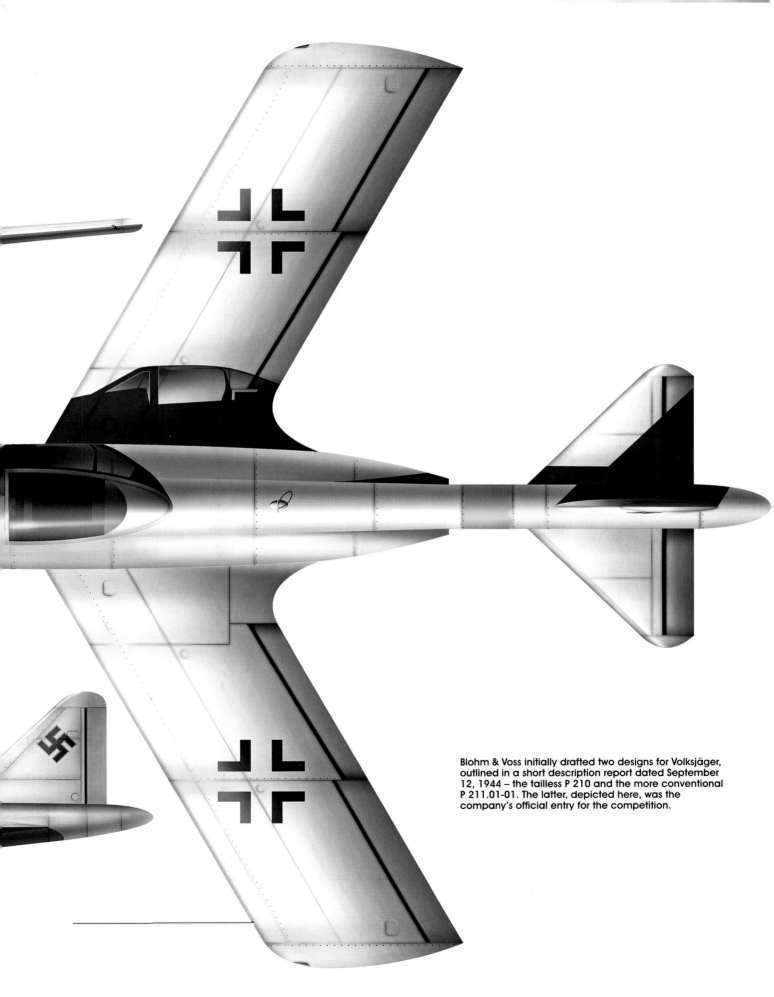

Blohm & Voss initially drafted two designs for Volksjäger, outlined in a short description report dated September 12, 1944 – the tailless P 210 and the more conventional P 211.01-01. The latter, depicted here, was the company's official entry for the competition.

It was clear from the demanding specification that the 1-TL-Jäger designs being worked on by the various manufacturers would take several years to reach full series production. And this was quite normal – even new conventional piston engine types such as the Ta 152 took at least two years to go from drawing board to active service.

But what if a less ambitious spec was put forward, one which would require performance only slightly better than that of existing piston engine types, and which would make use of an engine that was practically already in production? Surely such an aircraft could be ready in record time?

It was this line of thinking which resulted in the Volksjäger requirement of September 10, 1944.

Exactly whose idea it was to launch a second single-jet fighter competition before the presentations for the 1-TL-Jäger had even ended is uncertain – Heinkel director Carl Francke and Albert Speer's deputy Karl-Otto Saur are good candidates – but clearly a rapid turnaround was demanded.

The 1-TL-Jäger conference of September 8-10, 1944, was just winding down when, at around 11.40am, a telegram was sent to the offices of Arado, Blohm & Voss, Fieseler, Focke-Wulf, Heinkel, Junkers, Messerschmitt and Siebel outlining a new requirement. It called for a fighter "of the cheapest construction" powered by a single BMW 003 engine and made with "extensive use of wood and steel" that could reach a maximum speed of 750kph (466mph) and have an endurance of 30 minutes at full throttle. It also had to be able to operate from poor airfields, with a take-off roll of under 500m, and come equipped with two MK 108s or two MG 151s.

This was a much more achievable set of objectives compared to those of 1-TL-Jäger, which called for 1000kph (621mph) and a full hour's endurance with a single HeS 011 engine. However, the companies were only given between three and five days to complete the design work.

Only three of the eight companies had something to present when the first design conference was called on September 14, 1944 – Arado, Blohm & Voss and Heinkel.

The meeting took place at Berlin and was chaired by Heinkel technical director Carl Francke – who was also presenting the Heinkel design. He gave the delegates a detailed lecture which emphasised the fact that Heinkel had worked on its design

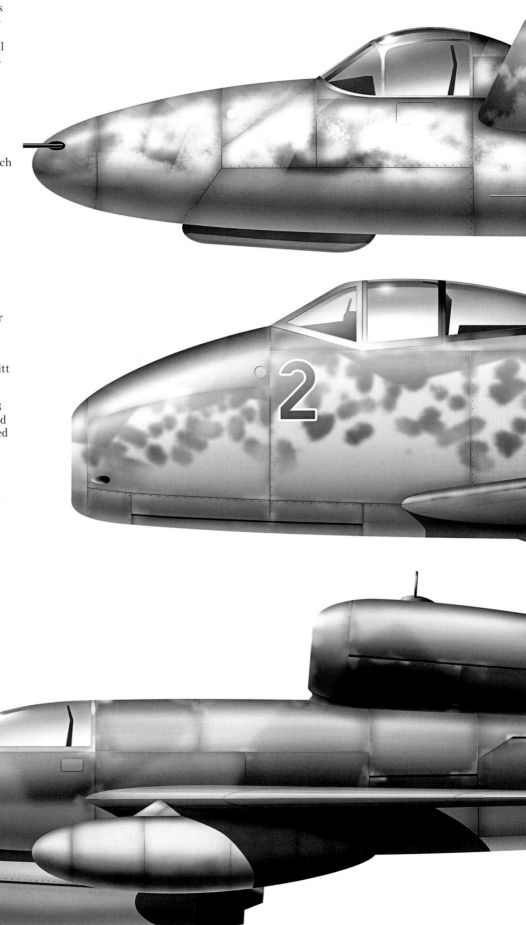

ABOVE: Arado's Volksjäger, the E 580, is somewhat reminiscent of the company's 1943 K-Jäger design and was universally rejected at the first competition design comparison.

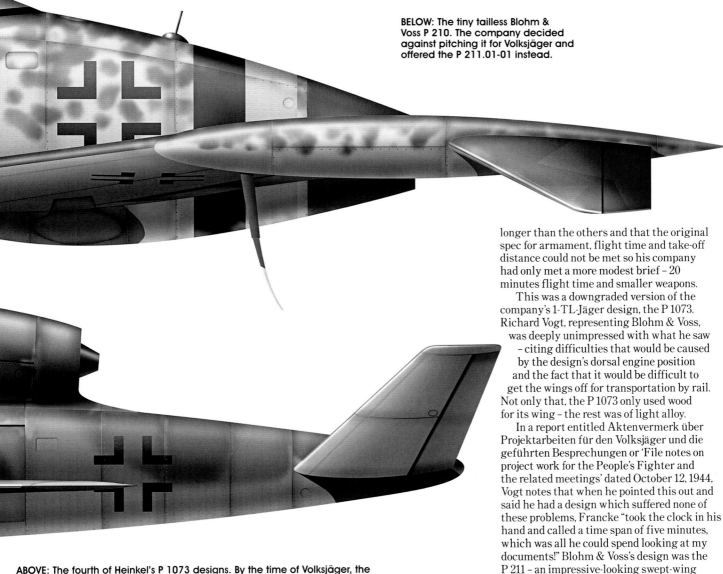

BELOW: The tiny tailless Blohm & Voss P 210. The company decided against pitching it for Volksjäger and offered the P 211.01-01 instead.

ABOVE: The fourth of Heinkel's P 1073 designs. By the time of Volksjäger, the company had evolved the design into a single-jet fighter that could be entered for 1-TL-Jäger. The Volksjäger P 1073 was just a simplified version of that design – with straight wings instead of swept, a twin-rudder tail instead of a V-tail and a BMW 003 instead of an HeS 011. This would become the He 162.

longer than the others and that the original spec for armament, flight time and take-off distance could not be met so his company had only met a more modest brief – 20 minutes flight time and smaller weapons.

This was a downgraded version of the company's 1-TL-Jäger design, the P 1073. Richard Vogt, representing Blohm & Voss, was deeply unimpressed with what he saw – citing difficulties that would be caused by the design's dorsal engine position and the fact that it would be difficult to get the wings off for transportation by rail. Not only that, the P 1073 only used wood for its wing – the rest was of light alloy.

In a report entitled Aktenvermerk über Projektarbeiten für den Volksjäger und die geführten Besprechungen or 'File notes on project work for the People's Fighter and the related meetings' dated October 12, 1944, Vogt notes that when he pointed this out and said he had a design which suffered none of these problems, Francke "took the clock in his hand and called a time span of five minutes, which was all he could spend looking at my documents!" Blohm & Voss's design was the P 211 – an impressive-looking swept-wing design based on a simple steel structure.

Arado's design was the E 580 – a small fighter with the turbojet mounted on its back like that of the P 1073 and the rear part of the cockpit canopy engine's intake. According to Vogt: "A project by the company Arado was also submitted, which was rejected by all involved. The company Focke-Wulf participated in the meeting only informally, because the time available was not sufficient to complete a project. The company Messerschmitt was uninterested in the model under discussion."

No decision was made but "after leaving Mr Francke, we were asked to Lieutenant-Colonel Knemeyer". Knemeyer was TLR Fl.-E-Chef – head of the RLM's development department – and a second discussion on the Volksjäger now commenced.

The TLR minutes of the meeting state: "Projects were submitted by the companies Arado, Blohm & Voss and Heinkel. According to the companies involved, the take-off requirement – rolling distance of 500m – is not achievable." Arado and Heinkel said they could meet the take-off distance but only by reducing flight time to 20 minutes. But "the project of the company Blohm & Voss is impressive in its construction and appears in this form extremely cheap and expedient for the intended construction. It also perfectly fulfils the demand for extensive use of wood and steel. Regardless of which company receives the final order, these aspects of Project B&V should be taken into account as much as possible.

"A production review of the B&V project will be carried out in the next few days. Everyone involved agreed at the final meeting with TLR Fl.-E-Chef that such an aircraft should be created without failing to deprive the Me 262 of any capacity. The project is particularly justified if it is possible to use large numbers of measures in the shortest possible time through special measures. The possible uses of such an aircraft are of course limited. The question of fuel quantity – 20 or 30 min. – is finally clarified between Chef-TLR [Diesing], TLR Fl-E-Chef [Knemeyer] and the General of Fighters [Adolf Galland]: 20 minutes flight time is probably too low."

Incredibly, on Saturday, September 16, Vogt received a telex from Heinkel "in which the visit of its chief designer, Mr Schwärzler, is announced to me on Sunday! He was instructed to determine to what extent my suggestions could be worked into his own project".

The next Volksjäger meeting was on September 19, at which projects drawn up by Arado, Blohm & Voss, Focke-Wulf, Fieseler, Junkers and Siebel were presented. Today, the design of the Fieseler and Siebel projects is lost – though Vogt's account confirms that they were presented at the meeting – while the Junkers design is known only from photographs of a model rather than drawings.

Precisely which Focke-Wulf design was presented is uncertain since the only known Focke-Wulf Volksjäger presentation document is dated September 20 – the day after the meeting – and

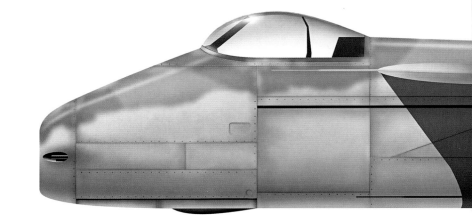

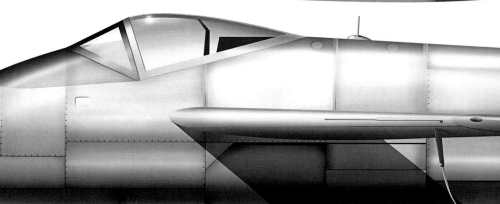

BELOW: Blohm & Voss quickly shed the 'riskier' design elements of its P 211.01-01 and produced the simplified P 211.01-02. This had straight wings, a straight tailfin and a straighter, easier to build nose section. This was how the design looked by September 29, 1944 – just as it was being defeated by the P 1073.

ABOVE: Focke-Wulf was late in delivering its Volksjäger designs but when it did eventually put them forward, a simplified Baubeschreibung Nr. 280 'Flitzer' was offered in much the same way that Heinkel offered a simplified P 1073.

ABOVE: Junkers was also late to the Volksjäger party and offered this small fighter as its entry – but was unsuccessful.

ABOVE: Another of Focke-Wulf's entries was the bespoke Volksflugzeug – evidently a new design for the competition rather than a rehash of an existing one.

day after the meeting – and features a Volksflugzeug, which is somewhat similar to the P 211, a downgraded version of the company's 1-TL-Jäger 'Flitzer' design and another 'option' in the form of a turboprop version of the 1-TL-Jäger design – known in other company documents as 'Peterle'.

During this meeting, chaired by Roluf Lucht, Vogt again raised his objections to the Heinkel design but "the way in which these important questions were dealt with at this commission meeting had a shattering effect on me. There was no question of an assessment of things, let alone a more serious examination. It remained with general discussion and remarks thrown over the table, which were for the most part untenable and worthless".

In return, Heinkel's representative Carl Frydag expressed doubt's about Vogt's design, "pointing out the difficulties involved in the production of removable skin panels. He did not say a word of appreciation for the unique assembly opportunity I could offer and not a word about the appropriate material types. No one contributed a single positive thought – only criticism".

Again, no decision was made. But on September 30, Knemeyer announced that a decision had been made and that Heinkel's He 162 would be built.

Vogt, convinced that this was a terrible error, went back to the RLM on October 2 and gave a convincing presentation to Knemeyer, demonstrating that his design was superior to that of Heinkel. All those present, including Heinrich Beauvais, the head of fighter testing at Rechlin, agreed that the P 211 ought to have won the contest.

Knemeyer "did not want to argue the decision and defended it with psychological reasons". He promised Vogt to put his design back up for discussion. In the afternoon, Vogt attended a meeting with the RLM's production specialists, who were also convinced that the P 211 would be better than the P 1073. Vogt rang Lucht and "informed him of my exasperation that he had committed himself to a model that, from a military and maintenance point of view, was bad". Lucht told him that the decision had been made following a personal presentation of the P 1073 by Frydag to Saur. Vogt was invited to present his grievance to Obersturmbahnführer Herbert Klemm, state secretary of the Reich Ministry of Justice in the Waffen-SS main office. He made the presentation but "expressly pointed out that no charge would be made by me" though Klemm was apparently also convinced that the wrong decision had been made.

Vogt was told that Saur would be asked to consider whether the wrong type had been approved for construction but it then transpired that Frydag had raised doubts about the P 211's intake duct. At this, Vogt enlisted the AVA to assess his design and after wind tunnel tests they found that there was no problem with it.

By now, however, it was far too late and the P 1073 went on to be built as the He 162. ●

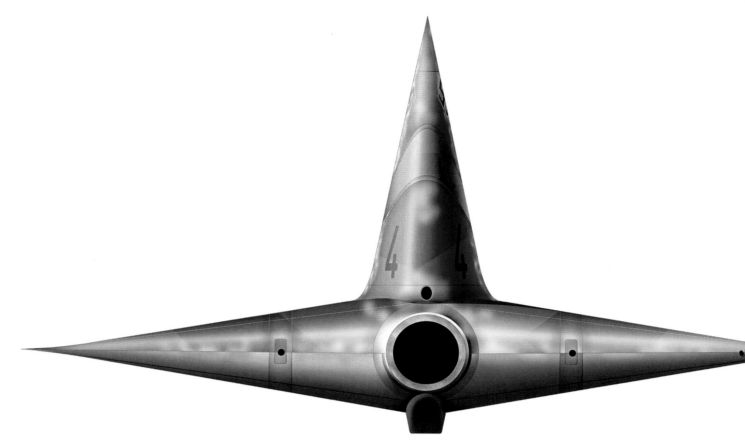

Lorin's legacy

Ramjet fighters

As resources dwindled, the ramjet became an increasingly appealing concept to German aircraft designers – in theory it could make phenomenal speeds achievable using only powdered coal for fuel. In theory.

Towards the end of 1944, Alexander Lippisch was heavily involved in designing this ramjet-powered rammer – the P 13. In artistic renderings, as here, the design is usually depicted with gun holes in its wings but this part of the wing was actually where it hinged up to allow access for refuelling the ramjet motor. If there were holes at these locations, they were most likely for cooling purposes – to prevent heat from the ramjet damaging the aircraft's structure.

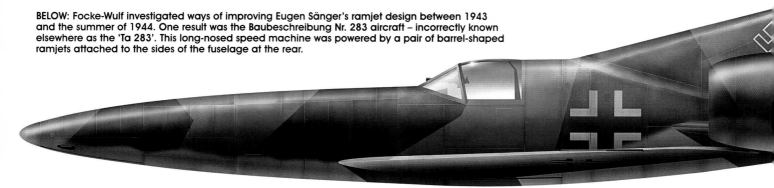

BELOW: Focke-Wulf investigated ways of improving Eugen Sänger's ramjet design between 1943 and the summer of 1944. One result was the Baubeschreibung Nr. 283 aircraft – incorrectly known elsewhere as the 'Ta 283'. This long-nosed speed machine was powered by a pair of barrel-shaped ramjets attached to the sides of the fuselage at the rear.

irst described as a concept by Frenchman René Lorin in 1908, the ramjet was nothing new, even at the beginning of the Second World War. Just as the Germans called the piston engine 'Otto' after the man they saw as its inventor, so they called the ramjet 'Lorin'. The British tended to refer to it as the athodyd instead – a contraction of Aero THermoDYnamic Duct.

A ramjet needs to be moving forwards before it can produce any thrust – with the air being 'rammed' into its intake by this motion acting like the compressor of a jet engine. Lorin couldn't get his engine moving quickly enough to work, nor did he have the necessary materials to build it. However, these problems were more easily overcome in Germany during the late 1930s and engineer Hellmuth Walter set to work on a ramjet in 1936 before switching to rocket propulsion instead.

BMW and Junkers also investigated the concept before Austrian inventor Eugen Sänger went a step further in 1941 by creating and testing working ramjets. He ran them on the back of Dornier Do 17s and 217s in flight with the specific goal of creating an example that could power an interceptor aircraft. The basic form of the aircraft itself was set down but the project was shelved in 1943 before the engines could be made to produce sufficient thrust, but in the meantime Focke-Wulf had taken notice and begun steps to start its own ramjet research.

Company aerodynamicist Dr Otto Ernst Pabst set up a new facility at Kirchhorsten in 1943 with the goal of cutting down the length of Sänger's duct – making it work more efficiently. The result was a new ramjet design that was proposed for at least two very different fighter projects. The more conventional of the two, outlined in the company's Baubeschreibung Nr. 283 dated August 4, 1944, and referred to as a

Strahlrohrjäger or 'Ray tube fighter', was a single-seater with a very long nose and sharply swept-back wing. The tailplane was swept back at both leading and trailing edges and two Pabst ramjet units were mounted one on either side. There was a Walter starter rocket at the end of the fuselage, below the tail.

Behind the guns in the nose there was a 20mm-thick armoured bulkhead protecting the forward ramjet fuel tank of 308 gallons capacity. The cockpit was in the middle and behind it were three more tanks – another one for ramjet fuel and the other two for the rocket motor's hydrazine hydrate and hydrogen peroxide.

The other Focke-Wulf ramjet design about which most is known is referred to as the Triebflugeljäger or 'Power-wing fighter'. It had three wings rotating around a cigar-shaped central fuselage, each with a ramjet at the tip. The pitch of the wings could be adjusted by the pilot and their maximum speed, which was to normally be used only while climbing, was 670ft/sec (455mph).

Having the ramjets spinning from the outset meant they could be activated while the aircraft fuselage itself was still sitting motionless on the ground.

For take-off the aircraft was to stand on its tail, which housed five wheels. Three small 660lb thrust Walter rocket engines, each incorporated into one of the ramjets, would be used to get the wings rotating and the ramjets started.

The wings would be at neutral pitch to begin with, then moved into fine pitch, creating lift. Once the aircraft reached the desired altitude and began to level out, the pitch would be increased and the speed of wing rotation therefore reduced to prevent the wing tips from exceeding Mach 0.9. At the aircraft's top speed in forward motion, the wings would be rotating at 220rpm.

The Focke-Wulf report on the Triebflugeljäger stated that the design had six key benefits: low fuel consumption, high altitude capability, no runway needed, low weight, simplicity and the ability to use any combustible gas or liquid that could be vaporised as fuel.

Neither design was submitted to the RLM and both remained strictly private ventures on Focke-Wulf's part. Similarly, neither reached the mock-up stage.

Alexander Lippisch had begun working on ramjets in parallel to his P 11, latterly renamed Delta VI, at the LFW during 1944. His first ramjet aircraft design was the curvy streamlined P 12, which would be brought up to speed either while carried on the back of another aircraft or with the aid of a rocket-powered launching sled. The P 12's ramjet was liquid-fuelled.

Improvements to the shape of the air intake and combustion chamber, combined with the decision to use powdered coal as a fuel, led to a new design during the summer of 1944: the wedge-shaped P 13. The aircraft had a tubular intake on its nose and the pilot sat within its huge fin. Rather than being a conventionally armed fighter, the P 13 was to be a rammer – its angular edges fitted with a hard edge to slice through the relatively thin metal of Allied bomber airframes.

Inside its short fuselage, the aircraft's fuel would take the form of either a wire mesh grate filled with powdered coal or pressed coal in plates and hollow cylindrical shapes. It would be brought up to ramjet ignition speed using either rockets or a catapult. Refuelling was a

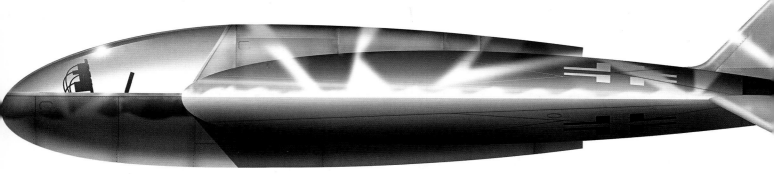

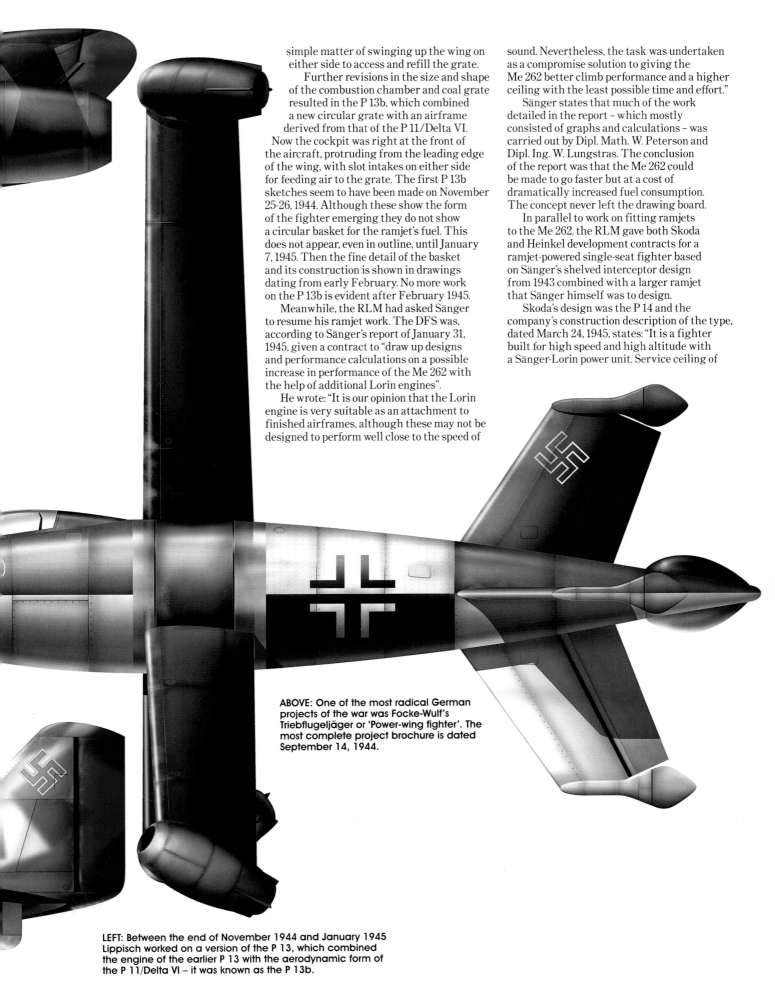

simple matter of swinging up the wing on either side to access and refill the grate.

Further revisions in the size and shape of the combustion chamber and coal grate resulted in the P 13b, which combined a new circular grate with an airframe derived from that of the P 11/Delta VI. Now the cockpit was right at the front of the aircraft, protruding from the leading edge of the wing, with slot intakes on either side for feeding air to the grate. The first P 13b sketches seem to have been made on November 25-26, 1944. Although these show the form of the fighter emerging they do not show a circular basket for the ramjet's fuel. This does not appear, even in outline, until January 7, 1945. Then the fine detail of the basket and its construction is shown in drawings dating from early February. No more work on the P 13b is evident after February 1945.

Meanwhile, the RLM had asked Sänger to resume his ramjet work. The DFS was, according to Sänger's report of January 31, 1945, given a contract to "draw up designs and performance calculations on a possible increase in performance of the Me 262 with the help of additional Lorin engines".

He wrote: "It is our opinion that the Lorin engine is very suitable as an attachment to finished airframes, although these may not be designed to perform well close to the speed of sound. Nevertheless, the task was undertaken as a compromise solution to giving the Me 262 better climb performance and a higher ceiling with the least possible time and effort."

Sänger states that much of the work detailed in the report – which mostly consisted of graphs and calculations – was carried out by Dipl. Math. W. Peterson and Dipl. Ing. W. Lungstras. The conclusion of the report was that the Me 262 could be made to go faster but at a cost of dramatically increased fuel consumption. The concept never left the drawing board.

In parallel to work on fitting ramjets to the Me 262, the RLM gave both Skoda and Heinkel development contracts for a ramjet-powered single-seat fighter based on Sänger's shelved interceptor design from 1943 combined with a larger ramjet that Sänger himself was to design.

Skoda's design was the P 14 and the company's construction description of the type, dated March 24, 1945, states: "It is a fighter built for high speed and high altitude with a Sänger-Lorin power unit. Service ceiling of

ABOVE: One of the most radical German projects of the war was Focke-Wulf's Triebflügeljäger or 'Power-wing fighter'. The most complete project brochure is dated September 14, 1944.

LEFT: Between the end of November 1944 and January 1945 Lippisch worked on a version of the P 13, which combined the engine of the earlier P 13 with the aerodynamic form of the P 11/Delta VI – it was known as the P 13b.

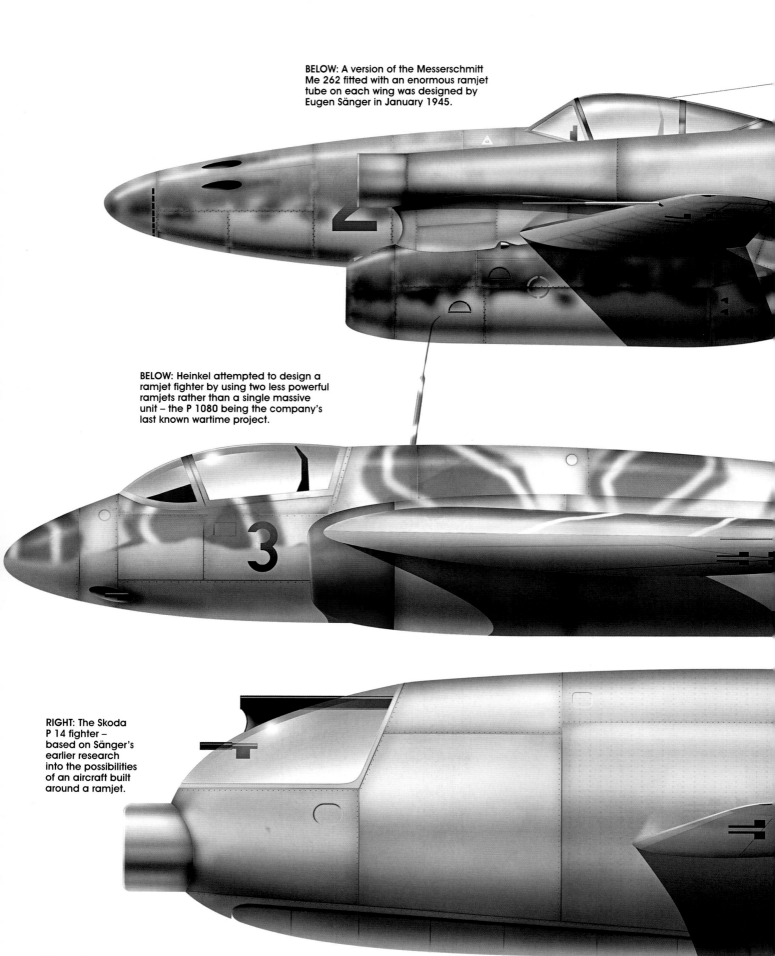

BELOW: A version of the Messerschmitt Me 262 fitted with an enormous ramjet tube on each wing was designed by Eugen Sänger in January 1945.

BELOW: Heinkel attempted to design a ramjet fighter by using two less powerful ramjets rather than a single massive unit – the P 1080 being the company's last known wartime project.

RIGHT: The Skoda P 14 fighter – based on Sänger's earlier research into the possibilities of an aircraft built around a ramjet.

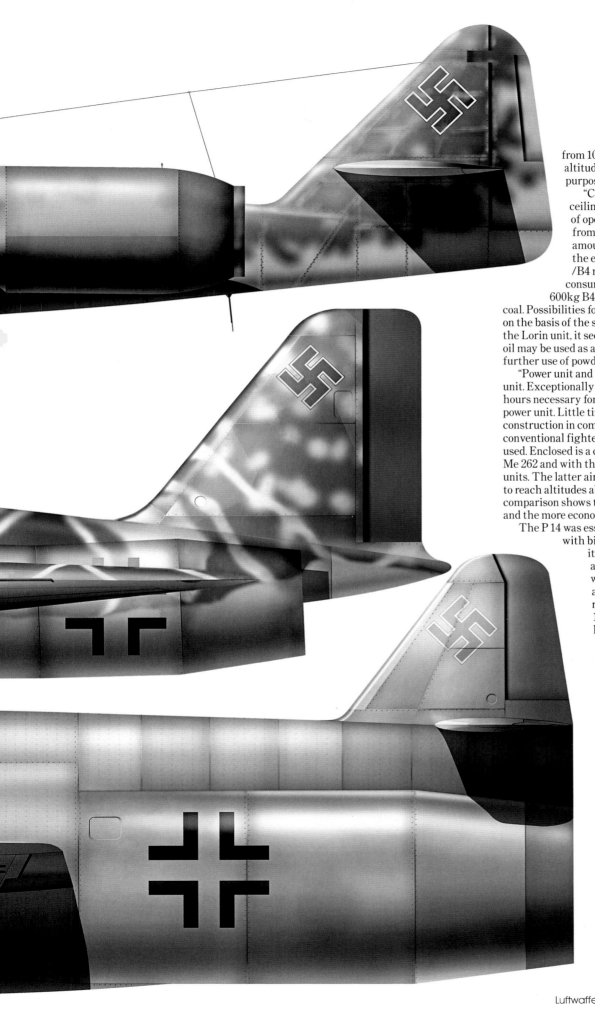

from 10,000 to 15,000m. Maximum altitude 18,500m, thus built for the purpose of counteracting the B-29.

"Climbing time to service ceiling is 5 to 6 minutes. Time of operation at service ceiling from 30 to 45 minutes. The amount of fuel necessary for the entire flight is 1200kg /B4 m I2/ measured fuel consumption. BEING TESTED: 600kg B4 or I2 + 850kg powdered coal. Possibilities for further development: on the basis of the special characteristics of the Lorin unit, it seems possible that crude oil may be used as a liquid fuel and that a further use of powdered coal is possible.

"Power unit and fuselage are a single unit. Exceptionally small number of man-hours necessary for construction of the power unit. Little time needed for total construction in comparison to that of conventional fighters. No critical materials used. Enclosed is a comparison with the Me 262 and with the Me 262 + 2 x Lorin units. The latter aircraft was developed to reach altitudes above 10,000m. This comparison shows the better performances and the more economical use of fuel."

The P 14 was essentially a ramjet tube with bits of aircraft stuck on to it. The pilot had to lie prone above it and the aircraft would be armed with just a single MK 103 with 70 rounds. Wing area was 12.5sqm, wingspan 7.9m, length 9.5m, height 4.2m.

Heinkel's competing aircraft design, the tailless P 1080, was aerodynamically cleaner and much more compact – though the project was incomplete when the war ended. The Heinkel team had worked out that it ought to be possible to get better results from a pair of smaller ramjet tubes than one large one, resulting in a simpler layout with the pilot given a conventional seated cockpit similar to that of the He 162. Wingspan was 8.9m, length is 8.15m and wing area is 20sqm. Its ramjets were each 90cm in diameter.

As with all the other ramjet projects – neither of these 'final fighters' got anywhere near the prototype stage. ●

Die ersten strahlbomber der welt

Work on the Arado Ar 234 demonstrated that a high-flying jet aircraft would be practically invulnerable to piston-engined interceptors – which meant that the jet engine was the perfect powerplant for a bomber.

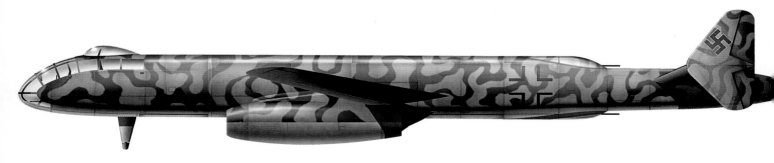

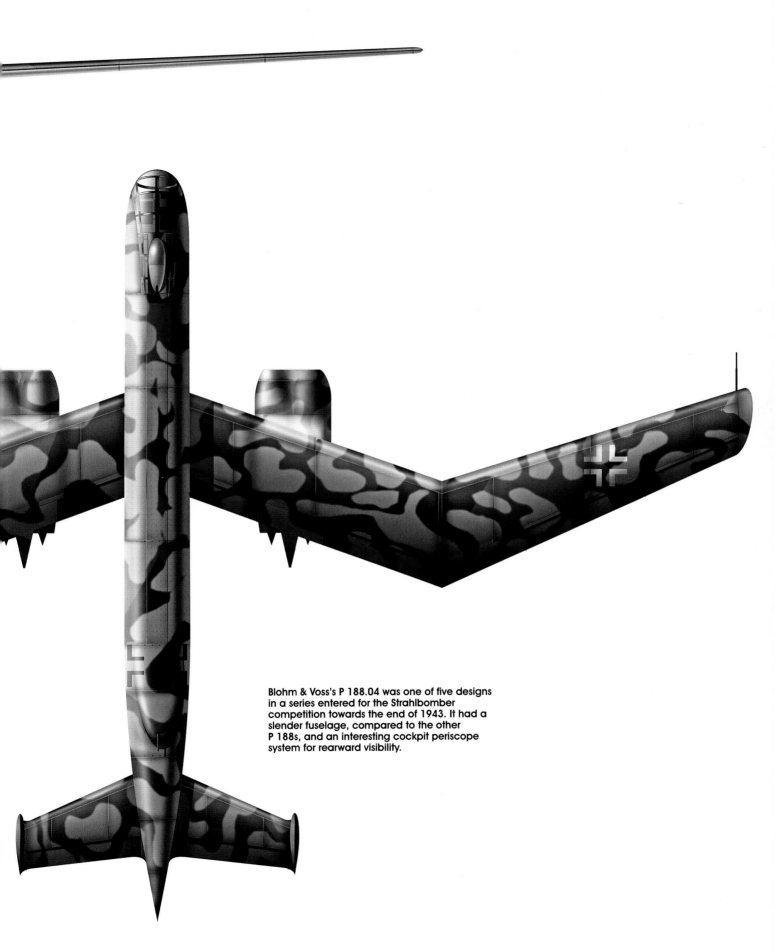

Blohm & Voss's P 188.04 was one of five designs in a series entered for the Strahlbomber competition towards the end of 1943. It had a slender fuselage, compared to the other P 188s, and an interesting cockpit periscope system for rearward visibility.

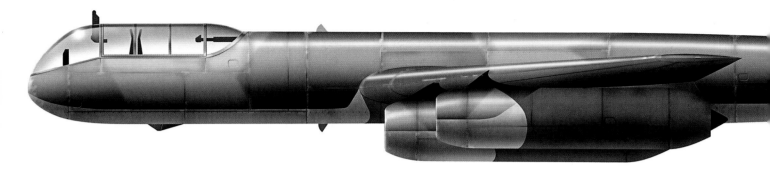

The Ar 234 had been designed with the most straightforward aerodynamic layout possible. It had a slender fuselage, conventional cruciform tail and straight wings with its engines held in nacelles beneath them. The result was a safe and unambitious aircraft well suited to the straight and level flying required for aerial reconnaissance.

Arado was well aware that there was room for improvement but it was aware, too, that the Ar 234's relatively small size and tightly packed fuselage would undoubtedly limit its potential. In November 1942, the company established a new experimental programme under the designation E 560 to assess the potential of different swept or pfeilflügel 'arrow wing' shapes.

It was hoped that a swept wing form, either straight or kinked, could be developed for use with future high-speed aircraft. From the outset, it was considered that E 560 wings might well be suitable for the next stage of the Ar 234's development too.

Extensive wind tunnel testing followed which concentrated on the relationship between an aircraft's fuselage, swept wings and jet engines. After nine months, on August 11, 1943, the company produced a report entitled Vorschlag für die Weiterentwicklung schneller Zweisitzer or 'Proposal for the development of a fast two-seater'.

This presented a series of potential layouts for future designs, including several powered by turbojets, and concentrated on the 16 tonne aircraft, the smallest jet-powered design. This, it was argued, represented the best possible power-to-weight ratio using a pair of Jumo 012 engines. The Jumo 012, only a drawing board project at this point, had an 11-stage axial compressor and a two-stage turbine.

The report features detailed illustrations of this aircraft design as a heavy fighter and as a heavy bomber and presents a version powered by six BMW 003s, since these engines were expected to be available sooner than the Jumo 012. Another illustration shows how the Arado design would be armed for the five different roles outlined in the report.

The report seems to have prompted the RLM into commencing a new competition to find the Luftwaffe a jet bomber in September 1943, with tenders for a new 'Strahlbomber'

being invited from Arado itself, Junkers and Blohm & Voss. Messerschmitt also designed a new jet bomber at this time – the P 1100, a twin-jet design – and although the company compared this to the other contenders, it is unclear whether it was actually entered for the competition.

STRAHL-BOMBER

The Arado entry, project E 395, abandoned the straight swept leading edge version of the E 560 wing and offered instead a two-seater with a choice of either unswept wings or a less sharply swept 'crescent' version of the E 560.

It was effectively a scaled-up version of the Ar 234 with aerodynamic improvements incorporated into the design. Where the Ar 234 was 12.64m long, the E 395 was 16.85m long, and where the Ar 234's wingspan was 14.41m, the E 395's was 17.6m.

This low-risk approach seems to have been under consideration since at least August 1943, the design pre-dating the competition itself, but it had changed little even by January 1944. The slightly bulged pressure cabin of the fast-two seater proposed in the Arado report that same month was rejected in favour of a smooth bullet-shaped nose.

There is a hint of the fast two-seater in the design's four engines, however. These are given as either HeS 011s or Jumo 012s – the type intended for the design with the sharply swept wings. The aircraft offered in January 1944 was presented alongside an alternative with a 'pfeilflügel'. This was one of the curving E 560 shapes, rather than the straight leading edge type.

The Junkers entry was the EF 122. Like Arado, Junkers had spent months investigating

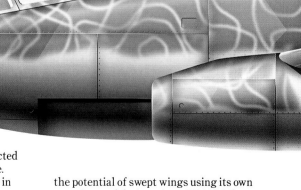

BELOW: This version of the P 1100 sacrificed defensive weaponry for the sake of internal bomb load and a speedy getaway.

the potential of swept wings using its own experimental designation – EF 116. Like some of the EF 116 arrangements, the EF 122 featured forward-swept wings but retained a conventional tailfin and unswept horizontal tail surfaces. From the outset its four engines were to be Jumo 004Cs rather than Heinkel HeS 011s or Jumo 012s. Two were to be attached directly to the fuselage, near the nose, and another would sit atop the trailing edge of each wing.

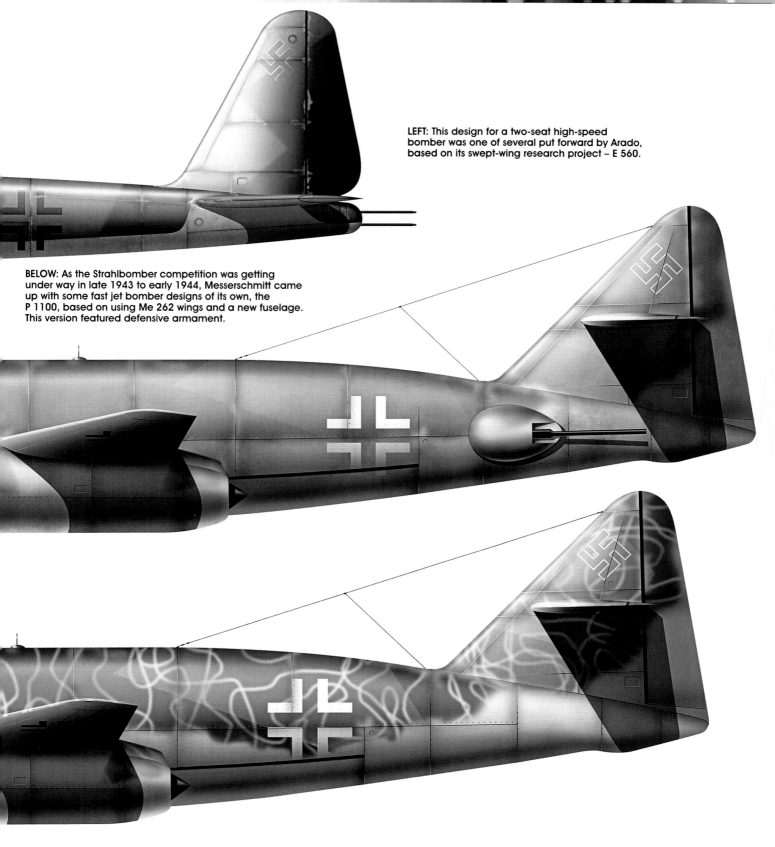

LEFT: This design for a two-seat high-speed bomber was one of several put forward by Arado, based on its swept-wing research project – E 560.

BELOW: As the Strahlbomber competition was getting under way in late 1943 to early 1944, Messerschmitt came up with some fast jet bomber designs of its own, the P 1100, based on using Me 262 wings and a new fuselage. This version featured defensive armament.

Blohm & Voss's Strahlbomber was the P 188. Presented to the RLM in four slightly different configurations, though a fifth was also later studied, the P 188 offered a host of novel features – landing gear retracting into the fuselage rather than the wings, with only small unstressed support wheels on the wings themselves; wings which rotated at their root so that the wings rather than the fuselage would pitch up on landing; and a highly unorthodox W-shaped wing planform

intended to provide the benefits of a swept-back wing at high speeds and the advantages of a swept-forward wing at low speeds. Power for all four versions of the P 188 would come from a quartet of Jumo 004Cs, although other engine types were not ruled out.

Despite also boasting a simple internal structure, the P 188 seems to have offered few advantages and some serious potential risks arising from its unusual configuration. As a result, it was dropped

and the EF 122 was approved for prototype construction under the designation Ju 287.

However, the RLM felt that the forward-swept wing configuration of the Ju 287 was still risky and decided to have a simpler second design built as insurance. Heinkel was approached and told to design a simple four-jet bomber as a matter of urgency. The company was told to take Arado's E 395 and use that as the basis of its new project, so Heinkel chief engineer Siegfried Günter went to collect the documents personally from Rüdiger Kosin at Arado's offices in Landeshut, Silesia, eastern Germany, on January 24, 1944.

Just over a week later, on February 1, Heinkel produced a report entitled 'Strabo 16 to'. This outlined the new Heinkel design, which was a combination of the firm's own four-jet project, the P 1068, and the scaled-up Ar 234, and emphasised the simple nature of the 'Strabo 16 to' aircraft and the rapidity with which it would be built. It quickly received the official RLM designation He 343.

JU 287 VS HE 343

Having been told to develop the He 343 as a matter of extreme urgency, Ernst Heinkel was surprised to find that days, weeks and then months passed without the necessary orders being given to set the work in motion.

He personally wrote a letter to Knemeyer in July 1944, emphasising the suitability of the He 343 for immediate mass production and arguing that the Ju 287 was a hazardous design that promised little in return for the risks involved.

He compared the two designs in great detail and took issue with Junkers' projected performance statistics. The additional cost of building the Ju 287 – the He 343 would be much cheaper to build – was simply not worthwhile, he argued.

The letter's combative tone prompted Knemeyer to forward it on to Heinrich Hertel, technical director at Junkers, for comment. Hertel refuted Heinkel's arguments and cast aspersions on Heinkel's own figures for the He 343. The disagreement ended without a clear winner – work on the Ju 287 was suspended at the end of September 1944 with a 'flying mock-up' having been constructed and test-flown. The He 343 was cancelled but the P 1068 project would go on to have a second life as a basis for supersonic research at the DFS.

FLYING WING BOMBERS

Arado may have been forced to hand over its work on the scaled-up Ar 234 to Heinkel in January 1944, but the state-owned company nevertheless continued its work on dedicated jet bomber designs. During the summer of 1943, it had launched a second experimental jet bomber study designated E 555. This ran in parallel with E 560 but rather than focusing on swept-wing designs, it looked at flying-wing layouts.

The earliest known document from the E 555 programme is dated July 14, 1943, and comprises a chart showing the horizontal top speeds of configurations E 555-6, -7, -8 and 10, each of which was to have been fitted with a trio of BMW 018 engines.

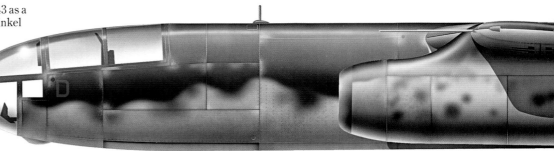

BELOW: Arado's Strahlbomber was the E 395. It came in two versions – one with crescent-shaped wings derived from the E 560 programme and one with straight wings. The fuselage of each was essentially scaled up from that of the Ar 234.

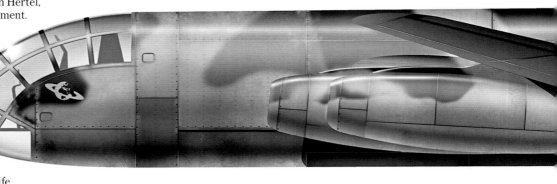

BELOW: The unarmed Blohm & Voss P 188.01 with aerodynamic cockpit and single fin.

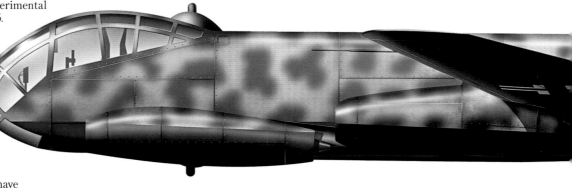

BELOW: Junkers' EF 122 would be redesignated Ju 287 after it won the Strahlbomber competition. Numerous different engine configurations were tried and versions with and without remote-controlled tail armament were drafted.

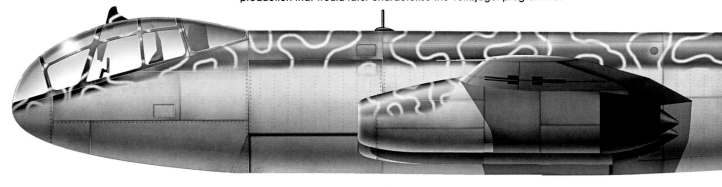

BELOW: Heinkel's He 343 – which started off as P 1068, then became the 'Strabo 16 to', then received its official RLM designation. It was a basic design intended for the sort of rapid mass production that would later characterise the Volksjäger programme.

The last known document relating directly to the E 555 'Nurflügelprojekt' as it is entitled in Arado company documents, a handwritten sheet of calculations, is dated August 15, 1944. However, activity on the project seems to have peaked between September 1943 and February 1944. Then, on October 18, 1944, Arado issued a report entitled Bomber für Höhe Geschwindigkeit und Grosse Reichweite or 'A high-speed long-range bomber' which offered up the E 555 flying wing designs that had existed in one form or another since the summer of 1943 configured as a selection of bombers without using the E 555 designation, just as the fast bomber proposal had not mentioned E 560.

It seems that at least a dozen E 555 configurations existed but some were passed over in choosing 10 to present with the report. These were forms 1, 2, 3, 4, 7, 8a, 8b, 9, 10 and 11.

They varied considerably in layout, ranging from just one engine to six, depending on the powerplant. Some had tail fins on their trailing edge, three had twin-boom tails and one had a conventional fuselage but with the characteristic E 555 wing shape superimposed over it.

Mirroring what happened after Arado put forward its proposal for a new two-seat fast bomber, a new jet bomber development competition was launched around a month after the publication of 'A high-speed long-range bomber'. It was entitled Langstreckenbomber - but this time there

would be no formal entry from Arado. Instead, Messerschmitt would compete against Junkers and rank outsiders the Horten brothers.

LANGSTRECKENBOMBER

Work on the Ju 287 had been suspended in September 1944 but in November, two months later, interest in a four-engined jet bomber was revived. Arado had just completed its E 555 report when Willy Messerschmitt offered the Entwicklungshauptkommission his new P 1107 project. His proposal was simple - build a fast four-engined jet bomber that could bypass Allied defences and deliver a heavy payload.

While this had previously been the basis of the Strahlbomber competition, it was now suggested that the Strahlbomber might actually be the solution to a very particular problem plaguing Germany at that time: a fleet of jet bombers could fly to Britain unassailed and destroy the Allied bomber fleets on the

ground – thereby halting the round-the-clock attacks being made by the USAAF and RAF.

The first full P 1107 brochure was published on January 26, 1945, and briefly outlined the project as a two-stage development. The first stage "vorläufige Lösung" or 'temporary solution' P 1107 was a bomber with a smooth cigar-shaped fuselage and swept wings with a 17.3m span. Its engines were to be grouped into two pairs of two and attached to the underside of its wings and its horizontal tail surfaces would be positioned at the top of its fin in a T-tail configuration. Its tricycle undercarriage would consist of a double nosewheel and two very large mainwheels – all of them retracting into the 18.4m long fuselage – and within the tail was room for a large reconnaissance camera. It would be unarmed save for its bomb load.

The second stage "endgültige Lösung" or 'final solution' as Messerschmitt put it, would

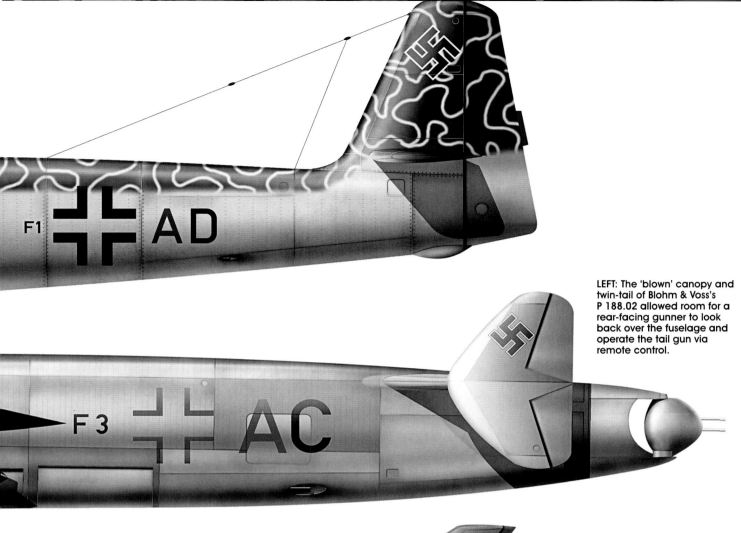

LEFT: The 'blown' canopy and twin-tail of Blohm & Voss's P 188.02 allowed room for a rear-facing gunner to look back over the fuselage and operate the tail gun via remote control.

ABOVE: The advanced version of Messerschmitt's P 1107 four-engined fast bomber. The quick-availability version had a T- rather than V-tail and engines attached to the underside of its wings rather than built into the wing roots.

utilise the same fuselage and undercarriage but with the engines now submerged into the wing roots and the T-tail replaced with a V-tail. Wingspan remained the same but the nature of the V-tail meant the overall length was slightly reduced, to 18m.

Neither stage was fully illustrated and only scant data was offered. Despite the date on the cover, the committee tasked with assessing the proposal did not receive it until some days later.

In the meantime, on January 27, Junkers issued its own report document, also brief, comparing the P 1107 to the Ju 287 and emphasising their similarities. At around this time, a date was set for a formal conference to fully examine the two designs and a third design was added, the Horten XVIII.

The mammoth four-day event was to take place from February 20-23 at Junkers' Dessau headquarters and would involve both the Sonderkommission 'Flugzeugzellenbau' or Special Commission for Airframe Construction and the EHK, the latter chaired by Junkers director Heinrich Hertel.

A panel of interested parties and independent experts was assembled to go over the designs, establish their relative merits and identify their flaws. These included Ludwig Bölkow, representing Messerschmitt; Hans Gropler, head of Junkers' project office; Reimar and Walter Horten, representing themselves; Rüdiger Kosin of Arado, production management specialist Senior Staff Engineer Kohl and Professor August Quick of the

Deutsche Versuchsanstalt für Luftfahrt (DVL).

By the time of the event, drawings of the P 1107 still had not been submitted and Bölkow was left attempting to outline his company's project with just the performance predictions and a description for his fellow delegates to go on. Little time was spent outlining the Ju 287's features at the beginning of the conference since most of those present were already intimately familiar with its design but the Hortens' XVIII was largely an unknown quantity.

The flying wing had been designed by Reimar Horten only a few months earlier, while he and his brother Walter were working on their large flying wing transport, the Horten VIII. The H XVIII had a fixed undercarriage and four HeS 011 turbojets. From the post-conference report itself, issued by the DVL at Berlin-Adlershof on February 25, 1945, it is clear that all the delegates were fascinated by the Horten XVIII's layout and were keen to explore its potential through detailed engineering calculations.

It was required that each of the three designs – the P 1107, Ju 287 and H XVIII – should be assessed with a fuel load of 15,000kg and a payload of 4000kg of bombs. It was found, on crunching the numbers, that Messerschmitt had been rather over-optimistic about the P 1107's weight but the Hortens had been overly pessimistic about the H XVIII, which would actually have been lighter than they anticipated.

RIGHT: The Horten H XVIII flying wing had huge fixed undercarriage 'legs' housing its enormous wheels beneath large doors at the base. The aircraft's shape meant it could contain sufficient fuel for an impressive range.

In terms of performance, at 7000m the Ju 287 was calculated to have a top speed of 885km/h, the P 1107 933km/h and the H XVIII 861km/h, range was Ju 287 4430km, P 1107 4850km (Messerschmitt had given a range of 7400km) and H XVIII 5350km. In fact, the H XVIII could go even further because the interior of the flying wing shape was extremely spacious, meaning more fuel could be carried for a range of 6500km.

On the face of it, the H XVIII seemed like a clear winner. However, the panel of experts considered that the positioning of its turbojets, in nacelles attached to the fixed undercarriage, would cause difficulties and the undercarriage itself would result in undue wear on the wheels. In addition, the amount of time required to properly test the H XVIII's unusual aerodynamic form would be disproportionately large and it was this more than anything else which seems to have determined the panel's decision to choose the Ju 287, which had already been thoroughly tested, for full series production. It is unknown whether any work was actually done to put this order into effect but it seems doubtful.

ABOVE: Even as the P 1107 was being discussed during a meeting on February 20-23, Messerschmitt's designers were pressing ahead with a closely related series of tailless bombers – the P 1108. Some versions of this design looked a little like the postwar Avro Vulcan.

P 1108 AND EF 130

Messerschmitt's official entry for Langstreckenbomber had been the conventional P 1107 but between November 1944 and February 1945 the firm had also worked on a flying-wing bomber design in parallel – the P 1108.

This looked something like a cross between the P 1107 and the H XVIII but Messerschmitt struggled with the same problem as the Hortens: where to put the engines and how to shape their intakes.

Designs were studied with intakes above, below or in the leading edge of the wing but no firm conclusion about which was best had been reached by the time of the Langstreckenbomber conference.

Evidently the RLM was aware of Messerschmitt's work on the P 1108, and was interested in it, but was also concerned that Messerschmitt lacked the capacity to complete the design. It would appear that the Messerschmitt P 1108 and Horten XVIII projects were both effectively handed over

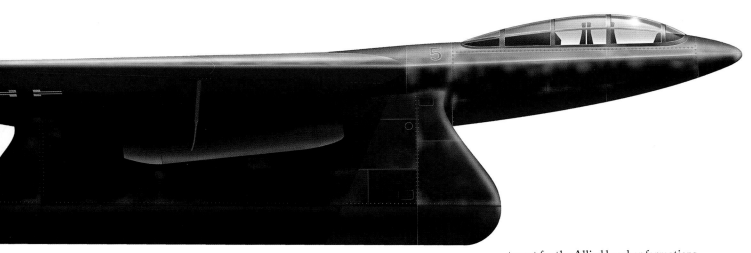

LEFT: The massive short-range carrier/launcher aircraft designed by Focke-Wulf at the behest of Daimler-Benz – complete with high-speed bomber.

LEFT: When the Ju 287 won the Langstreckenbomber/TL-Grossbomber competition, Junkers was handed the Messerschmitt P 1108 and Horten XVIII and told to combine them into a new flying wing project. The result was the Junkers EF 130.

to Junkers for further development as a single project – the Junkers EF 130 – with the Horten brothers retained as consultants.

According to German Aircraft: New and Projected Types: "Several different designs were submitted for the EF 130 and it was the subject of considerable controversy, particularly the positioning of the four jet units."

Only one period drawing of the EF 130 is known to exist and it has been suggested that even this may be either a very basic preliminary layout or a sketch drawn from someone's memory because the original documents were not available. Certainly, nothing else is known about the "considerable

controversy" regarding the different designs, nor what those designs actually looked like.

FOCKE-WULF AND DAIMLER-BENZ
When Messerschmitt set to work on the P 1107 back in November 1944, Focke-Wulf Oberingenieur Herbert Wolff of Flugmechanik L started to draw up a rival design. But by December he had encountered a seemingly insurmountable problem – getting it off the ground.

Swept wings generate less lift and given the sheer weight of the necessary payload the bomber would need a very long concrete runway – exactly the sort of runway that was proving to be such an easy and attractive

target for the Allied bomber formations. Focke-Wulf chief designer Kurt Tank himself evidently mentioned this problem to Daimler-Benz director Fritz Nallinger, who went away and gave it some serious thought.

From this brief exchange, Nallinger and his colleague Erich Übelacker formulated a proposal which could not only solve Tank's problem but also help to solve the much wider problem of the Allied bomber streams which at that time were inflicting severe damage on German industry and infrastructure.

A short while later, Nallinger came back to Tank and presented him with the idea – a second aircraft specifically designed for heavy lifting which could get the fast bomber off the ground and carry it up to an altitude from which it could be launched. Fitted with rugged fixed landing gear, powerful engines and large wings, the carrier would be able to operate from rough landing strips and could be moved easily from one area to another. Only a handful of these would be necessary, since each one would only fly short distances before turning round, landing and repeating the process.

Daimler-Benz as a company then commissioned Focke-Wulf to carry out the detailed design work and do the necessary sums to turn the proposal into a seemingly viable prospect for production. The resulting design was outlined in Focke-Wulf Kurzbeschreibung Nr. 28, dated February 10-February 17, 1945.

The Schnellbomber or 'fast bomber' would be able to carry a very heavy bomb load of 30,000kg at 1000km/h, with a range of 2000km. Attached to the Trägerflugzeug or 'carrier aircraft', take-off distance would be less than 500m – making it possible to launch the bomber from even small airstrips.

And since the bomber's own undercarriage would only be needed for landing, when all the bombs had been dropped and most of the fuel burned off, it could be relatively small.

There would be one launch aircraft for every three bombers and the launch aircraft could also be used to carry a number of either piloted or remote-controlled 'SO Flugzeug' – a self-destructing suicide aircraft. This was envisioned as a conventional-looking fighter-size aircraft carrying explosives in its nose. It was powered by a single turbojet beneath its rear fuselage and it had no undercarriage.

The carrier's wing area was to be 500 square metres with a wingspan of 54m. The aircraft was to be 35m long and 12m tall. As far as the engine was concerned: "The propulsion system consists of six engines with DB 603N motors. Four-blade propellers would be used which were 5m in diameter." A later drawing, dated March 19, 1945, shows a dramatically redesigned carrier with only a single fuselage compared to the earlier design's twin-boom. As a result, its length was increased from 35m to 36m and height was up from 12m to 12.5m. Wingspan remained the same however. This new design was to be propelled by four Daimler-Benz PTL 021 turboprops. Values are also given for a carrier powered by five or even six PTL 021s.

As well as alterations to the carrier, the SO Flugzeug also seems to have been revised. A drawing appears in German Aircraft: New and Projected Types which shows it reconfigured with its jet engine on top of its fuselage rather than underneath, and the pilot is seated much further back with only a tiny window to look out of between the engine above his head and the fuselage below.

As innovative and imaginative as it was, the Focke-Wulf/Daimler-Benz fast bomber/carrier concept came far too late in the day to be anything other than a paper exercise.

BMW BOMBER PROJECTS

In June 1944, BMW put forward two designs for tailless bombers that were to be powered by its own jet engine products. The first, known as 'Strabo I' was propelled by no fewer than six BMW 003 As – two in the nose and two under each wing – while the second, 'Strabo II' had two BMW 018s in its rear fuselage, fed by gaping nose intakes. It was expected that the former would reach a top speed of around 875km/h, while the latter would manage a much more impressive 990km/h.

Very little further detail is given in the brief report accompanying the two designs and it

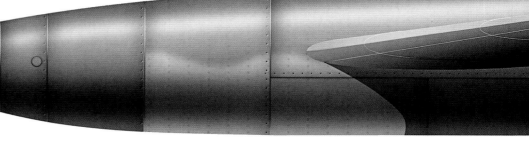

BELOW: Two different manned or guided flying bombers were designed to be launched from Focke-Wulf's enormous carrier/launcher aircraft. This version had its turbojet mounted almost on top of the cockpit.

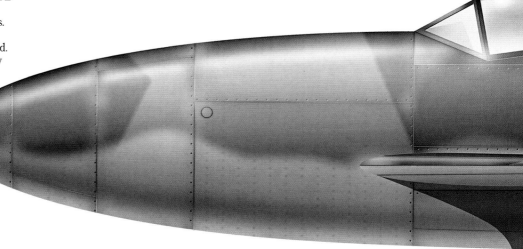

BELOW: The second manned or guided flying bomb designed by Focke-Wulf to be launched from the carrier/launcher aircraft it had designed for Daimler-Benz. This version looked like a slightly stout fighter but had no guns and no undercarriage – just a large quantity of explosives and a detonator in its nose.

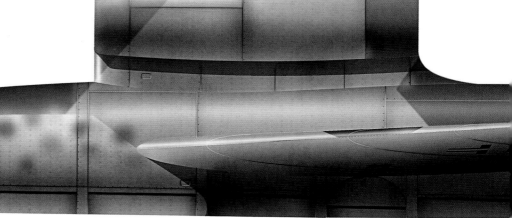

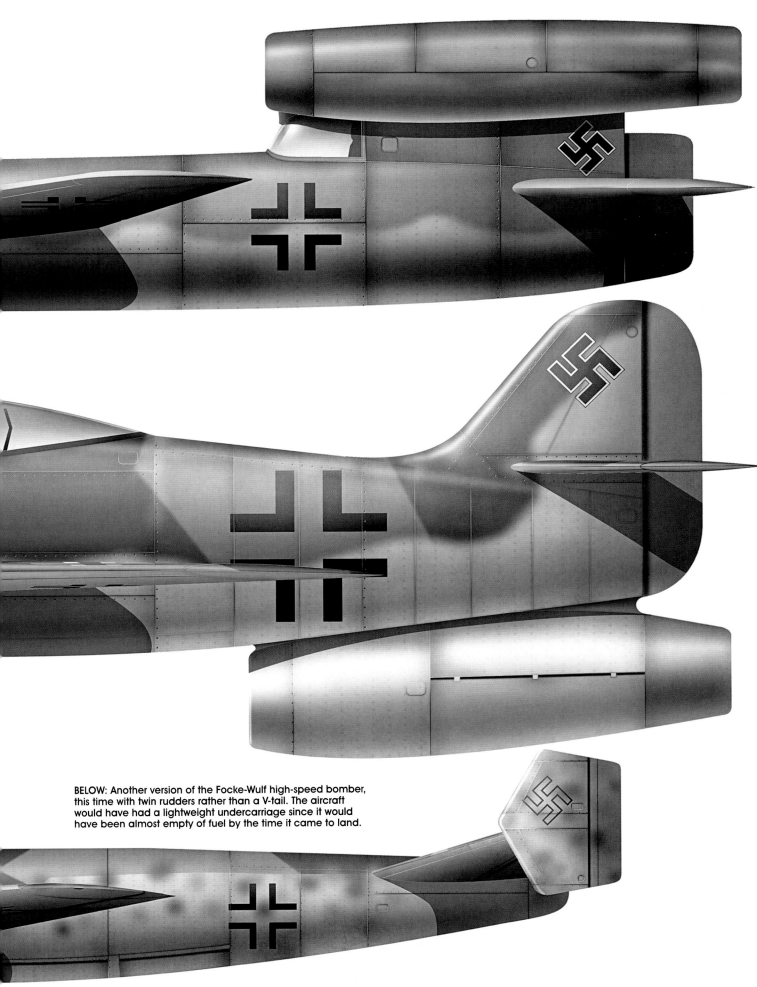

BELOW: Another version of the Focke-Wulf high-speed bomber, this time with twin rudders rather than a V-tail. The aircraft would have had a lightweight undercarriage since it would have been almost empty of fuel by the time it came to land.

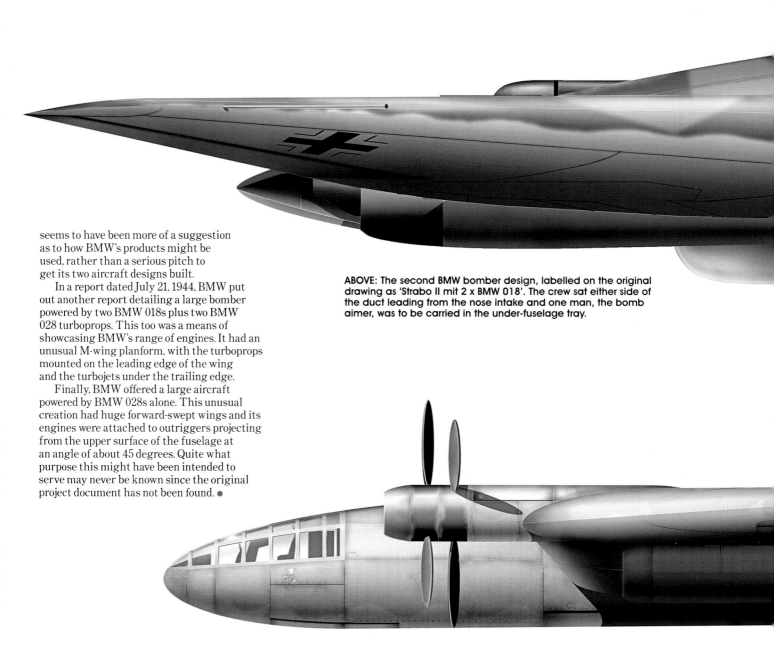

seems to have been more of a suggestion as to how BMW's products might be used, rather than a serious pitch to get its two aircraft designs built.

In a report dated July 21, 1944, BMW put out another report detailing a large bomber powered by two BMW 018s plus two BMW 028 turboprops. This too was a means of showcasing BMW's range of engines. It had an unusual M-wing planform, with the turboprops mounted on the leading edge of the wing and the turbojets under the trailing edge.

Finally, BMW offered a large aircraft powered by BMW 028s alone. This unusual creation had huge forward-swept wings and its engines were attached to outriggers projecting from the upper surface of the fuselage at an angle of about 45 degrees. Quite what purpose this might have been intended to serve may never be known since the original project document has not been found. ●

ABOVE: The second BMW bomber design, labelled on the original drawing as 'Strabo II mit 2 x BMW 018'. The crew sat either side of the duct leading from the nose intake and one man, the bomb aimer, was to be carried in the under-fuselage tray.

ABOVE: This BMW bomber design, produced a month after the others in July 1944, is labelled 'Schnellbomber mit kombiniertem PTL+TL-Antrieb'. It was powered by a pair of BMW 018 turbojets under its wings and a pair of BMW 028 turboprops on the leading edge of its wings. As a line drawing it looks odd, but fleshed out here it is a surprisingly attractive design.

RIGHT: BMW's design intended to showcase its 003 A engine – this bomber had a pair of engines built into its 'chin', plus two more built into each wing.

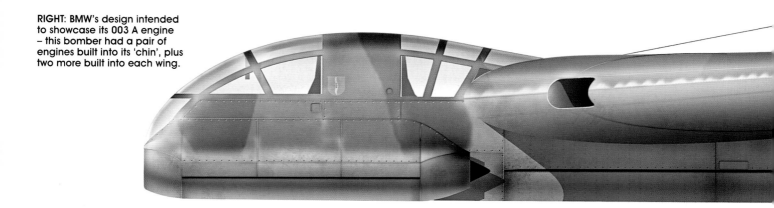

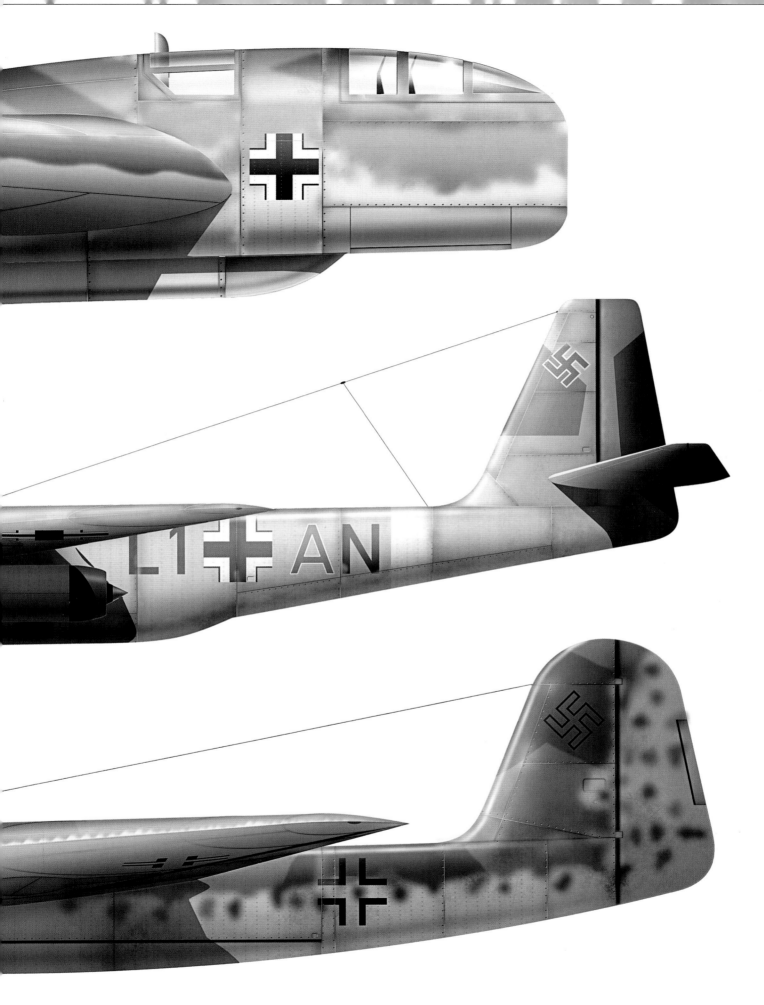

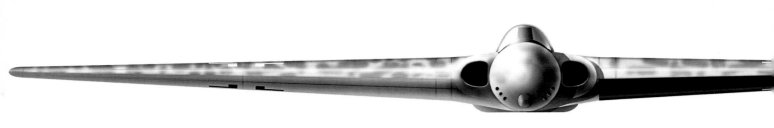

2-TL-Jäger

Advanced night fighters

With work on the interim night fighter types under way, a requirement was issued for a twin-jet night fighter – a '2-TL-Jäger' that would represent the state of the art in night fighter technology. And the designs tendered were nothing if not cutting edge...

The second Arado advanced night fighter design. The original drawing is dated March 8, 1945, and it is noted that the aircraft depicted has a "very short fuselage".

The introduction of ground-scanning radar at the end of 1942 allowed the RAF's bomber fleet to become steadily more effective at hitting key targets in Germany and occupied Europe under cover of darkness.

The need for better fighters to combat this threat had already resulted in first dedicated piston-engine night fighters, then a drive to convert existing jet types for night fighting.

During the summer of 1944, a third strand was begun – the development of the most technologically advanced dedicated night fighter the world had ever seen. Initially the requirement, issued on August 31, 1944, was for a piston-engined design with Jumo 222 E/Fs, As 413s, DB 603 Ls or DB 613s but "combination piston engine-jet must be looked at".

Weaponry was to be four MK 108s and two MK 213s fixed forward firing with space also allowed for Lichtenstein radar equipment and the Bremen airborne warning device. Oblique weaponry was to be two MK 108s angled at 70 degrees. The aircraft was also to be capable of carrying two 500kg bombs. A pressure cabin was to be fitted, along with armour for the crew, and top speed needed to be 800km/h at an altitude of 11km, with a flight time of four and a half hours without drop tanks.

Copies of this requirement were sent to Blohm & Voss, Focke-Wulf, Heinkel, Messerschmitt and Dornier. Arado and Gotha, who would both later submit designs, were not included at this stage.

The competition seems to have been delayed by first the 1-TL-Jäger conference on September 8-10, 1944, then the Volksjäger requirement of September 10, which demanded the immediate attention of the competing firms. The requirement was slightly altered on January 27, 1945, calling specifically for a two-seater machine that could achieve 900km/h at 9000m and fly on full throttle for four hours.

The first confirmed comparison meeting for what was dubbed 'Schlechtwetter und Nachtjäger' took place on February 26, 1945, and three companies submitted designs.

Blohm & Voss offered its radical tailless twin-jet P 215.01, Messerschmitt put forward two- and three-seater configurations of its Me 262 and Dornier put forward two conventional layout projects – the P 252/1 and P 254/1.

In two-seater form, the Me 262 B-2 or 'B2' as it appears in the project description document of January 18, 1945, featured a fuselage lengthened by 1.5m to provide room for a radar operator and equipment without compromising fuel load. The canopy over the men's heads was tall to accommodate the bulky FuG 350 Naxos Zc homing device scanner and the radar operator position had blackout curtains so the screen could be read more easily. Radar aerials would be fitted to the aircraft's nose.

The second option was an even longer fuselage to allow room for a navigator. In addition, the engines would be installed in the aircraft's wingroots, rather than underwing pods. The wings themselves would also have a 45-degree sweepback, compared to the standard Me 262's sweep of just 18.5 degrees.

Dornier's P 252/1, drafted on January 20, 1945, was perhaps the simplest of the four. It had unswept wings and a pair of DB 603 LA piston engines mounted in tandem within its fuselage, with two Jumo 213 Js

offered as an alternative option. The two crew sat side-by-side with the pilot slightly further forward on the left. Armament was given as two MK 108s fixed forward with another two at an oblique angle.

Set against the twin-jet Me 262, twin-jet P 215 and twin-piston engine P 252/1, the Dornier P 254/1 was unusual in being the only mixed propulsion design put forward. In design, the forward section and wings were similar to those of the Do 335 A series except for the installation of a DB 603 LA piston engine in place of the DB 603 A.

However, in the space where the second, pusher, DB 603 A would have been, aft of the main fuel tank, were a pair of oblique-firing MK 108s. To the rear of them was the radar operator's position. On either side of him was a wide intake for the HeS 011 jet engine positioned in the extreme rear of the fuselage, exhausting beneath the fin. Also unlike the Do 335, there was no lower tail fin – just the familiar horizontal tailplanes and fin arrangement.

Neither Dornier design came with a pressure cabin.

Finally, there was the Blohm & Voss P 215.01, the design apparently drawn up in a hurry on February 21, 1945 – just five days before the conference. It was essentially a scaled-up version of the company's P 212 design for 1-TL-Jäger.

It had a crew of three seated within a pressure cabin – two facing forwards and one to the rear. Armament was four MK 108s but these could evidently be fitted in a number of different arrangements since the side-view design drawing shows eight MK 108s – four in the upper nose, firing forward, two lower down on the sides of the nose air intake, angled slightly upwards, and a further two positioned towards the rear of the aircraft, firing upwards at an angle of 70 degrees.

REVISED SPEC

The day after the conference, February 27, 1945, a new set of specifications was issued which emphasised heavier armament, the ability to carry more equipment and the inclusion of a third crewman to manage all the

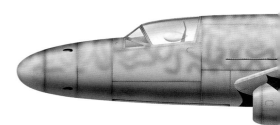

RIGHT: The Blohm & Voss P 215.02 as it appears in a brochure dated March 16, 1945. The wings are now a different shape and the whole aircraft has been enlarged compared to the P 215.01.

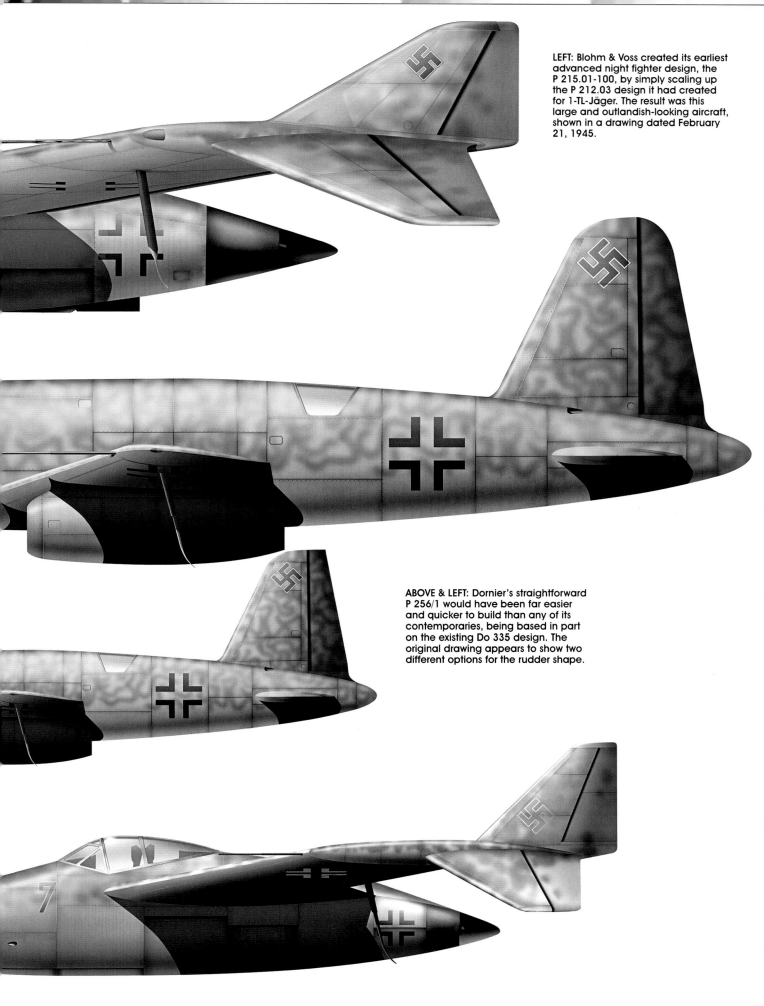

LEFT: Blohm & Voss created its earliest advanced night fighter design, the P 215.01-100, by simply scaling up the P 212.03 design it had created for 1-TL-Jäger. The result was this large and outlandish-looking aircraft, shown in a drawing dated February 21, 1945.

ABOVE & LEFT: Dornier's straightforward P 256/1 would have been far easier and quicker to build than any of its contemporaries, being based in part on the existing Do 335 design. The original drawing appears to show two different options for the rudder shape.

additional kit if one wasn't present already.

At this point Messerschmitt seems to have dropped out of contention, offering no designs for the new specification. Neither of Dornier's previous proposals was able to meet the revised specification and both were dropped. Only the Blohm & Voss P 215 remained of the original competitors. However, it was now set to face an even stiffer challenge. A new date was set for the discussion of Schlechtwetter und Nachtjäger designs – the next EHK meeting at Bad Eilsen on March 20-24.

There would now be seven competing designs: Blohm & Voss's slightly revised tailless P 215.02, Dornier's new P 256/1, two from Arado simply labelled 'Arado I' and 'Arado II', Gotha's tailless P-60 C and two designs from Focke-Wulf labelled 'Focke-Wulf II' and 'Focke-Wulf III'.

BLOHM & VOSS P 215

The Blohm & Voss P 215.02 appears almost identical to the P 215.01 at first glance but in fact it is a larger aircraft in almost every respect. The wingspan, including control surfaces, is 18.8m, compared to 17.6m; wing area is 63sq m compared to 59sq m and fuselage width is 2.2m compared to under 2m. The only dimension which remains the same is overall length at 11.6m.

According to the introduction to the P 215.02 brochure, dated March 1945: "The 215 project grew out of the P 212 design, a day fighter with only one turbojet." Comparing the P 215.02's dimensions to those of the P 212.03 reveals a startling difference in size however. The wingspan of the P 212.03 was only 9.5m – nearly half that of the P 215.02. Wing area was less than a quarter of the P 215.02's at just 14sq m, and overall length was 4.2m shorter at a relatively diminutive 7.4m.

As with the P 215.01, the aircraft had a tricycle undercarriage – with the nosewheel being borrowed from the He 219. The main wheels retracted directly into the fuselage.

A wide range of different armament options are outlined. The standard P 215 armament was to be five fixed forward-firing MK 108 cannon but this could be exchanged for five MK 108s with slightly

BELOW: Dated March 9, 1945 Arado's third design has smaller wings and a thicker fuselage compared to the two previous efforts. It also has broad vertical intakes for its engines and a rudder/fin part way along each wing.

BELOW: The fifth Arado night fighter. Now the engines are attached to the rear underside of the aircraft rather than being built into the wing at the rear. It features not only forward-firing and oblique-firing cannon, but also a pair of pivoting rear-facing cannon.

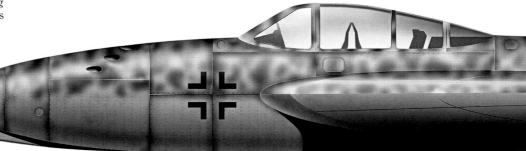

BELOW: Arado's sixth design, with a little modification to its undercarriage, was put forward for 2-TL-Jäger as 'Arado I'. It is basically a subtle refinement of the "5. Entwurf".

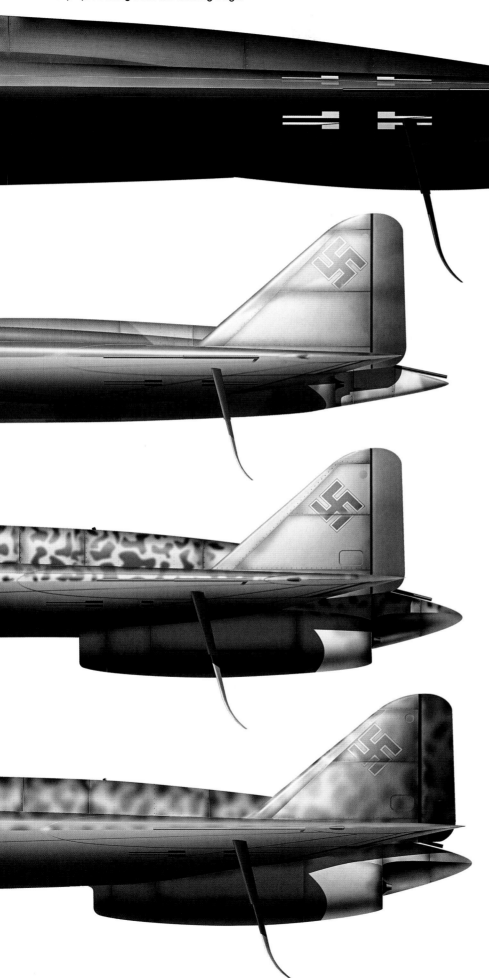

less ammunition that could be tilted upwards at an angle of between 0 and 15 degrees.

The third option was four MG 213/30s and the fifth was two massive MK 112 cannon. Finally, no fewer than 56 R4M unguided rockets could be installed in the P 215's nose – alongside either four MK 108s, four MG 213/30s or two MK 212/214s.

Like the P 215.01, the P 215.02 could also be fitted with a pair of MK 108s aimed to fire upwards. There was also an option to carry a pair of 500kg bombs semi-recessed within the fuselage. Where the P 215.02 differed most significantly from its predecessor was with the inclusion of a rear-facing FHL 151 remote controlled turret fitted with a single MG 151/20 20mm cannon. This was to be aimed and fired by the navigator.

DORNIER P 256/1

Where most of the other firms went for radical aerodynamic designs that might well have entailed long programmes of wind tunnel testing and refinement, Dornier opted for a simple and straightforward solution – basing its design loosely on the Do 335 push-pull piston engine fighter and installing the aircraft's two HeS 011 turbojets in under-wing nacelles.

The pilot and navigator sat almost side-by-side in the spacious cockpit with three large fuel tanks directly behind them. And behind the fuel tanks, in the aircraft's tail, sat the radar operator beneath a Perspex window. Armament was a quartet of MK 108s in the nose and two more firing upwards at an oblique angle – although exactly where the latter were to be positioned is unclear.

ARADO I AND II

While the other competitors had each worked through numerous earlier designs before finally producing the ones they entered for the contest, Arado apparently only got started designing its entry on March 7.

The first drawing in a series of nine, labelled 1. Entwurf zum Nacht- und Schlechtwetterjäger, shows a tailless design with no vertical control surfaces and the distinctive kinked wing that the company had developed during its E 560 project. This had an armament of six forward-firing MK 108s, two more firing upwards and a small rear turret set between its turbojet exhausts mounting two unspecified remote-control weapons.

The 2. Entwurf zum Nacht- und Schlechtwetterjäger (mit verkleinertem Rumpf) dated March 8, 1945, was another

tailless design which had, as the name suggests, a shortened fuselage. Again, it had six forward-firing MK 108s but no rear turret and its swept wings had a dead straight leading edge. 3. Entwurf zum Nacht- und Schlechtwetterjäger dated March 9 was again tailless but moved back to the longer fuselage. Now, however, it also featured a vertical fin towards the end of each wing. The forward-firing weaponry stayed the same but a rear turret mounted what appeared to be a pair of MK 103s on a pivot, allowing them to track left and right.

The fourth design is lost but the 5. Entwurf zum Nacht- und Schlechtwetterjäger, dated March 13, marked a substantial refinement on its predecessors. Forward armament was the same but now two oblique MK 108s made an appearance and the MK 103 rear turret could track up and down rather than left and right. The 6. Entwurf zum Nacht- und Schlechtwetterjäger was very similar to the fifth design but refined still further in the detail of its wings and fuselage.

The 6. Entwurf is dated March 14, whereas the 7. Entwurf is dated March 13. This design features a conventional layout – albeit with an extremely long fuselage, huge swept tailfin and engine nacelles integrated into its wings. There is no forward armament depicted – only oblique-firing cannon and a tail turret.

The 8. Entwurf is again missing and the 9. Entwurf zum Nacht- und Schlechtwetterjäger, dated March 17, 1945 – just three days before the conference – is another conventional layout design. Shorter than the 7. Entwurf, everything about it seems designed to be straightforward. The wings are only lightly swept and the engines are fitted into underwing nacelles for ease of access. The three crew sit together under a bubble canopy offering good visibility over the short nose and the tricycle undercarriage appears not dissimilar to the tried and tested undercarriage of the Ar 234 B-2. An optional V-tail was included on the drawing.

From these nine designs, Arado chose the 6. Entwurf to offer as its 'Arado I', albeit with a slightly modified undercarriage retraction arrangement, and the 9. Entwurf to offer unaltered as 'Arado II'.

BELOW: The seventh Arado night fighter design looks the most modern today. It consisted of a long stretched-out fuselage, a conventional cruciform tail and ordinary swept wings with the engines built into them.

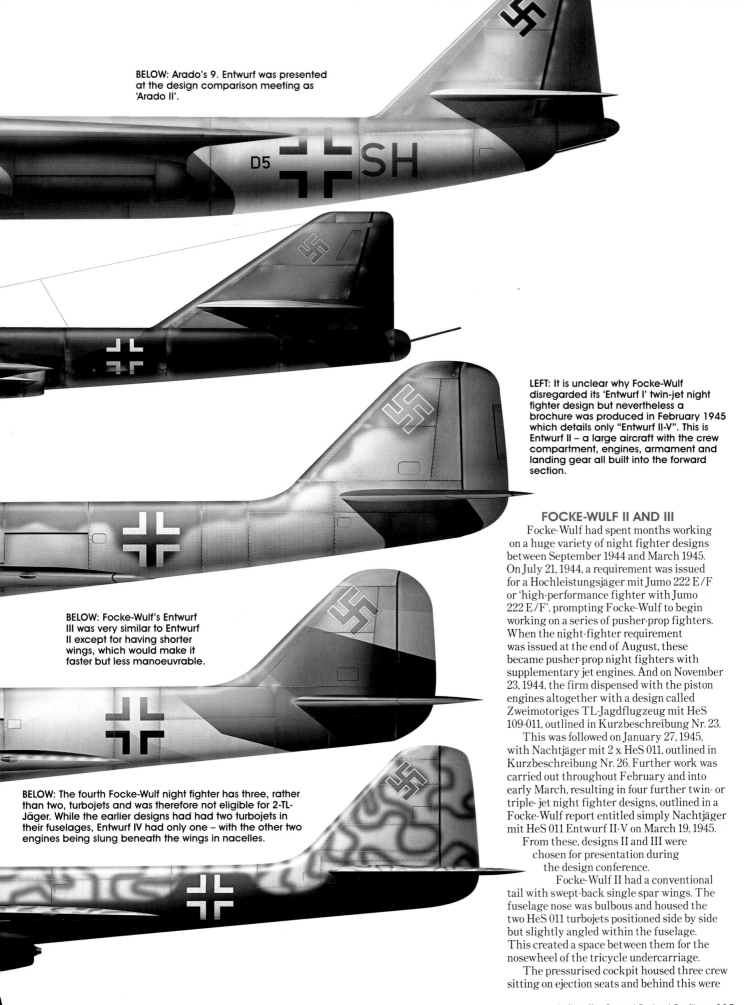

BELOW: Arado's 9. Entwurf was presented at the design comparison meeting as 'Arado II'.

LEFT: It is unclear why Focke-Wulf disregarded its 'Entwurf I' twin-jet night fighter design but nevertheless a brochure was produced in February 1945 which details only "Entwurf II-V". This is Entwurf II – a large aircraft with the crew compartment, engines, armament and landing gear all built into the forward section.

BELOW: Focke-Wulf's Entwurf III was very similar to Entwurf II except for having shorter wings, which would make it faster but less manoeuvrable.

BELOW: The fourth Focke-Wulf night fighter has three, rather than two, turbojets and was therefore not eligible for 2-TL-Jäger. While the earlier designs had had two turbojets in their fuselages, Entwurf IV had only one – with the other two engines being slung beneath the wings in nacelles.

FOCKE-WULF II AND III

Focke-Wulf had spent months working on a huge variety of night fighter designs between September 1944 and March 1945. On July 21, 1944, a requirement was issued for a Hochleistungsjäger mit Jumo 222 E/F or 'high-performance fighter with Jumo 222 E/F', prompting Focke-Wulf to begin working on a series of pusher-prop fighters. When the night-fighter requirement was issued at the end of August, these became pusher-prop night fighters with supplementary jet engines. And on November 23, 1944, the firm dispensed with the piston engines altogether with a design called Zweimotoriges TL-Jagdflugzeug mit HeS 109-011, outlined in Kurzbeschreibung Nr. 23.

This was followed on January 27, 1945, with Nachtjäger mit 2 x HeS 011, outlined in Kurzbeschreibung Nr. 26. Further work was carried out throughout February and into early March, resulting in four further twin- or triple- jet night fighter designs, outlined in a Focke-Wulf report entitled simply Nachtjäger mit HeS 011 Entwurf II-V on March 19, 1945.

From these, designs II and III were chosen for presentation during the design conference.

Focke-Wulf II had a conventional tail with swept-back single spar wings. The fuselage nose was bulbous and housed the two HeS 011 turbojets positioned side by side but slightly angled within the fuselage. This created a space between them for the nosewheel of the tricycle undercarriage.

The pressurised cockpit housed three crew sitting on ejection seats and behind this were two self-sealing fuel tanks. Armament was four fixed forward-firing MK 108s and two more firing upwards. Wingspan was 16m. Focke-Wulf III was the same but with larger main undercarriage wheels and a wingspan of 14.1m.

Even as the EHK sat down to discuss the night fighter designs on March 20, Focke-Wulf's Flugmechanik L department was still hard at work on the night fighter design series and drafted preliminary details of an Entwurf VI – labelled "Nurflügel" in the designer Pauselius's notes. The fuselage was to be 9.35m long, wingspan 17m and wing area 74.5sqm. The wings were to be swept back by 38 degrees. It was to have a pair of HeS 011 engines, carry 5400 litres of fuel and be armed with four MK 108s. Unfortunately, there is no known drawing of this design.

Finally, there was something called 'Entwurf Klages' which appears to belong to the same project. Even less is known about this design – only that it was to have a fuselage 12.5m long and was calculated to have been marginally faster than Entwurf VI. Again, there is no known drawing of the design.

GOTHA P-60 C
Gothaer Waggonfabrik aerodynamics specialist Dr Rudolf Göthert had originally designed the P-60 as an alternative to the Horten IX, which his company had been tasked with building. As his work progressed, however, he saw that the design had greater potential than originally envisioned.

The BMW 003-powered P-60 A was a direct H IX heavy fighter competitor, with a two-man prone crew, and the P-60 B was a revised version of the 'A', with greater equipment capacity and HeS 011 engines. The P-60 C, however, had a different wing centre section where the two crew had been seated in tandem rather than prone positions – freeing up space in the nose for a radar unit.

Just nine days before the conference however, Gotha's P-60 C was revised to become a three-seater. While the pilot remained seated in the central fuselage cockpit, his two fellow crewmen were given positions within the aircraft's wings themselves to his left and right. There is no mention of it in the documentation but drawings of the three-man P-60 C appear to show these two positions covered by a large curving sheet of Perspex – giving their occupants a reasonable degree of visibility. Armament remained the same: four fixed-forward MK 108s plus two more angled upwards.

DECISION-MAKING
According to a report on his interrogation by Allied investigators shortly after the war, the P-60 C's designer Dr Rudolf Göthert believed that his design "was shown to have the best performance of these aircraft, and Dr Göthert believed it would have won had not the war disrupted the competition".

However, Göthert appears to have been ill informed. None of the designs, tailless or conventional, came out on top in the end. According to the war diary of the TLR:

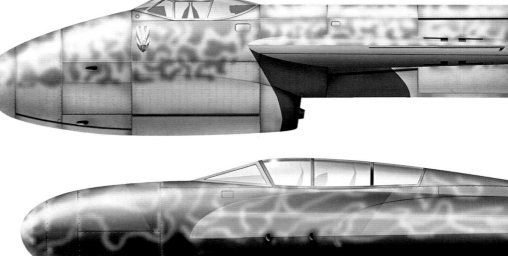

BELOW: The fifth and penultimate Focke-Wulf night fighter design. This also had three engines but all three were built into the fuselage – two in the nose and a third at the extreme rear, fed by slot intakes in the aircraft's sides.

BELOW: The last known version of the Gotha P 60 C was a revision of the earlier two-seater. The Nacht- und Schlechtwetter/2-TL-Jäger competition required two additional crewmen besides the pilot, so provision was made to house them in the inner wings under glazed panels – making the P 60 C a little more like the A and B, which both had fully glazed nose canopies for their prone crewmen.

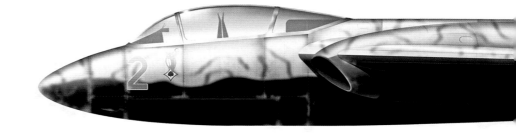

BELOW: Heinkel's P 1079 had a conventional fuselage and V-tail, with its engines housed in large nacelles built into its wing-roots. It looked very much like the postwar Vickers-Supermarine Type 508, which had almost the same configuration, except for the swept wings. Heinkel also designed at least two flying-wing versions of the P 1079 but it remains unclear whether these were designed while the war was still ongoing or not.

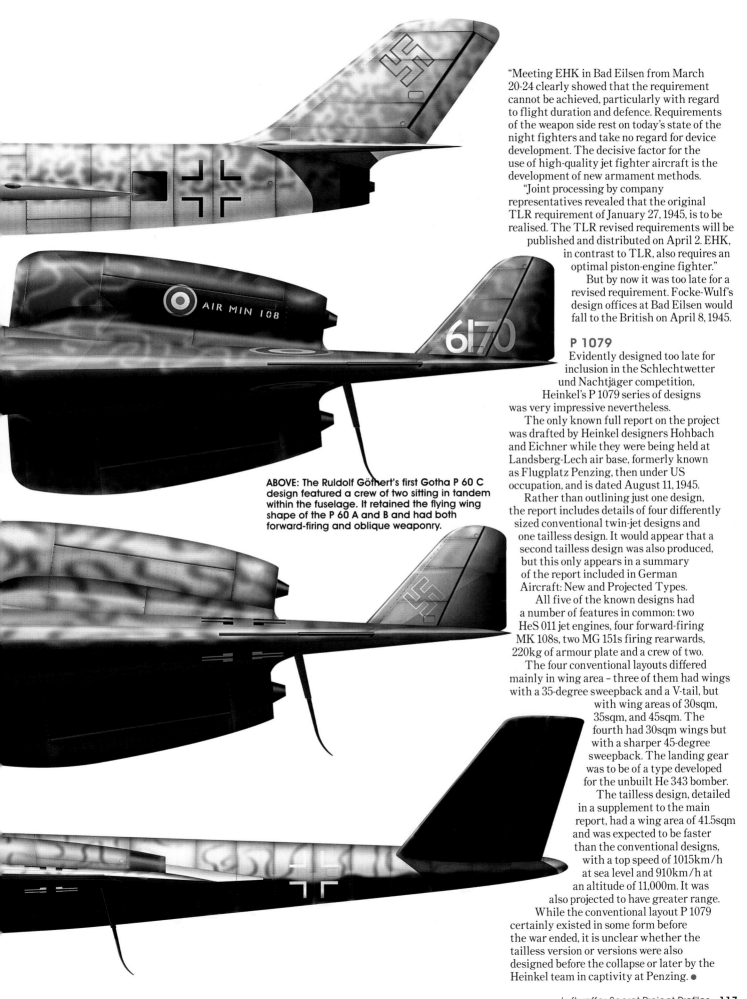

"Meeting EHK in Bad Eilsen from March 20-24 clearly showed that the requirement cannot be achieved, particularly with regard to flight duration and defence. Requirements of the weapon side rest on today's state of the night fighters and take no regard for device development. The decisive factor for the use of high-quality jet fighter aircraft is the development of new armament methods.

"Joint processing by company representatives revealed that the original TLR requirement of January 27, 1945, is to be realised. The TLR revised requirements will be published and distributed on April 2. EHK, in contrast to TLR, also requires an optimal piston-engine fighter."

But by now it was too late for a revised requirement. Focke-Wulf's design offices at Bad Eilsen would fall to the British on April 8, 1945.

P 1079

Evidently designed too late for inclusion in the Schlechtwetter und Nachtjäger competition, Heinkel's P 1079 series of designs was very impressive nevertheless.

The only known full report on the project was drafted by Heinkel designers Hohbach and Eichner while they were being held at Landsberg-Lech air base, formerly known as Flugplatz Penzing, then under US occupation, and is dated August 11, 1945.

Rather than outlining just one design, the report includes details of four differently sized conventional twin-jet designs and one tailless design. It would appear that a second tailless design was also produced, but this only appears in a summary of the report included in German Aircraft: New and Projected Types.

All five of the known designs had a number of features in common: two HeS 011 jet engines, four forward-firing MK 108s, two MG 151s firing rearwards, 220kg of armour plate and a crew of two.

The four conventional layouts differed mainly in wing area – three of them had wings with a 35-degree sweepback and a V-tail, but with wing areas of 30sqm, 35sqm, and 45sqm. The fourth had 30sqm wings but with a sharper 45-degree sweepback. The landing gear was to be of a type developed for the unbuilt He 343 bomber.

The tailless design, detailed in a supplement to the main report, had a wing area of 41.5sqm and was expected to be faster than the conventional designs, with a top speed of 1015km/h at sea level and 910km/h at an altitude of 11,000m. It was also projected to have greater range.

While the conventional layout P 1079 certainly existed in some form before the war ended, it is unclear whether the tailless version or versions were also designed before the collapse or later by the Heinkel team in captivity at Penzing. ●

ABOVE: The Ruldolf Göthert's first Gotha P 60 C design featured a crew of two sitting in tandem within the fuselage. It retained the flying wing shape of the P 60 A and B and had both forward-firing and oblique weaponry.

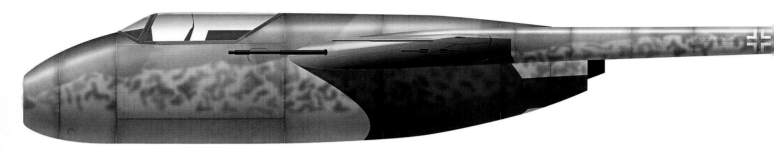

Loose ends

Miscellaneous jets

There are numerous Second World War German jet designs which don't fit easily into any particular competition or lineage. These oddities are collected here.

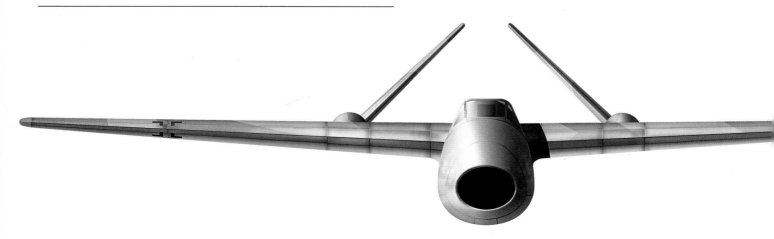

A centrally positioned turbojet and twin-boom tail are the main differences between the Strahljäger III and the two other BMW 003 designs from the November 3, 1944 report. The Strahljäger III also had an extremely short nosewheel leg, with the wheel itself barely clearing the bottom of the fuselage.

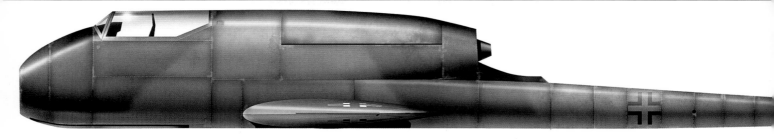

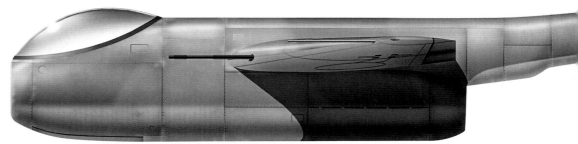

ABOVE: BMW's Strahljäger I design had its BMW 003 turbojet installed within the central section of the fuselage, fed by a nose intake. Dating from November 3, 1944, after the He 162 had already been chosen as the Volksjäger, it seems unlikely anyone ever expected it to be built.

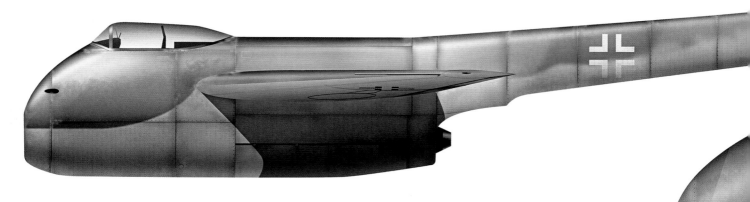

ABOVE: Similar in some ways to the Strahljäger III, the Strahljäger IV differed in having a much larger BMW 018 turbojet in its lower fuselage and in having swept wings. Overall, it was a substantially larger aircraft.

BMW SINGLE JET FIGHTERS

As one of the three biggest aero engine manufacturers in Germany during the Second World War, BMW was constantly in contact with the aircraft constructors – liaising over existing models and potential future designs.

In addition to the ongoing development of its war-critical BMW 801 piston engine, and piston engines it hoped would soon reach series production such as the BMW 802 and 803, the company was also at the forefront of developing both turbojet and rocket engines.

Towards the end of the war, the BMW 003 turbojet became increasingly important in the minds of those planning for the Luftwaffe's requirements and the troubled BMW 018 was also perceived to have great potential.

Just as the company had come up with a series of bomber designs to showcase its products, in EZS-Bericht Nr. 58 of November 3, 1944, it appears to have done the same with fighters – presenting four configurations which leaned on the latest aerodynamic forms being reported on by experimental institutions such as the AVA and LFA. While the four look quite different from one another at first glance, the first three all have exactly the same straight wing shape with swept leading edge and are all powered by the BMW 003. The second and fourth designs have a very similar fuselage and tail design, and all four have a nose intake and a tricycle undercarriage.

The first design, known as 'Strahljäger I', has a twin-tail with the high-position turbojet exhausting above it, 'Strahljäger II' has a conventional tail with the low-position

turbojet exhausting below it and 'Strahljäger III' has a centrally positioned turbojet exhausting between the fins of a twin-boom tail. The final design, known as 'Strahljäger IV', was powered by a BMW 018 and was somewhat larger than the other three.

None of these designs went any further than BMW's report.

MESSERSCHMITT P 12

It is possible to determine the origin and purpose of nearly every design worked on by Messerschmitt's Abteilung L during its more than four years in existence – with the exception of the P 12.

This extremely bulky fighter, appearing in a drawing dated September 30, 1942, was designed around BMW's enormous P 3303 turbojet project, later to be renamed the BMW 018, at a time when few other manufacturers were considering it.

At that time, Abteilung L was locked into an increasingly bitter disagreement with Professor Messerschmitt himself following the P 10/Me 329 debacle outlined elsewhere in this publication. As department head Alexander Lippisch and his two lieutenants Walter Stender and Dr Hermann Wurster argued among themselves and with Messerschmitt, the remainder of Abteilung L seems to have simply got on with its projects work.

Handrick produced the seminal P 11 on September 13, a fast bomber intended for the long-running Schnellbomber competition which was ongoing at that time, and one of Lippisch's longest-serving staff members, Josef Hubert, produced the P 12 some 17 days later.

Loosely resembling the earlier P 01 designs, it was offered with two different wing forms – either an 11m wingspan or 14.8m – and two different tailfins, a relatively conventional short one which gave the aircraft a length of 7m and a swept one which increased the overall length by 60cm. The pilot sat beneath a bubble canopy and above a huge, sharply angled intake for the massive engine.

Armament was a pair of long-barrelled MG 151s or possibly MK 103s and the drawing shows a cylindrical object under each wing – probably a bomb, although these are only shown in the forward view and not the side or top views. Large as it is for an Abteilung L design, the aircraft was intended to land on a skid and presumably would have had to take off using a catapult or trolley undercarriage since it lacks any other sort of undercarriage.

Exactly what the P 12 was intended to demonstrate or what requirement it was intended to meet is unclear. Lippisch would later return to the P 11 and rework it extensively

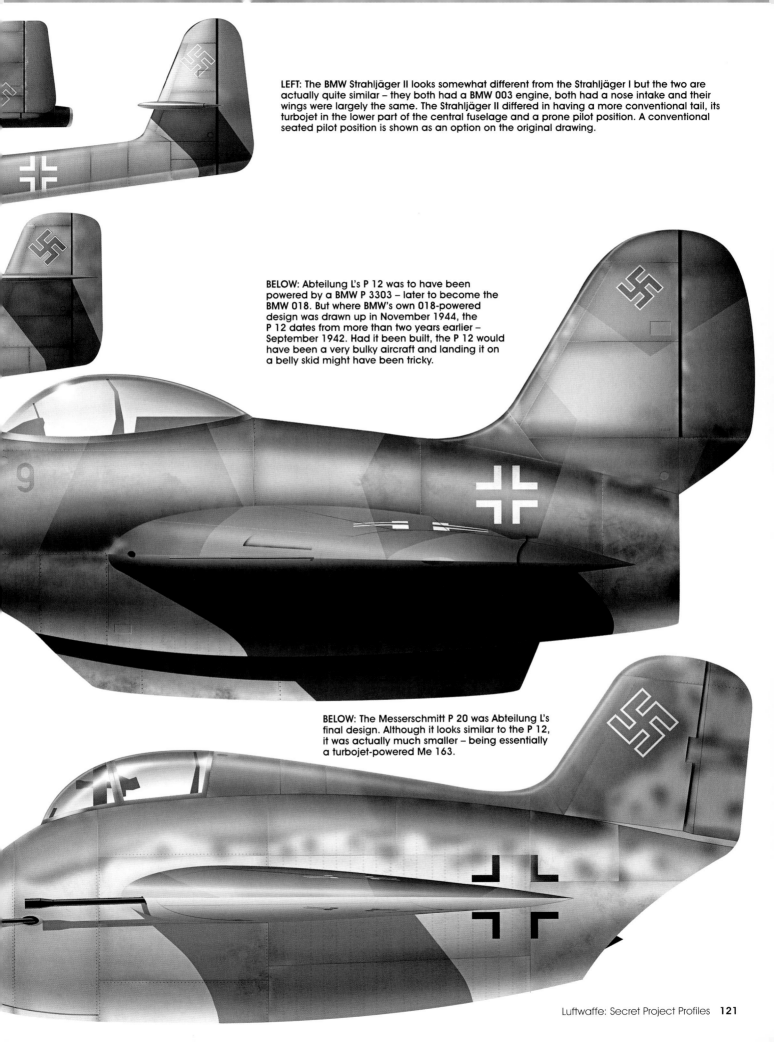

LEFT: The BMW Strahljäger II looks somewhat different from the Strahljäger I but the two are actually quite similar – they both had a BMW 003 engine, both had a nose intake and their wings were largely the same. The Strahljäger II differed in having a more conventional tail, its turbojet in the lower part of the central fuselage and a prone pilot position. A conventional seated pilot position is shown as an option on the original drawing.

BELOW: Abteilung L's P 12 was to have been powered by a BMW P 3303 – later to become the BMW 018. But where BMW's own 018-powered design was drawn up in November 1944, the P 12 dates from more than two years earlier – September 1942. Had it been built, the P 12 would have been a very bulky aircraft and landing it on a belly skid might have been tricky.

BELOW: The Messerschmitt P 20 was Abteilung L's final design. Although it looks similar to the P 12, it was actually much smaller – being essentially a turbojet-powered Me 163.

extensively but the P 12 was left on the shelf – perhaps because the BMW P 3303 never materialised as a viable production model, even after its redesignation as the BMW 018.

MESSERSCHMITT P 20 AND P 1092

Over six and a half months later, on April 19, 1943, the final Abteilung L design was detailed in a new report – the P 20. Like the P 12, this was a single jet fighter but unlike the P 12 it was much closer to the Me 163 B in scale thanks to the much more modestly sized Jumo 004 C fitted centrally within its stubby fuselage.

In fact, the report notes that the P 20 is effectively an Me 163 B with a jet, rather than rocket, engine. The drawing appended to the report is by Wurster. But at least the P 20 had a purpose – on June 23, nearly two months after Abteilung L's dissolution, it was included in a report comparing the qualities of single-jet fighters with those of the Me 262 alongside two versions of the P 1092. The latter was closer to the Me 262 in the shape of its fuselage and tail but with its single engine positioned much like that of the P 20, centrally on the underside of the fuselage, venting beneath the up-raised tail.

The P 20/P 1092/Me 262 report concluded that there was little to be gained from installing only a single Jumo 004 C since the engine was not quite powerful enough to produce the desired performance. This seems to have been where Messerschmitt's single-jet fighter development ground to a halt for almost a year – up to the beginning of the 1-TL-Jäger competition.

MESSERSCHMITT P 1112

Jumping forward to the very end of the 1-TL-Jäger, another series of Messerschmitt designs appeared right at the end of the war – P 1112. This was the company's final project. After the EHK meeting at the end of February, none of Messerschmitt's three entries had succeeded in defeating the other competitors. So Messerschmitt ditched all three and started a new project which combined the best elements of the most advanced two – the P 1110 and P 1111. The P 1112 has a refined version of the P 1111's tailless layout and in some versions the annular or side intakes of the P 1110.

The British summary of the project in German Aircraft: New and Projected Types reads: "The P 1112 was designed to correct some of the faults which became apparent after study of the P 1111.

"The wing area was reduced to 236.5sq ft since it was felt that the wing loading could be increased. The pilot's cockpit is situated at the extreme nose of the aircraft and 2 x MK 108 guns are fitted in the wing.

"The remainder of the design closely resembles the P 1111. Performance calculations were not completed."

Interviewed on September 7, 1945, by the British, the head of Messerschmitt's project office, Woldemar Voigt, said: "P 1101, P 1106, P 1110, P 1111, P 1112. A project investigation of the single-engined jet fighter was being carried out. The project drawings are known here, I assume.

"A final conclusion had not been drawn until the end of the war; the results secured by that time were: a speed of

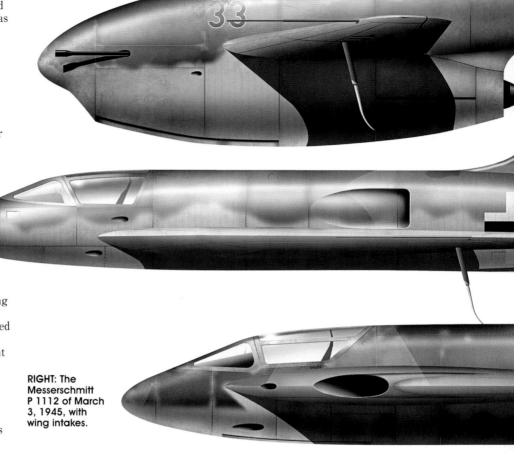

RIGHT: The Messerschmitt P 1112 of March 3, 1945, with wing intakes.

BELOW: This undated design with fuselage slot intakes presumably sits somewhere between the wing intake version of March 3 and the longer fuselage intake version of March 27.

RIGHT: Undated Messerschmitt P 1112 with long fuselage and wing intakes.

LEFT: Messerschmitt's single-jet P 1092 was compared against the Me 262 and P 20 but the Me 262 beat both of them on performance and overall cost – despite having two turbojets instead of one.

LEFT: Messerschmitt P 1112 of March 27, 1945, with fuselage intakes.

1000kph (620mph) is obtainable and had been guaranteed to the government.

"The tailless designs P 1111 and P 1112 showed the best performance out of the hitherto completed project series. They had the special advantage of combining best max speed with best landing speed. They seem to be dangerous at high Mach numbers (pitching moments). It seems to be possible to reach the same performance with more conventional designs (or even to exceed it) with less risk."

ARADO TL-JÄGER AND K-JÄGER

As previously mentioned, Arado put forward designs for a rocket fighter, jet fighter and combination rocket and jet fighter in its Vorschlag für die Weiterentwicklung schneller Zweisitzer or 'Proposal for the development of a fast two-seater' report of August 11, 1943.

The section of the report that deals with the interceptors, Appendix 2, begins: "Preview of future technical and tactical possibilities of next-step fighter aircraft. General requirements for a fighter to combat rapid aircraft.

"For rapid aircraft flying at high altitude, despite a well-organised reporting system, defensive fighters have little time to go on the attack. Therefore, a very large rate of climb is absolutely necessary and aircraft with Otto engines must be separated from those with more suitable propulsion.

"The fighter must be at least equipped with jet engines, but would not be significantly superior to the enemy in this arrangement. Above all, the rate of climb would still be regarded as insufficient, since the altitude greatly decreases the thrust of jet devices, which means a significant decrease in the rate of climb.

"By contrast, with a rocket-powered fighter (here called R-Jäger) large rates of climb and steep climb angle are possible, but due to the high specific fuel consumption has completely inadequate range, whereby the possibility of a dogfighting battle is called into question.

"If one wants to succeed with a fighter against a rapid opponent, one must combine high-altitude performance with climbing speed, long range and horizontal velocity. Even under these conditions, a successful interception will be possible only with excellent reporting and guidance to the target.

"These conditions are only applicable when the fighter is equipped both with a turbojet engine and an intermittently connectable rocket engine. This combination fighter (here called K-Jäger) alone has the potential to fight and destroy rapid opponents."

The report then goes on to outline the equipment, advantages and disadvantages of the TL-Jäger, R-Jäger and K-Jäger before concluding that the K-Jäger offers the best performance. However, the designs appear to have been drawn up to make a point – rather than to provide a basis for real aircraft.

ARADO'S E 581-4 AND -5

Little is known about Arado's outlandish single jet flying wing fighter series – E 581. The series seems to have begun in mid-November 1944 and the earliest known version is the E 581-2, which was to be powered by the

BMW 003. It had a wing sweepback of 46 degrees, mid-wing fins for control, a 740 litre fuel tank and two MK 108 cannon. By January 1945, the design had evolved into the E 581-4 and E 581-5, each of which was to be powered by a single HeS 011 – putting the small fighter into the same category as the 1-TL-Jäger designs.

However, no evidence has yet come to light suggesting that the E 581 was ever submitted or considered for the 1-TL-Jäger competition. The only surviving period documentation appears to be a bundle of notes and 3-view drawings of the latter two designs, produced by Arado designer Braun at Landeshut and dated March 1945.

HENSCHEL HS 132

The Hs 132 evidently resulted from Henschel's own experience with dive-bomber aircraft, rather than from a competition to design a jet-propelled Stuka. The company had realised that a small well-armoured ground-attack aircraft moving very fast would be almost impossible to intercept and extremely difficult for anti-aircraft fire to shoot down.

The aircraft bore a marked resemblance to Heinkel's He 162 with the notable exception of its prone pilot position cockpit. Inside, the pilot was to lie on a couch pressed out of 8mm thick armour, behind a 75mm thick disc of armoured glass. The cabin opened downwards normally but there was an emergency upper exit in the case of a belly landing. The fuel tanks, to the rear of the fuselage, were self-sealing and the wing roots could also house an unprotected tank each.

The aircraft was to be built mainly of wood and steel, with the use of light alloy kept to a minimum. Steel and wooden components were

to be joined by an intermediate layer of glued dural and wood, which was to be riveted to the steel part and glued to the wooden part.

A V-tail with end-plate rudders was to be fitted which were to be made entirely of wood. The engine, lying on the back of the aircraft, was to be either a BMW 003 or Jumo 004 with the HeS 011 replacing whichever was chosen when it became available.

The hydraulically actuated undercarriage was a tricycle arrangement and the main legs were to be wide gauge, folding into the wing roots. The nosewheel at the forward tip of the fuselage turned sideways while retracting to lie flat under the pilot's legs.

Armament varied according to the engine fitted. With a BMW 003, it would feature just two MG 151 cannon with 250 rounds each, plus a bomb load totalling 1250kg or 1500kg under the fuselage. The greater thrust provided by the HeS 011 however, would allow for four MG 151s with 250 rounds each and a bomb load of 1500kg or 2000kg.

The aircraft's safe dive speed was to be 950km/h (590mph). Top speed in level flight with a BMW 003 was to be a relatively meagre 650km/h (403mph) carrying a 500kg bomb load, or 780km/h (484mph) without the bombs. With a HeS 011 level flight without a bomb load would be 830km/h (515mph).

Work had begun on three prototypes of the Hs 132 when the war ended.

HENSCHEL P 135

Two tailless single-seat fighter projects were worked on in parallel by Henschel from late 1944 to early 1945. The first, P 130, was to be powered by a Jumo 213 piston engine but no drawing of it appears to have

RIGHT: The Arado E 581-5 has a similar appearance to the E 581-4 but with a reshaped intake.

RIGHT: The small single-jet Arado E 581-4 fighter. While it looks 'fat' when viewed side-on, from above the design is something like an arrow-shaped flying wing.

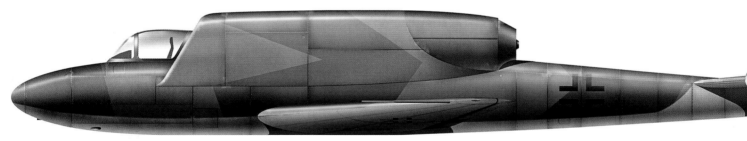

BELOW: The Arado TL-Jäger or 'turbojet fighter' was a simple design, looking something like the early fighter version of the Ar 234. Arado argued that turbojets alone would be insufficient for a truly high-performance fighter due to their slow acceleration.

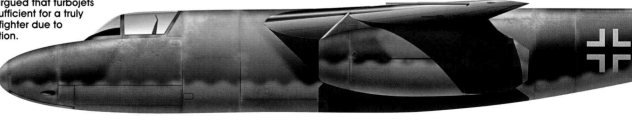

RIGHT: Another undated Messerschmitt P 1112, this time with V-tail as well as fuselage intakes.

LEFT: Arado Kombinationsjäger – abbreviated to 'K-Jäger' in the text of the 1943 report in which it appears. It had a combination of jet and rocket propulsion, giving it the best of both worlds according to Arado.

survived. The P 135, on the other hand, is known from at least two period drawings.

Like the Arado E 581, it was initially to have been fitted with the BMW 003 and later the HeS 011. The jet engine, whichever it ended up being, would be fitted centrally within the fuselage behind a straight cylindrical duct from a nose intake. The pilot was to be positioned on a seat which could be reclined very far back, to protect him from the effects of g-force during high-speed dogfighting.

The wing had an unusual double kink design. Early on the entirety of the wing was swept back, but the last design had forward-swept wingtips. The tricycle undercarriage all retracted into the fuselage so that the wing surfaces could be completely smooth and unaffected by the lumps and bumps of wheel wells and doors.

Top speed with the BMW 003 was expected to be 930km/h or 1010km/h with the HeS 011. Maximum ceiling with both was 14-15km (46,000-50,000ft).

It has been suggested that the P 135 was Henschel's entry for the 1-TL-Jäger competition but that the entry was too late to be considered. Certainly, none of the documentation for the competition up to

the beginning of March 1945 mentions a Henschel entry. However, according to the March 5 to March 15, 1945, section of the war diary of the Chef der Technische Luftrüstung or 'Head of Technical Air Force Armament', the office of General Ulrich Diesing, under the heading of '1 TL-Projekt': "FL-E required the following projects: 1) Junkers, B&V, and modified FW project. 2) Mtt. Optimal solution. Recently, EHK proposed that in addition to 2) Fa. Henschel be used as a second solution for the optimal solution (based on the work of Dr Zobel)."

The outcome of the February 27-28 1-TL-Jäger meeting had been Focke-Wulf's Nr. 279 design being chosen as an 'immediate solution' and shortly thereafter awarded the designation Ta 183, with Messerschmitt's design, presumably the P 1111, being chosen as an 'optimal solution' for longer term development. Now it appeared that Junkers' EF 128 design, the Blohm & Voss P 212 and the Ta 183 were all being regarded as 'immediate solutions' with Henschel being tacked on alongside Messerschmitt's fighter as a development for the future. Given the advanced state of development that several of the other projects had reached, it seems unlikely that Henschel's P 135 would ever have been a serious contender.

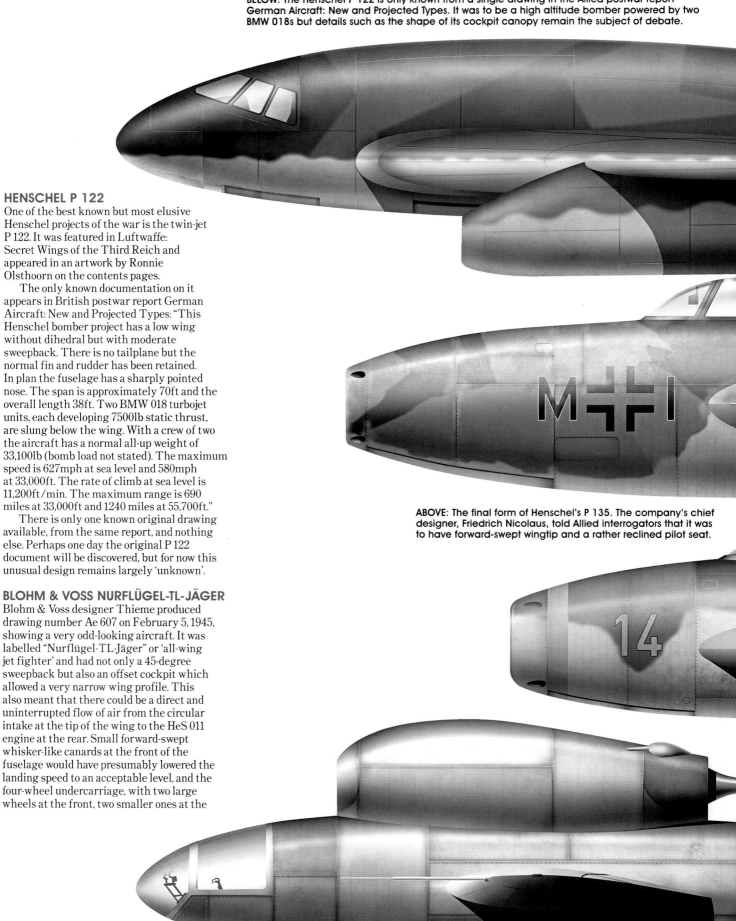

HENSCHEL P 122

One of the best known but most elusive Henschel projects of the war is the twin-jet P 122. It was featured in Luftwaffe: Secret Wings of the Third Reich and appeared in an artwork by Ronnie Olsthoorn on the contents pages.

The only known documentation on it appears in British postwar report German Aircraft: New and Projected Types: "This Henschel bomber project has a low wing without dihedral but with moderate sweepback. There is no tailplane but the normal fin and rudder has been retained. In plan the fuselage has a sharply pointed nose. The span is approximately 70ft and the overall length 38ft. Two BMW 018 turbojet units, each developing 7500lb static thrust, are slung below the wing. With a crew of two the aircraft has a normal all-up weight of 33,100lb (bomb load not stated). The maximum speed is 627mph at sea level and 580mph at 33,000ft. The rate of climb at sea level is 11,200ft/min. The maximum range is 690 miles at 33,000ft and 1240 miles at 55,700ft."

There is only one known original drawing available, from the same report, and nothing else. Perhaps one day the original P 122 document will be discovered, but for now this unusual design remains largely 'unknown'.

BLOHM & VOSS NURFLÜGEL-TL-JÄGER

Blohm & Voss designer Thieme produced drawing number Ae 607 on February 5, 1945, showing a very odd-looking aircraft. It was labelled "Nurflügel-TL-Jäger" or 'all-wing jet fighter' and had not only a 45-degree sweepback but also an offset cockpit which allowed a very narrow wing profile. This also meant that there could be a direct and uninterrupted flow of air from the circular intake at the tip of the wing to the HeS 011 engine at the rear. Small forward-swept whisker-like canards at the front of the fuselage would have presumably lowered the landing speed to an acceptable level, and the four-wheel undercarriage, with two large wheels at the front, two smaller ones at the

ABOVE: The final form of Henschel's P 135. The company's chief designer, Friedrich Nicolaus, told Allied interrogators that it was to have forward-swept wingtip and a rather reclined pilot seat.

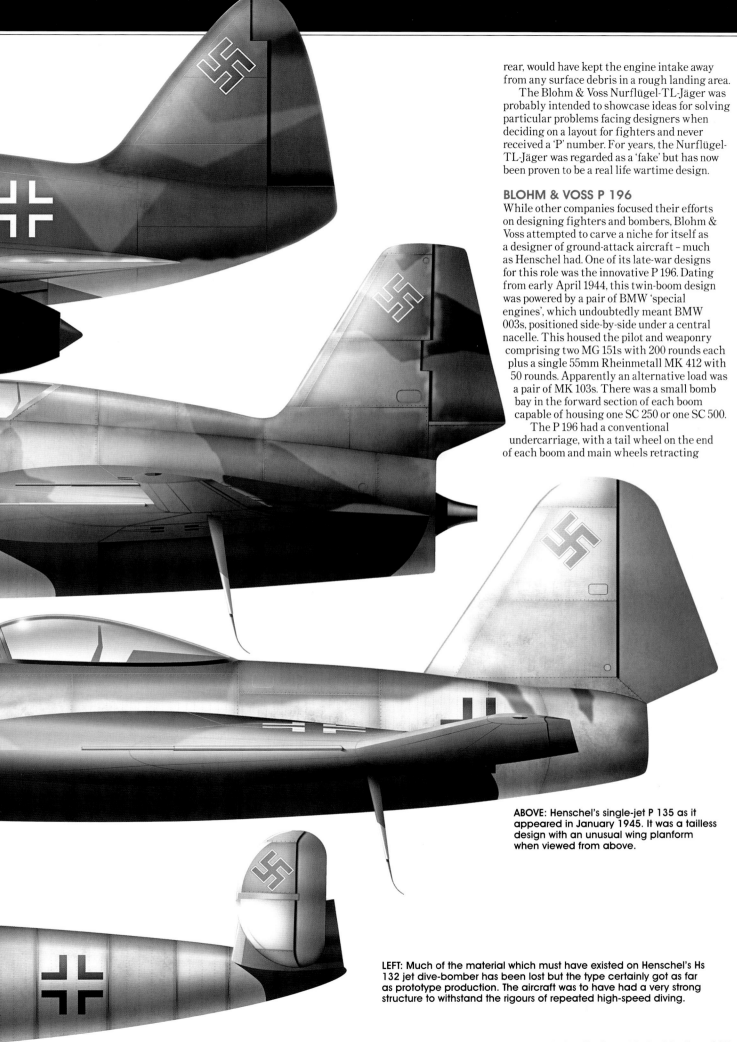

rear, would have kept the engine intake away from any surface debris in a rough landing area.

The Blohm & Voss Nurflügel-TL-Jäger was probably intended to showcase ideas for solving particular problems facing designers when deciding on a layout for fighters and never received a 'P' number. For years, the Nurflügel-TL-Jäger was regarded as a 'fake' but has now been proven to be a real life wartime design.

BLOHM & VOSS P 196

While other companies focused their efforts on designing fighters and bombers, Blohm & Voss attempted to carve a niche for itself as a designer of ground-attack aircraft – much as Henschel had. One of its late-war designs for this role was the innovative P 196. Dating from early April 1944, this twin-boom design was powered by a pair of BMW 'special engines', which undoubtedly meant BMW 003s, positioned side-by-side under a central nacelle. This housed the pilot and weaponry comprising two MG 151s with 200 rounds each plus a single 55mm Rheinmetall MK 412 with 50 rounds. Apparently an alternative load was a pair of MK 103s. There was a small bomb bay in the forward section of each boom capable of housing one SC 250 or one SC 500.

The P 196 had a conventional undercarriage, with a tail wheel on the end of each boom and main wheels retracting

ABOVE: Henschel's single-jet P 135 as it appeared in January 1945. It was a tailless design with an unusual wing planform when viewed from above.

LEFT: Much of the material which must have existed on Henschel's Hs 132 jet dive-bomber has been lost but the type certainly got as far as prototype production. The aircraft was to have had a very strong structure to withstand the rigours of repeated high-speed diving.

into the wing. All-up weight was 9120kg. Although these basic specifications concerning the P 196 can be verified from Blohm & Voss documents, little else is known about the type's background.

BLOHM & VOSS P 197

This advanced-looking single-seat fighter – probably dating from April to May 1944 – was powered by two Jumo 004s fitted side-by-side in the rear end of the fuselage. This arrangement was possible thanks to the sweepback of the low wing. According to German Aircraft: New and Projected Types: "Apart from the fact that the tailplane is mounted at the top of the fin the front elevation is rather like that of the Me 262." Armament consisted of two MK 103s underneath the cockpit and an MG 151/20 on either side. The intakes for the jet units were in the nose just forward of the leading edge. Unusually, they were positioned facing slightly downwards and were therefore partially masked when looked at directly from the front. Estimated maximum speed was 660mph. Again, little else is known about the P 197.

BLOHM & VOSS P 198

Powered by a single very large BMW 018, the P 198 was apparently designed as a high-altitude fighter. It had a relatively conventional layout except for a very deep fuselage to accommodate the turbojet and bulges on the underside of the wing roots to accommodate its undercarriage main wheels when retracted. The armoured cabin was in the aircraft's nose and the armament was a single MK 412 and a pair of MG 151/20s. It probably dated from mid-1944 but no other data about it has yet been discovered. ●

RIGHT: Another design disfigured by the enormous BMW 018 turbojet was Blohm & Voss's P 198 high-altitude fighter. The position of the wings relative to the underside of the fuselage meant that the aircraft would have needed to have extremely long undercarriage legs.

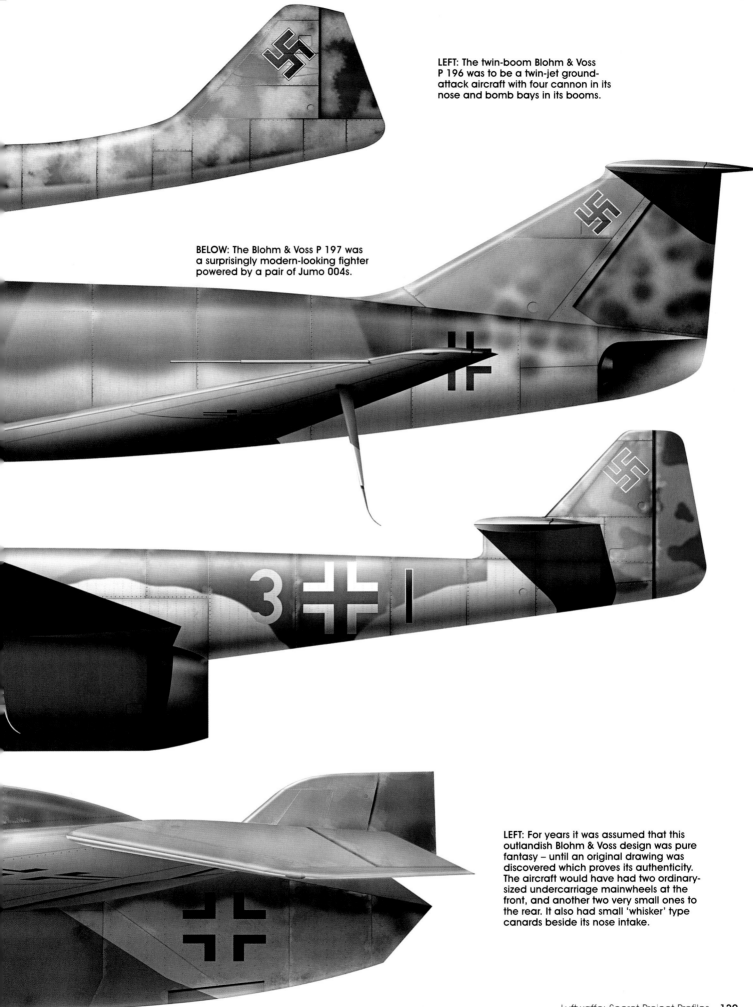

LEFT: The twin-boom Blohm & Voss P 196 was to be a twin-jet ground-attack aircraft with four cannon in its nose and bomb bays in its booms.

BELOW: The Blohm & Voss P 197 was a surprisingly modern-looking fighter powered by a pair of Jumo 004s.

LEFT: For years it was assumed that this outlandish Blohm & Voss design was pure fantasy – until an original drawing was discovered which proves its authenticity. The aircraft would have had two ordinary-sized undercarriage mainwheels at the front, and another two very small ones to the rear. It also had small 'whisker' type canards beside its nose intake.

AIRCRAFT	SQUADRON	SEASON
Me 262 early	Factory	Germany 43
P 01-116	VIII./JG 52	Eastern Front
P 01-111	I./JG 51	Germany, May 45
P 01-113	III./JG 1	Germany, 45
P 01-116 (June 41)	Test	Germany, 42
Me 262 Schnellbomber (Avia S. 92)	5. LP	CZ, 50
Me 262 Schnellbomber Ia	KG 54	Germany, Mar 45
Me 262 Schnellbomber II	JG 1	Germany, May 45
Me 262 Aufklarer I	KG 54	Captured by US troops
Me 262 Aufklarer Ia	2./KG 51	Germany, Feb 45
Me 262 Aufklarer II	JV 44	Germany, Feb 45
Me 262 Interzeptor I	III./EJG 2	Germany, Nov 44
Me 262 Interzeptor II	VII./EJG 2	Germany, Nov 44
Me 262 Interzeptor III	Eprobungs Kommando	Germany, 1944
Me 262 HG III	III./KG(J) 54	CZ, May 45
Ar 234 pfeilflügel	KG 76	Germany, 44
Ar 234 fighter	III./KG 26	Germany, Apr 45
Me P 01-114	N/A	Captured by Red Army
Me P 01-116	244th Sentai	Kofu, Japan, 45
Me P 01-117	101st Sentai	Okinawa, Japan, 44
Me P 01-118	2./ JG 400	Germany, 45
Me P 01-119	2./ JG 400	Germany, 45
Me P 05	N/A	Germany, Nov 43
Me P 09	N/A	Germany, Oct 42
Me P 1104	JG 54	Germany, 45
Fi 166 I	7./KG 54	Germany, 44
Fi 166 II	7./KG 54	Germany, 44
BP 20 Natter early	N/A	Germany, March 45
BP 20 Natter late	N/A	Germany, May 45
Ju EF 127 Walli	JG 2	Germany, May 45
He Julia I	N/A	Austria - Vienna, Dec 44
He Julia II	N/A	Austria - Vienna, Dec 44
Me 163 C late	RA 31 Gruppo 18 Stormo	Rome 44
Me 263 late	N/A	Sion, Switzerland, Nov 45
Ar 381	JG 1	Germany, 44
Ar R-Jäger	JG 11	Germany, 43
Stockel 1	JG 6	Germany, 45
Stockel 2	KG(J) 54	Germany, 45
Stockel 3	N/A	Germany, 45
Stockel 4	N/A	Germany, 44 (scheme from V2)
Stockel 5	JG 26	Germany, 44
Me 262 B-2	I/NJG 1	Germany, 45
Ar 234 P-5	II./NJG 1	Germany, 45
Do P 254	IV./NJG 5	Germany, 45
Me 262 3-seater	II./NJG 3	Germany, 44
Me P 09	JG 54	Germany, 42
Me P 010	JG 54	Western front, 44
Me P 11	III. / KG 54	Germany, 45
Me P 11	III. / KG 54	Germany, 44
Li P 11 early	III./ KG 76	Germany, 44
Li P 11 late	I./ (Jabo) JG 53	Hungary, 44/45
Ho 8-229 single seater	III./ KG 30	Germany, 44/45
Ho 8-229 two-seater	II. / KG 30	Germany, 44/45
Fw bomber early	I./ KG 51	Germany, 45
Fw bomber fuselage	10./ LG 1	Greece, 44
Fw bomber tailless	II./ KG 30	Germany, 44/45
Me 328 B	Test	Germany, 44
Me 328 swept	Test	Germany, 44
He Romeo	JV 44	Germany, 45
Ju EF 126 Elli	N/A	Germany, 45
B&V P 213	N/A	Germany, 45
He P 1073.02	SKJ	Iraq - Mosul, 45
He P 1073.11	JG 54	Germany, 45
He P 1073 (advanced)	I./ JG 77	Germany, 45
He P 1078 early	JG 54	Germany, 45
He P 1078 late	JG 54	Germany, 45
Fw 190 with turbojet	6./JG 4	Sweden 45
Fw Entwurf 1	I./ JG 51	Germany, 45
Fw Entwurf 2	I./ JG 51	Germany, 45
Fw 1. Entwurf	JG 6	Germany, 45
Fw 2. Entwurf	JG 3	Germany, 45
Fw 3. Entwurf	KG(J) 54	Germany, 45
Fw 4. Entwurf	JG 77	Tunisia, 45
Fw 5. Entwurf	III. /JG 54	Germany, 45
Fw 6. Entwurf (Flitzer)	F3 Flygflottilj	Sweden, 46
Fw II straight back	Flying Wing F10	Sweden, 46
Fw II curved back	2/HLeLv 24	Finnland, 44
Fw Ta 183	III. /JG 54	Germany, 45
Me P 1101 (early)	5/1 Puma Squadron	Hungary 45
Me P 1101 late	Escadrille GC II/6	France, 45
Me P 1106 early	Escuela de Caza	Spain, 46
Me P 1106 late	9./ JG 3 (Udet)	Germany, 45
Me P 1110 late	Flyglotilij F11	Sweden, 46
Me P 1111	JG51	Germany, 45

AIRCRAFT	SQUADRON	SEASON
B&V P 209.01	JG 52	Germany, 45
B&V P 209.02	JG 54	Germany, 45
B&V P 212.01	JG 7	Germany, 45
B&V P 212.02	JG 300	Germany, 45
B&V P 212.02-01	JG 53	Germany, 45
B&V P 212.03	JV 301	Germany, 45
B&V P 212.03	JV 44	Germany, 45
Ju EF 128 early	JG 2	Germany, 45
Ju EF 128 late	JG 52	Germany, 45
Ar 580	N/A	Germany, 44
Fw Volksflugzeug	KG(J) 6	Germany, 45
Fw Flitzer	JG 27	Libya, 44
Ju Projekte	JG 1	Germany, 45
He P 1073	N/A	Germany, Feb 45
B&V P 210	JG 5	Germany, 45
B&V P 211.01	JG 11	Germany, 45
B&V P 211.02	JG 53	Germany, 45
Skoda P.14	N/A	Germany, 45
He P 1080	III./JG 2	Germany, 45
Me 262 Lorin	III./JG 27	Germany, 45
Fw Triebflugeljäger	FW company	Germany,44
Fw Strahlrohrjäger	III. /JG 4	Germany, 44
Li P 13a	JG 26	Germany, 44
Ar E 560 1	II. /KG 200	Germany, 45
Ar E 395	KG 76	Germany, 45
Me P 1100	5. / KG 100	Denmark, 45
Me P 1100	5. / KG 100	Germany, 45
B&V P 188.01	13. / KG 40	Holland, 44
B&V P 188.02	N/A	Germany, 45
B&V P 188.04	4. /KG 100	France, 45
He 343	KG74	Germany, 45
Me P 1107/I	I. /KG 40	France, 45
Me P 1107/II	I. /KG 40	France, 45
Ju 287	6. KG 100	France, 45
H XVIII	KG 55	France, 45
Me P 1108	5. /KG 1	East Prussia, 45
Ju EF 130	I. /KG 40	France, 45
BMW bomber I	I/KG 4	Germany, 45
BMW bomber II	II/LG 1	Crete, 45
DB projects 1	N/A	Germany, 45
DB projects 2	N/A	Germany, 45
Fw SO Flugzeug I	N/A	Germany, 45
B&V P 215.01	NJG 2	Germany, 45
B&V P 215.02	NJG 1	Germany, 45
He P 1079	(N)JG 53	Germany, 45
Ar 1. Entwurf	NJG 1	Germany, 45
Ar 2. Entwurf	NJG 1	Germany, 45
Ar 3. Entwurf	II./ NJG 4	Germany, 45
Ar 5. Entwurf	I./ JG 300	Germany, 45
Ar 6. Entwurf	NJG 1	Germany, 45
Ar 7. Entwurf	NJG 1	Germany, 45
Ar 9. Entwurf	4./ NJG 3	Denmark, 45
Fw Nachtjäger Entwurf II	3./ NJG 3	Germany, 45
Fw Nachtjäger Entwurf III	I. /NJG 4	Germany, 45
Fw Nachtjäger Entwurf IV	JG 300	Germany, 45
Fw Nachtjäger Entwurf V	10./ (N)JG 77	Germany, 45
Do P 256	NJG 2	Germany, 45
Go P-60 C two-seater	2./ NJG 1	RAE, summer 1946
Go P-60 C three-seater	2./ NJG 1	Germany, 45
Me P 01-115	III./JG 27	Germany, 44
Me P 12	EJG 1	Germany, 45
Me P 20	JG 4	Germany, 44
Me P 1092	3. /JG 51	Germany, 44
Me P 1112	JG 77	Germany, 44
Me P 1112 (V1)	3. /JG 26	Germany, 45
Me P 1112 (S2)	N/A	Germany, 45
Me P 1112 (Mar 27 45)	JG 4	Germany, 45
Me P 1112 (Mar 3 45)	KG(J) 54	Germany, 45
Me P 1073	N/A	Germany, 45
BMW Strahljäger I	14. /JG 54	Germany, 45
BMW Strahljäger II	JG 301	Germany, 45
BMW Strahljäger III	7. /JG 26	France, 45
BMW Strahljäger IV	III. JG 3	Germany, 45
Ar E 581-4	I. JG 3	Germany, 45
Ar E 581-5	JG 53	Germany, 45
Ar TL-Jäger	3./ JG 27	Germany, 44
Ar K-Jäger	3./ JG 27	Germany, 44
Hs P 122	6. KG 77	Germany, 45
Hs P 135 early	II./SG 2	Germany, May 45
Hs P 135 late	III./JG 3	Luftwaffe in Sweden, May 45
Hs 132	Test	Germany, 45
B&V Nurflügel	7. /JG 26	Germany, 45
B&V P 196	6. /JG 5	Finland, 45
B&V P 197	III. /EJG 2	Germany, 45
B&V P 198	I./JG 3	Germany, Apr 45

LUFTWAFFE
Secret Project Profiles

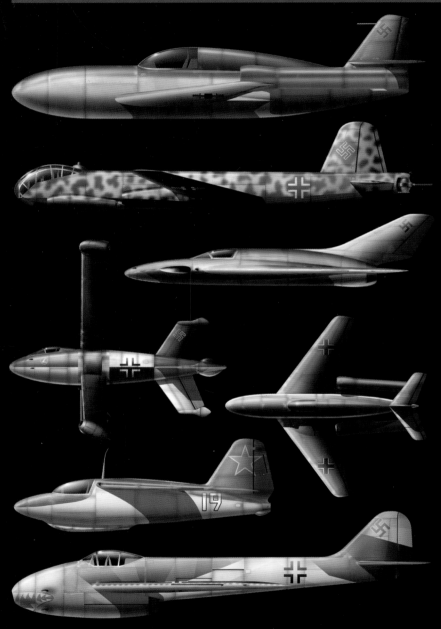

The constantly evolving nature of the air war from 1939 to 1945 meant existing aircraft types on all sides required constant upgrades and requirements for new types were regularly passed on to aircraft manufacturers.

The German government had already put huge resources into aviation research and development before the war – resulting in significant technological progress. So when the Luftwaffe asked for new aircraft, firms such as Messerschmitt, Focke-Wulf, Heinkel and Henschel were able to draw on cutting-edge aerodynamic research in formulating their designs to meet those requirements.

Competitions were held and the firms' designs were measured against one another and against the German government's strict standards – and the result was further evolution and development of even the most advanced aircraft proposals.

Luftwaffe: Secret Project Profiles focuses on the jet-propelled aircraft designs of the German aircraft manufacturers during the Second World War, beautifully illustrated by aviation artist Daniel Uhr.

More than 200 high-detailed full colour profiles cover the full range of German jet 'secret projects' from the war years, accompanied by details of why the designs were produced and how they fared against their competitors – based on the latest archival research.

Offering a host of different colour schemes and detailed notes, this is indispensable reading for enthusiasts and modellers alike.